ALEX HALEY, *Alex* >

"ROOTS /

VOLUME I

Contents:—v.1 **KUNTA KINTE**

929.2

④ 3 v.

G.K.HALL&CO.
Boston, Massachusetts
1979

Library of Congress Cataloging in Publication Data

Haley, Alex.
  Roots.

  Large print ed.
  1. Haley, Alex. 2. Haley family. 3. Kinte
family. 4. Large type books. L. Title.
E185.97.H24A33 1979   929'.2'0973   78-26753
  ISBN 0-8161-6639-0

A condensed version of a portion of this work first appeared in
Reader's Digest. Copyright © 1974 by Reader's Digest
Association, Inc.

Published in Large Print by arrangement with Doubleday &
Company, Inc.

Set in Compugraphic 18 pt English Times

DEDICATION

*It wasn't planned
that* Roots' *researching and writing
finally would take twelve years.
Just by chance it is being published
in the Bicentennial Year
of the United States.
So I dedicate* Roots *as a birthday
offering to my country
within which most of* Roots *happened.*

ACKNOWLEDGMENTS

I owe deep gratitude to so many people for their help with *Roots* that pages would be required simply to list them all. The following are pre-eminent:

George Sims, my lifelong friend from our Henning, Tennessee, boyhood, is a master researcher who often traveled with me, sharing both the physical and emotional adventures. His dedicated combing through volumes by the hundreds, and other kinds of documents by the thousands — particularly in the U. S. Library of Congress and the U. S. National Archives — supplied much of the historical and cultural material that I have woven around the lives of the people in this book.

Murray Fisher had been my editor for

years at *Playboy* magazine when I solicited his clinical expertise to help me structure this book from a seeming impassable maze of researched materials. After we had established *Roots'* pattern of chapters, next the story line was developed, which he then shepherded throughout. Finally, in the book's pressurized completion phase, he even drafted some of *Roots'* scenes, and his brilliant editing pen steadily tightened the book's great length.

The Africa section of this book exists in its detail only because at a crucial time Mrs. DeWitt Wallace and the editors of the *Reader's Digest* shared and supported my intense wish to explore if my maternal family's treasured oral history might possibly be documented back into Africa where all black Americans began.

Nor would this book exist in its fullness without the help of those scores of dedicated librarians and archivists in some fifty-seven different repositories of information on three continents. I found that if a librarian or archivist becomes excited with your own fervor of research, they can turn into sleuths to aid your quests.

I owe a great debt to Paul R. Reynolds, doyen of literary agents — whose client I have the pleasure to be — and to Doubleday Senior Editors Lisa Drew and Ken McCormick, all of whom have patiently shared and salved my frustrations across the years of producing *Roots*.

Finally, I acknowledge immense debt to the griots of Africa — where today it is rightly said that when a griot dies, it is as if a library has burned to the ground. The griots symbolize how all human ancestry goes back to some place, and some time, where there was no writing. Then, the memories and the mouths of ancient elders was the only way that early histories of mankind got passed along . . . for all of us today to know who we are.

VOLUME I

KUNTA KINTE

CHAPTER 1

Early in the spring of 1750, in the village of Juffure, four days upriver from the coast of The Gambia, West Africa, a manchild was born to Omoro and Binta Kinte. Forcing forth from Binta's strong young body, he was as black as she was, flecked and slippery with Binta's blood, and he was bawling. The two wrinkled midwives, old Nyo Boto and the baby's Grandmother Yaisa, saw that it was a boy and laughed with joy. According to the forefathers, a boy firstborn presaged the special blessings of Allah not only upon the parents but also upon the parents' families; and there was the prideful knowledge that the name of Kinte would thus be both distinguished and perpetuated.

It was the hour before the first crowing of the cocks, and along with Nyo Boto and Grandma Yaisa's chatterings, the first sound the child heard was the muted, rhythmic *bomp-a-bomp-a-bomp* of wooden pestles as the other women of the village pounded couscous grain in their mortars, preparing the traditional breakfast of porridge that was cooked in earthen pots over a fire built among three rocks.

The thin blue smoke went curling up, pungent and pleasant, over the small dusty village of round mud huts as the nasal wailing of Kajali Demba, the village alimamo, began, calling men to the first of the five daily prayers that had been offered up to Allah for as long as anyone living could remember. Hastening from their beds of bamboo cane and cured hides into their rough cotton tunics, the men of the village filed briskly to the praying place, where the alimamo led the worship: *"Allahu Akbar! Ashadu an lailahailala!"* (God is great! I bear witness that there is only one God!) It was after this, as the men were returning toward

2

their home compounds for breakfast, that Omoro rushed among them, beaming and excited, to tell them of his firstborn son. Congratulating him, all of the men echoed the omens of good fortune.

Each man, back in his own hut, accepted a calabash of porridge from his wife. Returning to their kitchens in the rear of the compound, the wives fed next their children, and finally themselves. When they had finished eating, the men took up their short, bent-handled hoes, whose wooden blades had been sheathed with metal by the village blacksmith, and set off for their day's work of preparing the land for farming of the groundnuts and the couscous and cotton that were the primary men's crops, as rice was that of the women, in this hot, lush savanna country of The Gambia.

By ancient custom, for the next seven days, there was but a single task with which Omoro would seriously occupy himself: the selection of a name for his firstborn son. It would have to be a name rich with history and with promise, for the people of his tribe — the Mandinkas —

believed that a child would develop seven of the characteristics of whomever or whatever he was named for.

On behalf of himself and Binta, during this week of thinking, Omoro visited every household in Juffure, and invited each family to the naming ceremony of the newborn child, traditionally on the eighth day of his life. On that day, like his father and his father's father, this new son would become a member of the tribe.

When the eighth day arrived, the villagers gathered in the early morning before the hut of Omoro and Binta. On their heads, the women of both families brought calabash containers of ceremonial sour milk and sweet munko cakes of pounded rice and honey. Karamo Silla, the jaliba of the village, was there with his tan-tang drums; and the alimamo, and the arafang, Brima Cesay, who would some day be the child's teacher; and also Omoro's two brothers, Janneh and Saloum, who had journeyed from far away to attend the ceremony when the drumtalk news of their nephew's birth had reached them.

As Binta proudly held her new infant, a small patch of his first hair was shaved off, as was always done on this day, and all of the women exclaimed at how well formed the baby was. Then they quieted as the jaliba began to beat his drums. The alimamo said a prayer over the calabashes of sour milk and munko cakes, and as he prayed, each guest touched a calabash brim with his or her right hand, as a gesture of respect for the food. Then the alimamo turned to pray over the infant, entreating Allah to grant him long life, success in bringing credit and pride and many children to his family, to his village, to his tribe — and, finally, the strength and the spirit to deserve and to bring honor to the name he was about to receive.

Omoro then walked out before all of the assembled people of the village. Moving to his wife's side, he lifted up the infant and, as all watched, whispered three times into his son's ear the name he had chosen for him. It was the first time the name had ever been spoken as this child's name, for Omoro's people felt that each human being should be the first to know who he was.

The tan-tang drum resounded again; and now Omoro whispered the name into the ear of Binta, and Binta smiled with pride and pleasure. Then Omoro whispered the name to the arafang, who stood before the villagers.

"The first child of Omoro and Binta Kinte is named *Kunta!*" cried Brima Cesay.

As everyone knew, it was the middle name of the child's late grandfather, Kairaba Kunta Kinte, who had come from his native Mauretania into The Gambia, where he had saved the people of Juffure from a famine, married Grandma Yaisa, and then served Juffure honorably till his death as the village's holy man.

One by one, the arafang recited the names of the Mauretanian forefathers of whom the baby's grandfather, old Kairaba Kinte, had often told. The names, which were great and many, went back more than two hundred rains. Then the jaliba pounted on his tan-tang and all of the people exclaimed their admiration and respect at such a distinguished lineage.

Out under the moon and the stars, alone with his son that eighth night, Omoro completed the naming ritual. Carrying little Kunta in his strong arms, he walked to the edge of the village, lifted his baby up with his face to the heavens, and said softly, *"Fend kiling dorong leh warrata ka iteh tee."* (Behold — the only thing greater than yourself.)

CHAPTER 2

It was the planting season, and the first rains were soon to come. On all their farming land, the men of Juffure had piled tall stacks of dry weeds and set them afire so that the light wind would nourish the soil by scattering the ashes. And the women in their rice fields were already planting green shoots in the mud.

While she was recovering from childbirth, Binta's rice plot had been attended by Grandma Yaisa, but now Binta was ready to resume her duties. With Kunta cradled across her back in a cotton sling, she walked with the other women — some of them, including her friend Jankay Touray, carrying their own newborns, along with the bundles they all balanced on their heads — to the dugout canoes on the bank of the village bolong, one of the many tributary canals that came twisting inland from the Gambia River, known as the Kamby Bolongo. The canoes went skimming down the bolong with five or six women in each one, straining against their short, broad paddles. Each time Binta bent forward to dip and pull, she felt Kunta's warm softness pressing against her back.

The air was heavy with the deep, musky fragrance of the mangroves, and with the perfumes of the other plants and trees that grew thickly on both sides of the bolong. Alarmed by the passing canoes, huge families of baboons, roused from sleep, began bellowing, springing about and shaking palm-tree fronds. Wild pigs grunted and snorted, running to hide themselves among the weeds and bushes. Covering the muddy banks, thousands of pelicans, cranes, egrets, herons, storks, gulls, terns, and spoonbills interrupted their breakfast feeding to watch nervously as the canoes glided by. Some of the smaller birds took to the air — ringdoves, skimmers, rails, darters, and kingfishers

— circling with shrill cries until the intruders had passed.

As the canoes arrowed through rippling, busy patches of water, schools of minnows would leap up together, perform a silvery dance, and then splash back. Chasing the minnows, sometimes so hungrily that they flopped right into a moving canoe, were large, fierce fish that the women would club with their paddles and stow away for a succulent evening meal. But this morning the minnows swam around them undisturbed.

The twisting bolong took the rowing women around a turn into a wider tributary, and as they came into sight, a great beating of wings filled the air and a vast living carpet of seafowl — hundreds of thousands of them, in every color of the rainbow — rose and filled the sky. The surface of the water, darkened by the storm of birds and furrowed by their flapping wings, was flecked with feathers as the women paddled on.

As they neared the marshy faros where generations of Juffure women had grown their rice crops, the canoes passed through swarming clouds of mosquitoes and then, one after another, nosed in against a walkway of thickly matted weeds. The weeds bounded and identified each woman's plot, where by now the emerald shoots of young rice stood a hand's height above the water's surface.

Since the size of each woman's plot was decided each year by Juffure's Council of Elders, according to how many mouths each woman had to feed with rice, Binta's plot was still a small one. Balancing herself carefully as she stepped from the canoe with her new baby, Binta took a few steps and then stopped short, looking with surprise and delight at a tiny thatch-roofed bamboo hut on stilts. While she was in labor, Omoro had come here and built it as a shelter for their son. Typical of men, he had said nothing about it.

Nursing the baby, then nestling him inside his shelter, Binta changed into the working clothes she had brought in the bundle on her head, and waded out to work. Bending nearly double in the water, she pulled up by the roots the young weeds that, left alone, would outgrow and

11

choke the rice crop. And whenever Kunta cried, Binta waded out, dripping water, to nurse him again in the shadow of his shelter.

Little Kunta basked thus every day in his mother's tenderness. Back in her hut each evening, after cooking and serving Omoro's dinner, Binta would soften her baby's skin by greasing him from head to toe with shea tree butter, and then — more often than not — she would carry him proudly across the village to the hut of Grandma Yaisa, who would bestow upon the baby still more cluckings and kissings. And both of them would set little Kunta to whimpering in irritation with their repeated pressings of his little head, nose, ears, and lips, to shape them correctly.

Sometimes Omoro would take his son away from the women and carry the blanketed bundle to his own hut — husbands always resided separately from their wives — where he would let the child's eyes and fingers explore such attractive objects as the saphie charms at the head of Omoro's bed, placed there to ward off evil spirits. Anything colorful intrigued little Kunta — especially his father's leather huntsman's bag, nearly covered by now with cowrie shells, each for an animal that Omoro had personally brought in as food for the village. And Kunta cooed over the long, curved bow and quiver of arrows hanging nearby. Omoro smiled when a tiny hand reached out and grasped the dark, slender spear whose shaft was polished from so much use. He let Kunta touch everything except the prayer rug, which was sacred to its owner. And alone together in his hut, Omoro would talk to Kunta of the fine and brave deeds his son would do when he grew up.

Finally he would return Kunta to Binta's hut for the next nursing. Wherever he was, Kunta was happy most of the time, and he always fell asleep either with Binta rocking him on her lap or bending over him on her bed, singing softly such a lullaby as,

My smiling child,
Named for a noble ancestor.
Great hunter or warrior

You will be one day,
Which will give your papa pride.
But always I will remember you thus.

However much Binta loved her baby and her husband, she also felt a very real anxiety, for Moslem husbands, by ancient custom, would often select and marry a second wife during that time when their first wives had babies still nursing. As yet Omoro had taken no other wife; and since Binta didn't want him tempted, she felt that the sooner little Kunta was able to walk alone, the better, for that was when the nursing would end.

So Binta was quick to help him as soon as Kunta, at about thirteen moons, tried his first unsteady steps. And before long, he was able to toddle about without an assisting hand. Binta was as relieved as Omoro was proud, and when Kunta cried for his next feeding, Binta gave her son not a breast but a sound spanking and a gourd of cow's milk.

CHAPTER 3

Three rains had passed, and it was that lean season when the village's store of grain and other dried foods from the last harvest was almost gone. The men had hunted, but they had returned with only a few small antelopes and gazelle and some clumsy bushfowl, for in this season of burning sun, so many of the savanna's waterholes had dried into mud that the bigger and better game had moved into deep forest — at the very time when the people of Juffure needed all their strength to plant crops for the new harvest. Already, the wives were stretching their staple meals of couscous and rice with the tasteless seeds of bamboo cane and with the bad-tasting dried leaves of the baobab tree. The days of hunger had begun so early that five goats and two bullocks — more than last time — were sacrificed to strengthen everyone's prayers that Allah might spare the village from starvation.

Finally the hot skies clouded, the light breezes became brisk winds and, abruptly as always, the little rains began, falling warmly and gently as the farmers hoed the softened earth into long, straight rows in readiness for the seeds. They knew the planting must be done before the big rains came.

The next few mornings, after breakfast, instead of canoeing to their rice fields, the farmers' wives dressed in the traditional fertility costumes of large fresh leaves, symbolizing the green of growing things, and set out for the furrowed fields of the men. Their voices would be heard rising and falling even before they appeared as they chanted ancestral prayers that the couscous and groundnuts and other seeds in the earthen bowls balanced on their heads would take strong roots and grow.

With their bare feet moving in step, the line of women walked and sang three times around every farmer's field. Then they separated, and each woman fell in behind a farmer as he moved along each row, punching a hole in the earth every few inches with his big toe. Into each hole a woman dropped a seed, covered it over with her own big toe, and then moved on. The women worked even harder than the men, for they not only had to help their husbands but also tend both the rice fields and the vegetable gardens they cultivated near their kitchens.

While Binta planted her onions, yams, gourds, cassava, and bitter tomatoes, little Kunta spent his days romping under the watchful eyes of the several old grandmothers who took care of all the children of Juffure who belonged to the first kafo, which included those under five rains in age. The boys and girls alike scampered about as naked as young animals — some of them just beginning to say their first words. All, like Kunta, were growing fast, laughing and squealing as they ran after each other around the giant trunk of the village baobab, played hide-and-seek, and scattered the dogs and chickens into masses of fur and feathers.

But all the children — even those as small as Kunta — would quickly scramble to sit still and quiet when the telling of a story was promised by one of the old grandmothers. Though unable yet to understand many of the words, Kunta would watch with wide eyes as the old women acted out their stories with such gestures and noises that they really seemed to be happening.

As little as he was, Kunta was already familiar with some of the stories that his own Grandma Yaisa had told him alone when he had been visiting in her hut. But along with his first-kafo playmates, he felt that the best story-teller of all was the beloved, mysterious, and peculiar old Nyo Boto. Bald-headed, deeply wrinkled, as black as the bottom of a cooking pot, with her long lemongrass-root chewstick sticking out like an insect's feeler between the few teeth she had left — which were deep orange from the countless kola nuts she had gnawed on — old Nyo Boto would settle herself with much grunting on her low stool. Though she acted gruff, the children knew that she loved them as if they were her own, which she claimed they all were.

Surrounded by them, she would growl, "Let me tell a story . . ."

"Please!" the children would chorus, wriggling in anticipation.

And she would begin in the way that all Mandinka story tellers began: "At this certain time, in this certain village, lived this certain person." It was a small boy, she said, of about their rains, who walked to the riverbank one day and found a crocodile trapped in a net.

"Help me!" the crocodile cried out.

"You'll kill me!" cried the boy.

"No! Come nearer!" said the crocodile.

So the boy went up to the crocodile — and instantly was seized by the teeth in that long mouth.

"Is this how you repay my goodness — with badness?" cried the boy.

"Of course," said the crocodile out of the corner of his mouth. "That is the way of the world."

The boy refused to believe that, so the crocodile agreed not to swallow him without getting an opinion from the first three witnesses to pass by. First was an old donkey.

When the boy asked his opinion, the donkey said, "Now that I'm old and can no longer work, my master has driven me out for the leopards to get me!"

"See?" said the crocodile. Next to pass by was an old horse, who had the same opinion.

"See?" said the crocodile. Then along came a plump rabbit who said, "Well, I can't give a good opinion without seeing this matter as it happened from the beginning."

Grumbling, the crocodile opened his mouth to tell him — and the boy jumped out to safety on the riverbank.

"Do you like crocodile meat?" asked the rabbit. The boy said yes. "And do your parents?" He said yes again. "Then here is a crocodile ready for the pot."

The boy ran off and returned with the men of the village, who helped him to kill the crocodile. But they brought with them a wuolo dog, which chased and caught and killed the rabbit, too.

"So the crocodile was right," said Nyo Boto. "It *is* the way of the world that goodness is often repaid with badness. This is what I have told you as a story."

"May you be blessed, have strength and prosper!" said the children gratefully.

Then the other grandmothers would pass among the children with bowls of freshly toasted beetles and grasshoppers. These would have been only tasty tidbits at another time of year, but now, on the eve of the big rains, with the hungry season already beginning, the toasted insects had to serve as a noon meal, for only a few handfuls of couscous and rice remained in most families' storehouses.

CHAPTER 4

Fresh, brief showers fell almost every morning now, and between the showers Kunta and his playmates would dash about excitedly outside. "Mine! Mine!" they would shout at the pretty rainbows that would arc down to earth, seeming never very far away. But the showers also brought swarms of flying insects whose vicious stinging and biting soon drove the children back indoors.

Then, suddenly, late one night, the big rains began, and the people huddled inside their cold huts listening to the water pound on their thatch roofs, watching the lightning flash and comforting their children as the frightening thunder rumbled through the night. Between cloudbursts, they heard only the barking of the jackals, the howling of the hyenas, and the croaking of the frogs.

The rains came again the next night, and the next, and the next — and only at night — flooding the lowlands near the river, turning their fields into a swamp and their village into a mudhole. Yet each morning before breakfast, all the farmers struggled through the mud to Juffure's little mosque and implored Allah to send still *more* rain, for life itself depended upon enough water to soak deeply into the earth before the hot suns arrived, which would wither those crops whose roots could not find enough water to survive.

In the damp nursery hut, dimly lighted and poorly heated by the burning dry sticks and cattle-dung patties in the earthen floor's shallow firehole, old Nyo Boto told Kunta and the other children of the terrible time she remembered when there were not enough big rains. No matter how bad anything was, Nyo Boto would always remember a time when it was worse. After two days of big rain, she told them, the burning suns had come. Although the people prayed very hard to

23

Allah, and danced the ancestral rain dance, and sacrificed two goats and a bullock every day, still everything growing in the ground began to parch and die. Even the forest's waterholes dried up, said Nyo Boto, and first wild fowl, and then the forest's animals, sick from thirst, began to appear at the village well. In crystal-clear skies each night, thousands of bright stars shone, and a cold wind blew, and more and more people grew ill. Clearly, evil spirits were abroad in Juffure.

Those who were able continued their prayers and their dances, and finally the last goat and bullock had been sacrificed. It was as if Allah had turned His back on Juffure. Some — the old and the weak and the sick — began to die. Others left town, seeking another village to beg someone who had food to accept them as slaves, just to get something into their bellies, and those who stayed behind lost their spirit and lay down in their huts. It was then, said Nyo Boto, that Allah had guided the steps of marabout Kairaba Kunta Kinte into the starving village of

Juffure. Seeing the people's plight, he kneeled down and prayed to Allah — almost without sleep and taking only a few sips of water as nourishment — for the next five days. And on the evening of the fifth day came a great rain, which fell like a flood, and saved Juffure.

When she finished her story, the other children looked with new respect at Kunta, who bore the name of that distinguished grandfather, husband of Kunta's Grandma Yaisa. Even before now, Kunta had seen how the parents of the other children acted toward Yaisa, and he had sensed that she was an important woman, just as old Nyo Boto surely was.

The big rains continued to fall every night until Kunta and the other children began to see grown-ups wading across the village in mud up to their ankles and even to their knees, and even using canoes to paddle from place to place. Kunta had heard Binta telling Omoro that the rice fields were flooded in the bolong's high waters. Cold and hungry, the children's fathers sacrificed precious goats and bullocks to Allah almost every day, patched leaking roofs, shored up sagging huts and prayed that their disappearing stock of rice and couscous would last until the harvest.

But Kunta and the others, being yet little children, paid less attention to the hunger pangs in their bellies than to playing in the mud, wrestling each other and sliding on their naked bottoms. Yet in their longing to see the sun again, they would wave up at the slate-colored sky and shout — as they had seen their parents do — "Shine, sun, and I will kill you a goat!"

The life-giving rain had made every growing thing fresh and luxuriant. Birds sang everywhere. The trees and plants were explosions of fragrant blossoms. The reddish-brown, clinging mud underfoot was newly carpeted each morning, with the bright-colored petals and green leaves beaten loose by the rain of the night before. But amid all the lushness of nature, sickness spread steadily among the people of Juffure, for none of the richly growing crops was ripe enough to eat. The adults and children alike would stare hungrily at the thousands of plump mangoes and monkey apples hanging heavy on the trees, but the green fruits were as hard as rocks, and those who bit into them fell ill and vomited.

"Nothing but skin and bones!" Grandma Yaisa would exclaim, making a loud clicking noise with her tongue every time she saw Kunta. But in fact his grandma was almost as thin as he; for every storehouse in Juffure was now completely empty. What few of the village's cattle and goats and chickens had not been eaten or sacrificed had to be kept alive — and fed — if there was to be a next year's crop of kids and calves and baby chicks. So the people began to eat rodents, roots, and leaves foraged from in and around the village on searchings that began when the sun rose and ended when it set.

If the men had gone to the forests to hunt wild game, as they frequently did at other times of the year, they wouldn't have had the strength to drag it back to the village. Tribal taboos forbade the Mandinkas to eat the abounding monkeys and baboons; nor would they touch the many hens' eggs that lay about, or the millions of big green bullfrogs that Mandinkas regarded as poisonous. And as devout Moslems, they would rather have died than eat the flesh of the wild pigs that often came rooting in herds right through the village.

For ages, families of cranes had nested in the topmost branches of the village's silk-cotton tree, and when the young hatched, the big cranes shuttled back and forth bringing fish, which they had just caught in the bolong, to feed their babies. Watching for the right moment, the grandmothers and the children would rush beneath the tree, whooping and hurling small sticks and stones upward at the nest. And often, in the noise and confusion, a young crane's gaping mouth would miss the fish, and the fish would miss the nest and come slapping down among the tall tree's thick foliage to the ground. The children would struggle over the prize, and someone's family would have a feast for dinner. If one of the stones thrown up by the children happened to hit a gawky, pin-feathered young crane, it would sometimes fall from the high nest along with the fish, killing or injuring itself in the crash against the ground; and that night a few families would have crane soup. But such meals were rare.

By the late evening, each family would meet back at their hut, bringing whatever each individual had found — perhaps even a mole or a handful of large grubworms, if they were lucky — for that night's pot of soup, heavily peppered and spiced to improve the taste. But such fare filled their bellies without bringing nourishment. And so it was that the people of Juffure began to die.

CHAPTER 5

More and more often now, the high-pitched howling of a woman would be heard throughout the village. The fortunate were those babies and toddlers yet too young to understand, for even Kunta was old enough to know that the howling meant a loved one had just died. In the afternoons, usually, some sick farmer who had been out cutting weeds in his field would be carried back to the village on a bullock's hide, lying very still.

And disease had begun to swell the legs of some adults. Yet others developed fevers with heavy perspiration and trembling chills. And among all the children, small areas on their arms or legs would puff up, rapidly grow larger and painfully sore; then the puffed areas would split, leaking a pinkish fluid that soon became a full, yellow, stinking pus that drew buzzing flies.

The hurting of the big open sore on Kunta's leg made him stumble while trying to run one day. Falling hard, he was picked up by his playmates, stunned and yelling, with his forehead bleeding. Since Binta and Omoro were away farming, they rushed him to the hut of Grandma Yaisa, who for a number of days now had not appeared in the nursery hut.

She looked very weak, her black face gaunt and drawn, and she was sweating under her bullock hide on her bamboo pallet. But when she saw Kunta, she sprang up to wipe his bleeding forehead. Embracing him tightly, she ordered the other children to run and bring her some kelelalu ants. When they returned, Grandma Yaisa tightly pressed together the skin's split edges, then pressed one struggling driver ant after another against the wound. As each ant angrily clamped its strong pincers into the flesh on each side of the cut, she deftly snapped off its body, leaving the head in place, until the

31

wound was stitched together.

Dismissing the other children, she told Kunta to lie down and rest alongside her on the bed. He lay and listened to her labored breathing as she remained silent for some time. Then Grandma Yaisa's hand gestured toward a pile of books on the shelf beside her bed. Speaking slowly and softly, she told Kunta more about his grandfather, whose books she said those were.

In his native country of Mauretania, Kairaba Kunta Kinte had thirty-five rains of age when his teacher, a master marabout, gave him the blessing that made him a holy man, said Grandma Yaisa. Kunta's grandfather had followed a family tradition of holy men that dated back many hundreds of rains into Old Mali. As a man of the fourth kafo, he had begged the old marabout to accept him as a student, and for the next fifteen rains had traveled with his party of wives, slaves, students, cattle and goats as he pilgrimaged from village to village in the service of Allah and his subjects. Over dusty foot trails and muddy creeks, under hot suns

32

and cold rains, through green valleys and windy wastelands, said Grandma Yaisa, they had trekked southward from Mauretania.

Upon receiving his ordination as a holy man, Kairaba Kunta Kinte had himself wandered for many moons alone, among places in Old Mali such as Keyla, Djeela, Kangaba, and Timbuktu, humbly prostrating himself before very great old holy men and imploring their blessings for his success, which they all freely gave. And Allah then guided the young man's footsteps in a southerly direction, finally to The Gambia, where he stopped first in the village of Pakali N'Ding.

In a short while, the people of this village knew, by the quick results from his prayers, that this young holy man had upon him Allah's special favor. Talking drums spread the news, and soon other villages tried to lure him away, sending messengers with offers of prime maidens for wives, and slaves and cattle and goats. And before long he did move, this time to the village of Jiffarong, but only because Allah had called him there, for the people of Jiffarong had little to offer him but their gratitude for his prayers. It was here that he heard of the village of Juffure, where people were sick and dying for lack of a big rain. And so at last he came to Juffure, said Grandma Yaisa, where for five days, ceaselessly, he had prayed until Allah sent down the big rain that saved the village.

Learning of Kunta's grandfather's great deed, the King of Barra himself, who ruled this part of The Gambia, personally presented a choice virgin for the young holy man's first wife, and her name was Sireng. By Sireng, Kairaba Kunta Kinte begot two sons — and he named them Janneh and Saloum.

By now, Grandma Yaisa had sat up on her bamboo pallet. "It was then," she said with shining eyes, "that he saw Yaisa, dancing the seoruba! My age was fifteen rains!" She smiled widely, showing her toothless gums. "He needed no king to choose his next wife!" She looked at Kunta. "It was from my belly that he begot your papa Omoro."

That night, back in his mother's hut,

Kunta lay awake for a long time, thinking of the things Grandma Yaisa had told him. Many times, Kunta had heard about the grandfather holy man whose prayers had saved the village, and whom later Allah had taken back. But Kunta had never truly understood until now that this man was his father's father, that Omoro had known him as he knew Omoro, that Grandma Yaisa was Omoro's mother as Binta was his own. Some day, he too would find a woman such as Binta to bear him a son of his own. And that son, in turn . . .

Turning over and closing his eyes, Kunta followed these deep thoughts slowly into sleep.

CHAPTER 6

Just before sundown for the next few days, after returning from the rice field, Binta would send Kunta to the village well for a calabash of fresh water, which she would use to boil a soup from whatever scraps she could find. Then she and Kunta would take some of the soup across the village to Grandma Yaisa. Binta moved more slowly than usual, it seemed to Kunta, and he noticed that her belly was very big and heavy.

While Grandma Yaisa protested weakly that she would soon feel well again, Binta would clean up the hut and arrange things. And they would leave Grandma Yaisa propped up on her bed, eating a bowl of soup along with some of Binta's hungry-season bread, made from the yellow powder that covered the dry black beans of the wild locust tree.

Then one night, Kunta awakened to find himself being shaken roughly by his father. Binta was making low, moaning sounds on her bed, and also within the hut, moving quickly about, were Nyo Boto and Binta's friend Jankay Touray. Omoro hurried across the village with Kunta, who, wondering what all of this was about, soon drifted back to sleep on his father's bed.

In the morning, Omoro again awakened Kunta and said, "You have a new brother." Scrambling sleepily onto his knees and rubbing his eyes, Kunta thought it must be something very special to so please his usually stern father. In the afternoon, Kunta was with his kafo mates, looking for things to eat, when Nyo Boto called him and took him to see Binta. Looking very tired, she sat on the edge of her bed gently caressing the baby in her lap. Kunta stood a moment studying the little wrinkly black thing; then he looked at the two women smiling at it, and he noticed that the familiar bigness of Binta's stomach was suddenly gone. Going back outside without a word, Kunta stood for a long moment and then, instead of rejoining his friends, went off to sit by himself behind his father's hut and think about what he had seen.

Kunta continued sleeping in Omoro's hut for the next seven nights — not that anyone seemed to notice or care, in their concern for the new baby. He was beginning to think that his mother didn't want him any more — or his father, either — until, on the evening of the eighth day, Omoro called him before his mother's hut, along with everyone else in Juffure who was physically able, to hear the new baby given his chosen name, which was Lamin.

That night Kunta slept peacefully and well — back in his own bed beside his mother and his new brother. But within a few days, as soon as her strength had returned, Binta began to take the baby, after cooking and serving something for Omoro's and Kunta's breakfast, and spent most of each day in the hut of Grandma Yaisa. From the worried expressions that both Binta and Omoro wore, Kunta knew that Grandma Yaisa was very sick.

Late one afternoon, a few days later, he and his kafo mates were out picking mangoes, which had finally ripened. Bruising the tough, orange-yellow skin against the nearest rock, they would bite open one plump end to squeeze and suck out the soft sweet flesh within. They were collecting basketfuls of monkey apples and wild cashew nuts when Kunta suddenly heard the howling of a familiar voice from the direction of his grandma's hut. A chill shot through him, for it was the voice of his mother, raised in the death wail that he had heard so often in recent weeks. Other women immediately joined in a keening cry that soon spread all the way across the village. Kunta ran blindly toward his grandmother's hut.

Amid the milling confusion, Kunta saw an anguished Omoro and a bitterly weeping old Nyo Boto. Within moments, the tobalo drum was being beaten and the jaliba was loudly crying out the good deeds of Grandma Yaisa's long life in Juffure. Numb with shock, Kunta stood watching blankly as the young, unmarried women of the village beat up dust from the ground with wide fans of plaited grass, as was the custom on the occasion of a death. No one seemed to notice Kunta.

As Binta and Nyo Boto and two other shrieking women entered the hut, the crowd outside fell to their knees and bowed their heads. Kunta burst suddenly into tears, as much in fear as in grief. Soon men came with a large, freshly split log and set it down in front of the hut. Kunta watched as the women brought out and laid on the log's flat surface the body of his grandmother, enclosed from her neck to her feet in a white cotton winding cloth.

Through his tears, Kunta saw the mourners walk seven circles around Yaisa, praying and chanting as the alimamo wailed that she was journeying to spend eternity with Allah and her ancestors. To give her strength for that journey, young unmarried men tenderly placed cattle horns filled with fresh ashes all around her body.

After most of the mourners had filed away, Nyo Boto and other old women took up posts nearby, huddling and weeping and squeezing their heads with their hands. Soon, young women brought the biggest ciboa leaves that could be found, to protect the old women's heads from rain through their vigil. And as the old women sat, the village drums talked about Grandma Yaisa far into the night.

In the misty morning, according to the custom of the forefathers, only the men of Juffure — those who were able to walk — joined the procession to the burying place, not far past the village, where otherwise none would go, out of the Mandinkas' fearful respect for the spirits of their ancestors. Behind the men who bore Grandma Yaisa on the log came Omoro, carrying the infant Lamin and holding the hand of little Kunta, who was too frightened to cry. And behind them came the other men of the village. The stiff, white-wrapped body was lowered into the freshly dug hole, and over her went a thick woven cane mat. Next were thorn bushes, to keep out the digging hyenas, and the rest of the hole was packed tight with stones and a mound of fresh earth.

Afterward, for many days, Kunta hardly ate or slept, and he would not go anywhere with his kafo mates. So grieved was he that Omoro, one evening, took him to his own hut, and there beside his bed, speaking to his son more softly and gently than he ever had before, told him something that helped to ease his grief.

He said that three groups of people lived in every village. First were those you could see — walking around, eating, sleeping, and working. Second were the ancestors, whom Grandma Yaisa had now joined.

"And the third people — who are they?" asked Kunta.

"The third people," said Omoro, "are those waiting to be born."

CHAPTER 7

The rains had ended, and between the bright blue sky and the damp earth, the air was heavy with the fragrance of lush wild blooms and fruits. The early morning echoed with the sound of the women's mortars pounding millet and couscous and groundnuts — not from the main harvest, but from those early-growing seeds that the past year's harvest had left living in the soil. The men hunted, bringing back fine, plump antelope, and after passing out the meat, they scraped and cured the hides. And the women busily collected the ripened reddish mangkano berries, shaking the bushes over cloths spread beneath, then drying the berries in the sun before pounding them to separate the delicious futo flour from the seeds. Nothing was wasted. Soaked and boiled with pounded millet, the seeds were cooked into a sweetish breakfast gruel that Kunta and everyone else welcomed as a seasonal change of diet from their usual morning meal of couscous porridge.

As food became more plentiful each day, new life flowed into Juffure in ways that could be seen and heard. The men began to walk more briskly to and from their farms, pridefully inspecting their bountiful crops, which would soon be ready for harvesting. With the flooded river now subsiding rapidly, the women were rowing daily to the faro and pulling out the last of the weeds from among the tall, green rows of rice.

And the village rang again with the yelling and laughing of the children back at play after the long hungry season. Bellies now filled with nourishing food, sores dried into scabs and falling away, they dashed and frolicked about as if possessed. One day they would capture some big scarab dung beetles, line them up for a race, and cheer the fastest to run outside a circle drawn in the dirt with a stick. Another day, Kunta and Sitafa Silla, his special friend, who lived in the hut next to Binta's, would raid a tall earth mound to dig up the blind, wingless termites that lived inside, and watch them pour out by the thousands and scurry frantically to get away.

Sometimes the boys would rout out little ground squirrels and chase them into the bush. And they loved nothing better than to hurl stones and shouts at passing schools of small, brown, long-tailed monkeys, some of which would throw a stone back before swinging up to join their screeching brothers in the topmost branches of a tree. And every day the boys would wrestle, grabbing each other, sprawling down, grunting, scrambling, and springing up to start all over again, each one dreaming of the day when he might become one of Juffure's champion wrestlers and be chosen to wage mighty battles with the champions of other villages during the harvest festivals.

Adults passing anywhere near the children would solemnly pretend not to see nor hear as Sitafa, Kunta, and the rest of their kafo growled and roared like lions, trumpeted like elephants, and grunted like wild pigs, or as the girls — cooking and tending their dolls and beating their couscous — played mothers and wives among themselves. But however hard they were playing, the children never failed to pay every adult the respect their mothers had taught them to show always toward their elders. Politely looking the adults in the eyes, the children would ask, *"Kerabe?"* (Do you have peace?) And the adults would reply, *"Kera dorong."* (Peace only.) And if an adult offered his hand, each child in turn would clasp it with both hands, then stand with palms folded over his chest until that adult passed by.

Kunta's home-training had been so strict that, it seemed to him, his every move drew Binta's irritated finger-snapping — if, indeed, he wasn't grabbed and soundly whipped. When he was eating, he would get a cuff on the head if Binta caught his eyes on anything except his own food. And unless he washed off every bit of dirt when he came into the hut from a hard day's play, Binta would snatch up her scratchy sponge of dried plant stems and her bar of homemade soap and make Kunta think she was going to scrape off his very hide.

For him ever to stare at her, or at his father, or at any other adult, would earn him a slap as quickly as when he committed the equally serious offense of interrupting the conversation of any grown-up. And for him ever to speak anything but truth would have been unthinkable. Since there never seemed any reason for him to lie, he never did.

Though Binta didn't seem to think so, Kunta tried his best to be a good boy, and soon began to practice his home-training lessons with the other children. When disagreements occurred among them, as they often did — something fanning into exchanges of harsh words and finger-snapping — Kunta would always turn and walk away, thus displaying the dignity and self-command that his mother had taught him were the proudest traits of the Mandinka tribe.

But almost every night, Kunta got

spanked for doing something bad to his baby brother — usually for frightening him by snarling fiercely or by dropping on all fours like a baboon, rolling his eyes, and stomping his fists like forepaws upon the ground. "I will bring the toubob!" Binta would yell at Kunta when he had tried her patience to the breaking point, scaring Kunta most thoroughly, for the old grandmothers spoke often of the hairy, red-faced, strange-looking white men whose big canoes stole people away from their homes.

CHAPTER 8

Though Kunta and his mates were tired and hungry from play by the time of each day's setting sun, they would still race one another to climb small trees and point at the sinking crimson ball. "He will be even lovelier tomorrow!" they would shout. And even Juffure's adults ate dinner quickly so that they might congregate outside in the deepening dusk to shout and clap and pound on drums at the rising of the crescent moon, symbolic of Allah.

But when clouds shrouded that new moon, as they did this night, the people dispersed, alarmed, and the men entered the mosque to pray for forgiveness, since a shrouded new moon meant that the heavenly spirits were displeased with the people of Juffure. After praying, the men led their frightened families to the baobab, where already on this night the jaliba squatted by a small fire, heating to its utmost tautness the goatskin head of his talking drum.

Rubbing at his eyes, which smarted from the smoke of the fire, Kunta remembered the times that drums talking at night from different villages had troubled his sleep. Awakening, he would lie there, listening hard; the sounds and rhythms were so like those of speech that he would finally understand some of the words, telling of a famine or a plague, or of the raiding and burning of some village, with its people killed or stolen away.

Hanging on a branch of the baobab, beside the jaliba, was a goatskin inscribed with the marks that talk, written there in Arabic by the arafang. In the flickering firelight, Kunta watched as the jaliba began to beat the knobby elbows of his crooked sticks very rapidly and sharply against different spots on the drumhead. It was an urgent message for the nearest magic man to come to Juffure and drive out evil spirits.

Not daring to look up at the moon, the people hurried home and fearfully went to bed. But at intervals through the night, the talk of distant drums echoed the appeal of Juffure for a magic man in other villages as well. Shivering beneath his cowskin, Kunta guessed that their new moon was shrouded, too.

The next day, the men of Omoro's age had to help the younger men of the village to guard their nearly ripened fields against the seasonal plague of hungry baboons and birds. The second-kafo boys were told to be especially vigilant as they grazed the goats, and the mothers and grandmothers hovered closer than they normally would over the toddlers and the babies. The first kafo's biggest children, those the size of Kunta and Sitafa, were instructed to play a little way out past the village's tall fence, where they could keep a sharp lookout for any stranger approaching the travelers' tree, not far distant. They did, but none came that day.

He appeared on the second morning — a very old man, walking with the help of a wooden staff and bearing a large bundle on his bald head. Spotting him, the children raced shouting back through the village gate. Leaping up, old Nyo Boto hobbled over and began to beat on the big tobalo drum that brought the men rushing back to the village from their fields a moment before the magic man reached the gate and entered Juffure.

As the villagers gathered around him, he walked over to the baobab and set down his bundle carefully on the ground. Abruptly squatting, he then shook from a wrinkled goatskin bag a heap of dried objects — a small snake, a hyena's jawbone, a monkey's teeth, a pelican's wingbone, various fowls' feet, and strange roots. Glancing about, he gestured impatiently for the hushed crowd to give him more room; and the people moved back as he began to quiver all over — clearly being attacked by Juffure's evil spirits.

The magic man's body writhed, his face contorted, his eyes rolled wildly, as his trembling hands struggled to force his resisting wand into contact with the heap of mysterious objects. When the wand's tip, with a supreme effort, finally touched, he fell over backward and lay as if struck by lightning. The people gasped. But then he slowly began to revive. The evil spirits had been driven out. As he struggled weakly to his knees, Juffure's adults — exhausted but relieved — went running off to their huts and soon returned with gifts to press upon him. The magic man added these to his bundle which was already large and heavy with gifts from previous villages, and soon he was on his way to answer the next call. In his mercy, Allah had seen fit to spare Juffure once again.

CHAPTER 9

Twelve moons had passed, and with the big rains ended once again, The Gambia's season for travelers had begun. Along the network of walking paths between its villages came enough visitors — passing by or stopping off in Juffure — to keep Kunta and his playmates on the lookout almost every day. After alerting the village when a stranger appeared, they would rush back out to meet each visitor as he approached the travelers' tree. Trooping boldly alongside him, they would chatter away inquisitively as their sharp eyes hunted for any signs of his mission or profession. If they found any, they would abruptly abandon the visitor and race back ahead to tell the grown-ups in that day's hospitality hut. In accordance with

54

ancient tradition, a different family in each village would be chosen every day to offer food and shelter to arriving visitors at no cost for as long as they wished to stay before continuing their journey.

Having been entrusted with the responsibility of serving as the village lookouts, Kunta, Sitafa, and their kafo mates began to feel and act older than their rains. Now after breakfast each morning, they would gather by the arafang's schoolyard and kneel quietly to listen as he taught the older boys — those of the second kafo, just beyond Kunta's age, five to nine rains old — how to read their Koranic verses and to write with grass-quill pens dipped in the black ink of bitter-orange juice mixed with powdered crust from the bottom of cooking pots.

When the schoolboys finished their lessons and ran off — with the tails of their cotton dundikos flapping behind them — to herd the village's goats out into the brushlands for the day's grazing, Kunta and his mates tried to act very unconcerned, but the truth was that they envied the older boys' long shirts as much as they did their important jobs. Though he said nothing, Kunta was not alone in feeling that he was too grown up to be treated like a child and made to go naked any longer. They avoided suckling babies like Lamin as if they were diseased, and the toddlers they regarded as even more unworthy of notice, unless it was to give them a good whack when no adults were watching. Shunning even the attentions of the old grandmothers who had taken care of them for as long as they could remember, Kunta, Sitafa, and the others began to hang around grown-ups of their parents' age in hopes of being seen underfoot and perhaps sent off on an errand.

It was just before the harvest came that Omoro told Kunta very casually, one night after dinner, that he wanted him up early the next day to help guard the crops. Kunta was so excited he could hardly sleep. After gulping down his breakfast in the morning, he almost burst with joy when Omoro handed him the hoe to carry when they set out for the fields. Kunta and his mates fairly flew up and down the ripe rows, yelling and waving sticks at the wild pigs and baboons that came grunting from the brush to root or snatch up groundnuts. With dirt clods and shouts, they routed whistling flocks of blackbirds as they wheeled low over the couscous, for the grandmothers' stories had told of ripened fields ruined as quickly by hungry birds as by any animal. Collecting the handfuls of couscous and groundnuts that their fathers had cut or pulled up to test for ripeness, and carrying gourds of cool water for the men to drink, they worked all through the day with a swiftness equaled only by their pride.

Six days later, Allah decreed that the harvest should begin. After the dawn's suba prayer, the farmers and their sons — some chosen few carrying small tan-tang and souraba drums — went out to the fields and waited with heads cocked, listening. Finally, the village's great tobalo drum boomed and the farmers leaped to the harvesting. As the jaliba and the other drummers walked among them, beating out a rhythm to match their movements, everyone began to sing. In exhilaration now and then, a farmer would fling his hoe, whirling up on one drumbeat and catch it on the next.

Kunta's kafo sweated alongside their fathers, shaking the groundnut bushes free of dirt. Halfway through the morning came the first rest — and then, at midday, happy shouts of relief as the women and girls arrived with lunch. Walking in single file, also singing harvest songs, they took the pots from their heads, ladled the contents into calabashes, and served them to the drummers and harvesters, who ate and then napped until the tobalo sounded once again.

Piles of the harvest dotted the fields at the end of that first day. Streaming sweat and mud, the farmers trudged wearily to the nearest stream, where they took off their clothes and leaped into the water, laughing and splashing to cool and clean themselves. Then they headed home, swatting at the biting flies that buzzed around their glistening bodies. The closer they came to the smoke that drifted toward them from the women's kitchens, the more tantalizing were the smells of the roasted meats that would be served three times daily for however long it took to finish the harvest.

After stuffing himself that night, Kunta noticed — as he had for several nights — that his mother was sewing something. She said nothing about it, nor did Kunta ask. But the next morning, as he picked up his hoe and began to walk out the door, she looked at him and said gruffly, "Why don't you put on your clothes?"

Kunta jerked around. There, hanging from a peg, was a brand-new dundiko. Struggling to conceal his excitement, he matter-of-factly put it on and sauntered out the door — where he burst into a run. Others of his kafo were already outside — all of them, like him, dressed for the first time in their lives, all of them leaping, shouting, and laughing because their nakedness was covered at last. They were now officially of the second kafo. They were becoming men.

CHAPTER 10

By the time Kunta sauntered back into his mother's hut that night, he had made sure that everyone in Juffure had seen him in his dundiko. Though he hadn't stopped working all day, he wasn't a bit tired, and he knew he'd never be able to go to sleep at his regular bedtime. Perhaps now that he was a grown-up, Binta would let him stay up later. But soon after Lamin was asleep, the same as always, she sent him to bed — with a reminder to hang up his dundiko.

As he turned to go, sulking as conspicuously as he thought he could get away with, Binta called him back — probably to reprimand him for sulking, Kunta thought, or maybe she'd taken pity on him and changed her mind. "Your Fa

60

wants to see you in the morning," she said casually. Kunta knew better than to ask why, so he just said, "Yes, Mama," and wished her good night. It was just as well he wasn't tired, because he couldn't sleep now anyway, lying under his cowhide coverlet wondering what he had done now that was wrong, as it seemed he did so often. But racking his brain, he couldn't think of a single thing, especially nothing so bad that Binta herself wouldn't have whacked him for it, since a father would involve himself only with something pretty terrible. Finally he gave up worrying and drifted off to sleep.

At breakfast the next morning, Kunta was so subdued that he almost forgot the joy of his dundiko, until naked little Lamin happened to brush up against it. Kunta's hand jerked up to shove him away, but a flashing look from Binta prevented that. After eating, Kunta hung around for a while hoping that something more might be said by Binta, but when she acted as if she hadn't even told him anything, he reluctantly left the hut and made his way with slow steps to Omoro's hut, where he stood outside with folded hands.

When Omoro emerged and silently handed his son a small new slingshot, Kunta's breath all but stopped. He stood looking down at it, then up at his father, not knowing what to say. "This is yours as one of the second kafo. Be sure you don't shoot the wrong thing, and that you hit what you shoot at."

Kunta just said, "Yes, Fa," still tongue-tied beyond that.

"Also, as you are now second kafo," Omoro went on, "it means you will begin tending goats and going to school. You go goat-herding today with Toumani Touray. He and the other older boys will teach you. Heed them well. And tomorrow morning you will go to the schoolyard." Omoro went back into his hut, and Kunta dashed away to the goat pens, where he found his friend Sitafa and the rest of his kafo, all in their new dundikos and clutching their new slingshots — uncles or older brothers having made them for boys whose fathers were dead.

The older boys were opening the pens

and the bleating goats were bounding forth, hungry for the day's grazing. Seeing Toumani, who was the first son of the couple who were Omoro's and Binta's best friends, Kunta tried to get near him, but Toumani and his mates were all herding the goats to bump into the smaller boys, who were trying to scramble out of the way. But soon the laughing older boys and the wuolo dogs had the goats hurrying down the dusty path with Kunta's kafo running uncertainly behind, clutching their slingshots and trying to brush the dirtied spots off their dundikos.

As familiar with goats as Kunta was, he had never realized how fast they ran. Except for a few walks with his father, he had never been so far beyond the village as the goats were leading them — to a wide grazing area of low brush and grass with the forest on one side and the fields of village farmers on the other. The older boys each nonchalantly set their own herds to grazing in separate grassy spots, while the wuolo dogs walked about or lay down near the goats.

Toumani finally decided to take notice

of Kunta tagging along behind him, but he acted as if the smaller boy was some kind of insect. "Do you know the value of a goat?" he asked, and before Kunta could admit he wasn't sure, he said, "Well, if you lose one, your father will let you know!" And Toumani launched into a lecture of warnings about goatherding. Foremost was that if any boy's attention or laziness let any goat stray away from its herd, no end of horrible things could happen. Pointing toward the forest, Toumani said that, for one thing, living just over there, and often creeping on their bellies through the high grass, were lions and panthers, which, with but a single spring from the grass, could tear a goat apart. "But if a boy is close enough," said Toumani, "he is tastier than a goat!"

Noting Kunta's wide eyes with satisfaction, Toumani went on: Even a worse danger than lions and panthers were toubob and their black slatee helpers, who would crawl through the tall grass to grab people and take them off to a distant place where they were eaten. In his own five rains of goatherding, he said, nine boys from Juffure had been taken, and many more from neighboring villages. Kunta hadn't known any of the boys who had been lost from Juffure, but he remembered being so scared when he heard about them that for a few days he wouldn't venture more than a stone's throw from his mother's hut.

"But you're not safe even inside the village gates," said Toumani, seeming to read his thoughts. A man he knew from Juffure, he told Kunta, deprived of everything he owned when a pride of lions killed his entire herd of goats, had been caught with toubob money soon after the disappearance of two third-kafo boys from their own huts one night. He claimed that he had found the money in the forest, but the day before his trial by the Council of Elders, he himself had disappeared. "You would have been too young to remember this," said Toumani. "But such things still happen. So never get out of sight of somebody you trust. And when you're out here with your goats, never let them go where you might have to chase them into deep bush, or your family may never see you again."

As Kunta stood quaking with fear, Toumani added that even if a big cat or a toubob didn't get him, he could still get into serious trouble if a goat got away from the herd, because a boy could never catch a dodging goat once it got onto someone's nearby farm of couscous and groundnuts. And once the boy and his dog were both gone after it, the remaining flock might start running after the strayed one, and hungry goats could ruin a farmer's field quicker even than baboons, antelopes, or wild pigs.

By noontime, when Toumani shared the lunch his mother had packed for him and Kunta, the entire new second kafo had gained a far greater respect for the goats they had been around all of their lives. After eating, some of Toumani's kafo lounged under small trees nearby, and the rest walked around shooting birds with their students' untried slingshots. While Kunta and his mates struggled to look after the goats, the older boys yelled out cautions and insults and held their sides with laughter at the younger boys' frantic shoutings and dashings toward any goat that as much as raised its head to look around. When Kunta wasn't running after the goats, he was casting nervous glances toward the forest in case anything was lurking there to eat him.

In the midafternoon, with the goats nearing their fill of grass, Toumani called Kunta over to him and said sternly, "Do you intend me to collect your wood for you?" Only then did Kunta remember how many times he had seen the goatherds returning in the evening, each of them bearing a headload of light wood for the night fires of the village. With the goats and the forest to keep an eye on, it was all Kunta and his mates could do to run around looking for and picking up light brush and small fallen limbs that had become dry enough to burn well. Kunta piled his wood up into a bundle as large as he thought his head could carry, but Toumani scoffed and threw on a few more sticks. Then Kunta tied a slender green liana vine about the wood, doubtful that he could get it onto his head, let alone all the distance to the village.

With the older boys observing, he and his mates somehow managed to hoist their headloads and to begin more or less following the wuolo dogs and the goats, who knew the homeward trail better than their new herdsmen did. Amid the older boys' scornful laughter, Kunta and the others kept grabbing at their headloads to keep them from falling off. The sight of the village had never been prettier to Kunta, who was bone-weary by now; but no sooner had they stepped inside the village gates when the older boys set up a terrific racket, yelling out warnings and instructions and jumping around so that all of the adults within view and hearing would know that they were doing their job and that their day of training these clumsy younger boys had been a most trying experience for them. Kunta's headload somehow safely reached the yard of Brima Cesay, the arafang, whose education of Kunta and his new kafo would begin the next morning.

Just after breakfast, the new herdsmen — each, with pride, carrying a cottonwood writing slate, a quill, and a section of bamboo cane containing soot to mix with water for ink — trooped anxiously into the schoolyard. Treating them as if they were even more stupid than their goats, the arafang ordered the boys to sit down. Hardly had he uttered the words when he began laying about among them with his limber stick, sending them scrambling — their first obedience to his command not having come as quickly as he wanted. Scowling, he further warned them that for as long as they would attend his classes, anyone who made so much as a sound, unless asked to speak, would get more of the rod — he brandished it fiercely at them — and be sent home to his parents. And the same would be dealt out to any boy who was ever late for his classes, which would be held after breakfast and again just after their return with the goats.

"You are no longer children, and you have responsibilities now," said the arafang. "See to it that you fulfill them." With these disciplines established, he announced that they would begin that evening's class with his reading certain verses of the Koran, which they would be expected to memorize and recite before proceeding to other things. Then he excused them, as his older students, the former goatherds, began arriving. They looked even more nervous than Kunta's kafo, for this was the day for their final examinations in Koranic recitations and in the writing of Arabic, the results of which would bear heavily upon their being formally advanced into the status of third kafo.

That day, all on their own for the first time in their lives, Kunta's kafo managed to get the goats unpenned and trotting in a ragged line along the trail out to the grazing area. For a good while to come, the goats probably got less to eat than usual, as Kunta and his mates chased and yelled at them every time they took a few steps to a new clump of grass. But Kunta felt even more hounded than his herd. Every time he sat down to sort out the meaning of these changes in his life, there seemed to be somethng he had to do, someplace he had to go. What with the goats all day, the arafang after breakfast and after herding, and then whatever slingshot practice he could fit in before darkness, he could never seem to find the time for any serious thinking any more.

CHAPTER 11

The harvesting of groundnuts and couscous was complete, and the women's rice came next. No men helped their wives; even boys like Sitafa and Kunta didn't help their mothers, for rice was women's work alone. The first light of dawn found Binta with Jankay Touray and the other women bending in their ripe fields and chopping off the long golden stalks, which were left to dry for a few days on the walkway before being loaded into canoes and taken to the village, where the women and their daughters would stack their neat bundles in each family's storehouse. But there was no rest for the women even when the rice harvesting was done, for then they had to help the men to pick the cotton, which had been left until last so that it would dry as long as possible under the hot sun and thus make better thread for the women's sewing.

With everyone looking forward to Juffure's annual seven-day harvest festival, the women hurried now to make new clothes for their families. Though Kunta knew better than to show his irritation, he was forced for several evenings to tend his talky, pesty little brother Lamin while Binta spun her cotton. But Kunta was happy again when she took him with her to the village weaver, Dembo Dibba, whom Kunta watched in fascination as her rickety hand-and-foot loom wove the spindles of thread into strips of cotton cloth. Back at home, Binta let Kunta trickle water through wood ashes to make the strong lye into which she mixed finely pounded indigo leaves to dye her cloth deep blue. All of Juffure's women were doing the same, and soon their cloth was spread across low bushes to dry, festooning the village with splashes of rich color — red, green, and yellow as well as blue.

While the women spun and sewed, the men worked equally hard to finish their own appointed tasks before the harvest festival — and before the hot season made heavy work impossible. The village's tall bamboo fence was patched where it was sagging or broken from the back-scratching of the goats and bullocks. Repairs were made on mud huts that had been damaged by the big rains, and new thatching replaced the old and worn. Some couples, soon to marry, required new homes, and Kunta got the chance to join the other children in stomping water-soaked dirt into the thick, smooth mud that the men used to mold walls for the new huts.

Since some muddy water had begun to appear in the buckets that were pulled up from the well, one of the men climbed down and found that the small fish that was kept in the well to eat insects had died in the murky water. So it was decided that a new well must be dug. Kunta was watching as the men reached shoulder depth in the new hole, and passed upward several egg-sized lumps of a greenish-white clay. They were taken immediately to those women of the village whose bellies were big, and eaten eagerly. That clay,

Binta told him, would give a baby stronger bones.

Left to themselves, Kunta, Sitafa, and their mates spent most of their free hours racing about the village playing hunter with their new slingshots. Shooting at nearly everything — and fortunately hitting almost nothing — the boys made enough noise to scare off a forest of animals. Even the smaller children of Lamin's kafo romped almost unattended, for no one in Juffure was busier than the old grandmothers, who worked often now until late at night to supply the demands of the village's unmarried girls for hair-pieces to wear at the harvest festival. Buns, plaits, and full wigs were woven of long fibers picked carefully from rotting sisal leaves or from the soaked bark of the baobab tree. The coarser sisal hairpieces cost much less than those made from the softer, silkier fiber of the baobab whose weaving took so much longer that a full wig might cost as much as three goats. But the customers always haggled long and loudly, knowing that the grandmothers charged less if they enjoyed an hour or so of good, tongue-clacking bargaining before each sale.

Along with her wigs, which were especially well made, old Nyo Boto pleased every woman in the village with her noisy defiance of the ancient tradition that decreed women should always show men the utmost of respect. Every morning found her squatted comfortably before her hut, stripped to the waist, enjoying the sun's heat upon her tough old hide and busily weaving hairpieces — but never so busily that she failed to notice every passing man. "Hah!" she would call out, "Look at that! They call themselves men! Now, in *my* day, men were *men!*" And the men who passed — expecting what always came — would all but run to escape her tongue, until finally Nyo Boto fell asleep in the afternoon, with her weaving in her lap and the toddlers in her care laughing at her loud snoring.

The second-kafo girls, meanwhile, were helping their mothers and big sisters to collect bamboo baskets full of ripe medicinal roots and cooking spices, which they spread under the sun to dry. When grains were being pounded, the girls brushed away the husks and chaff. They helped also with the family washing, beating against rocks the soiled clothing that had been lathered with the rough, reddish soap the mothers had made from lye and palm oil.

The men's main work done — only a few days before the new moon that would open the harvest festival in all of The Gambia's villages — the sounds of musical instruments began to be heard here and there in Juffure. As the village musicians practiced on their twenty-four-stringed koras, their drums, and their balafons — melodious instruments made of gourds tied beneath wooden blocks of various lengths that were struck with mallets — little crowds would gather around them to clap and listen. While they played, Kunta and Sitafa and their mates, back from their goatherding, would troop about blowing bamboo flutes, ringing bells, and rattling dried gourds.

Most men relaxed now, talking and squatting about in the shade of the baobab. Those of Omoro's age and younger kept respectfully apart from the Council of Elders, who were making their annual prefestival decisions on important village business. Occasionally two or three of the younger men would rise, stretch themselves, and go ambling about the village with their small fingers linked loosely in the age-old yayo manner of African men.

But a few of the men spent long hours alone, patiently carving on pieces of wood of different sizes and shapes. Kunta and his friends would sometimes even put aside their slings just to stand watching as the carvers created terrifying and mysterious expressions on masks soon to be worn by festival dancers. Others carved human or animal figures with the arms and legs very close to the body, the feet flat, and the heads erect.

Binta and the other women snatched what little relaxation they could around the village's new well, where they came every day for a cool drink and a few minutes of gossip. But with the festival now upon them, they still had much to do. Clothing had to be finished, huts to be cleaned, dried foods to be soaked, goats to be slaughtered for roasting. And above all, the women had to make themselves look their very best for the festival.

Kunta thought that the big tomboyish girls he had so often seen scampering up trees looked foolish now, the way they went about acting coy and fluttery. They couldn't even walk right. And he couldn't see why the men would turn around to watch them — clumsy creatures who couldn't even shoot a bow and arrow if they tried.

Some of these girls' mouths, he noticed, were swelled up to the size of a fist, where the inner lips had been pricked with thorns and rubbed black with soot. Even Binta, along with every other female in the village over twelve rains old, was nightly boiling and then cooling a broth of freshly pounded fudano leaves in which she soaked her feet — and the pale palms of her hands — to an inky blackness. When Kunta asked his mother why, she told him to run along. So he asked his father, who told him, "The more blackness a woman has, the more beautiful she is."

"But why?" asked Kunta.

"Someday," said Omoro, "you will understand."

CHAPTER 12

Kunta leaped up when the tobalo sounded at dawn. Then he, Sitafa, and their mates were running among grown-ups to the silk-cotton tree, where the village drummers were already pounding on the drums, barking and shouting at them as if they were live things, their hands a blur against the taut goatskins. The gathering crowd of costumed villagers, one by one, soon began to respond with slow movements of their arms, legs, and bodies, then faster and faster, until almost everyone had joined the dancing.

Kunta had seen such ceremonies for many plantings and harvests, for men leaving to hunt, for weddings, births, and deaths, but the dancing had never moved him — in a way he neither understood nor was able to resist — as it did now. Every adult in the village seemed to be saying with his body something that was in his or her mind alone. Among the whirling, leaping, writhing people, some of them wearing masks, Kunta could scarcely believe his eyes when he saw tough old Nyo Boto suddenly shrieking wildly, jerking both of her hands before her face, then lurching backward in fear at some unseen terror. Snatching up an imaginary burden, she thrashed and kicked the air until she crumpled down.

Kunta turned this way and that, staring at different people he knew among the dancers. Under one of the horrifying masks, Kunta recognized the alimamo, flinging and winding himself again and again like some serpent around a tree trunk. He saw that some of those he had heard were even older than Nyo Boto had left their huts, stumbling out on spindly legs, their wrinkled arms flapping, their rheumy eyes squinting in the sun, to dance a few unsteady steps. Then Kunta's eyes widened as he caught sight of his own father. Omoro's knees were churning high, his feet stomping up dust. With ripping cries, he reared backward, muscles trembling, then lunged forward, hammering at his chest, and went leaping and twisting in the air, landing with heavy grunts.

The pounding heartbeat of the drums seemed to throb not only in Kunta's ears but also in his limbs. Almost without knowing it, as if it were a dream, he felt his body begin to quiver and his arms to flail, and soon he was springing and shouting along with the others, whom he had ceased to notice. Finally he stumbled and fell, exhausted.

He picked himself up and walked with weak knees to the sidelines — feeling a deep strangeness that he had never known before. Dazed, frightened, and excited, he saw not only Sitafa but also others of their kafo out there dancing among the grown-ups, and Kunta danced again. From the very young to the very old, the villagers danced on through the entire day, they and the drummers stopping for neither food nor drink but only to catch fresh breath. But the drums were still beating when Kunta collapsed into sleep that night.

The festival's second day began with a parade for the people of honor just after the noon sun. At the head of the parade were the arafang, the alimamo, the senior elders, the hunters, the wrestlers, and those others whom the Council of Elders had named for their important deeds in Juffure since the last harvest festival. Everyone else came trailing behind, singing and applauding, as the musicians led them out in a snaking line beyond the village. And when they made a turn around the travelers' tree, Kunta and his kafo dashed ahead, formed their own parade, and then trooped back and forth past the marching adults, exchanging bows and smiles as they went, stepping briskly in time with their flutes, bells, and rattles. The parading boys took turns at being the honored person; when it was Kunta's turn, he pranced about, lifting his knees high, feeling very important indeed. In passing the grown-ups, he caught both Omoro's and Binta's eyes and knew they were proud of their son.

The kitchen of every woman in the village offered a variety of food in open invitation to anyone who passed by and wished to stop a moment and enjoy a plateful. Kunta and his kafo gorged themselves from many calabashes of delicious stews and rice. Even roasted meats — goats and game from the forest — were in abundance; and it was the young girls' special duty to keep bamboo baskets filled with every available fruit.

When they weren't stuffing their bellies, the boys darted out to the travelers' tree to meet the exciting strangers who now entered the village. Some stayed overnight, but most tarried only a few hours before moving on to the next village's festival. The visiting Senegalese set up colorful displays with bolts of decorated cloth. Others arrived with heavy sacks of the very best-quality Nigerian kola nuts, the grade and size of each determining the price. Traders came up the bolong in boats laden with salt bars to exchange for indigo, hides, beeswax, and honey. Nyo Boto was herself now busily selling — for a cowrie shell apiece — small bundles of cleaned and trimmed lemongrass roots, whose regular rubbing against the teeth kept the breath sweet and the mouth fresh.

Pagan traders hurried on past Juffure, not even stopping, for their wares of tobacco and snuff and mead beer were for infidels only, since the Moslem Mandinkas never drank nor smoked. Others who seldom stopped, bound as they were for bigger villages, were numerous footloose young men from other villages — as some young men had also left Juffure during the harvest season. Spotting them as they passed on the path beyond the village, Kunta and his mates would run alongside them for a while trying to see what they carried in their small bamboo headbaskets. Usually it was clothing and small gifts for new friends whom they expected to meet in their wanderings, before returning to their home villages by the next planting season.

Every morning the village slept and awakened to the sound of drums. And every day brought different traveling musicians — experts on the Koran, the balafon, and the drums. And if they were flattered enough by the gifts that were pressed upon them, along with the dancing and the cheers and clapping of the crowds, they would stop and play for a while before moving on to the next village.

When the story-telling griots came, a quick hush would fall among the villagers as they sat around the baobab to hear of ancient kings and family clans, of warriors, of great battles, and of legends of the past. Or a religious griot would shout prophecies and warnings that Almighty Allah must be appeased, and then offer to conduct the necessary — and by now, to Kunta, familiar — ceremonies in return for a small gift. In his high voice, a singing griot sang endless verses about the past splendors of the kingdoms of Ghana, Songhai, and Old Mali, and when he finished, some people of the village would often privately pay him to sing the praises of their own aged parents at their huts. And the people would applaud when the old ones came to their doorways and stood blinking in the bright sunshine with wide, toothless grins. His good deeds done, the singing griot reminded everyone that a drumtalk message — and a modest offering — would quickly bring him to Juffure any time to sing anyone's praises at funerals, weddings, or other special occasions. And then he hurried on to the next village.

It was during the harvest festival's sixth afternoon when suddenly the sound of a strange drum cut through Juffure. Hearing the insulting words spoken by the drum, Kunta hurried outside and joined the other villagers as they gathered angrily beside the baobab. The drum, obviously quite nearby, had warned of oncoming wrestlers so mighty that any so-called wrestlers in Juffure should hide. Within minutes, the people of Juffure cheered as their own drum sharply replied that such foolhardy strangers were asking to get crippled, if not worse.

The villagers rushed now to the wrestling place. As Juffure's wrestlers slipped into their brief dalas with the rolled-cloth handholds on the sides and buttocks, and smeared themselves with a slippery paste of pounded baobab leaves and wood ashes, they heard the shouts that meant that their challengers had arrived. These powerfully built strangers never glanced at the jeering crowd. Trotting behind their drummer, they went directly to the wrestling area, clad already in their dalas, and began rubbing one another with their own slippery paste. When Juffure's wrestlers appeared behind the village drummers, the crowd's shouting and jostling became so unruly that both drummers had to implore them to remain calm.

Then both drums spoke: "Ready!" The rival teams paired off, each two wrestlers crouching and glaring face to face. "Take hold! Take hold!" the drums ordered, and each pair of wrestlers began a catlike circling. Both of the drummers now went darting here and there among the stalking men; each drummer was pounding out the names of that village's ancestral champion wrestlers, whose spirits were looking on.

With lightning feints, one after another pair finally seized hold and began to grapple. Soon both teams struggled amid the dust clouds their feet kicked up, nearly hiding them from the wildly yelling spectators. Dogfalls or slips didn't count; a victory came only when one wrestler pulled another off balance, thrust him bodily upward, and hurled him to the ground. Each time there came a fall — first one of Juffure's champions, then one of the challengers — the crowd jumped and screamed, and a drummer pounded out that winner's name. Just beyond the excited crowd, of course, Kunta and his mates were wrestling among themselves.

At last it was over, and Juffure's team had won by a single fall. They were awarded the horns and hooves of a freshly slaughtered bullock. Big chunks of the meat were put to roast over a fire, and the brave challengers were invited warmly to join the feasting. The people congratulated the visitors on their strength, and unmarried maidens tied small bells around all of the wrestlers' ankles and upper arms. And during the feasting that followed, Juffure's third-kafo boys swept and brushed to smoothness the wrestling area's reddish dust to prepare it for a seoruba.

The hot sun had just begun to sink when the people again assembled around the wrestling area, now all dressed in their best. Against a low background of drums, both wrestling teams leaped into the ring and began to crouch and spring about, their muscles rippling and their little bells tinkling as the onlookers admired their might and grace. The drums suddenly pounded hard; now the maidens ran out into the ring, weaving coyly among the wrestlers as the people clapped. Then the drummers began to beat their hardest and fastest rhythm — and the maidens' feet kept pace.

One girl after another, sweating and exhausted, finally stumbled from the ring, flinging to the dust her colorfully dyed tiko headwrap. All eyes watched eagerly to see if the marriageable man would pick up that tiko, thus showing his special appreciation of that maiden's dance — for it could mean he meant soon to consult her father about her bridal price in goats and cows. Kunta and his mates, who were too young to understand such things, thought the excitement was over and ran off to play with their slingshots. But it had just begun, for a moment later, everyone gasped as a tiko was picked up by one of the visiting wrestlers. This was a major event — and a happy one — but the lucky maiden would not be the first who was lost through marriage to another village.

CHAPTER 13

On the final morning of the festival, Kunta was awakened by the sound of screams. Pulling on his dundiko, he went dashing out, and his stomach knotted with fright. Before several of the nearby huts, springing up and down, shrieking wildly and brandishing spears, were half a dozen men in fierce masks, tall headdresses, and costumes of leaf and bark. Kunta watched in terror as one man entered each hut with a roar and emerged jerking roughly by the arm a trembling boy of the third kafo.

Joined by a cluster of his own equally terrified second-kafo mates, Kunta peered with wide eyes around the corner of a hut. A heavy white cotton hood was over the head of each third-kafo boy. Spying Kunta, Sitafa, and their group of little

93

boys, one of the masked men dashed toward them waving his spear and shouting fearfully. Though he stopped short and turned back to his hooded charge, the boys scattered, squealing in horror. And when all of the village's third-kafo boys had been collected, they were turned over to slaves, who took them by the hand and led them, one by one, out the village gate.

Kunta had heard that these older boys were going to be taken away from Juffure for their manhood training, but he had no idea that it would happen like this. The departure of the third-kafo boys, along with the men who would conduct their manhood training, cast a shadow of sadness upon the entire village. In the days that followed, Kunta and his mates could talk of nothing but the terrifying things they had seen, and of the even more terrifying things they had overheard about the mysterious manhood training. In the mornings, the arafang rapped their heads for their lack of interest in memorizing the Koranic verses. And after school, trooping along behind their goats out into the bush,

Kunta and his mates each tried not to think about what each could not forget — that he would be among Juffure's next group of hooded boys jerked and kicked out through the village gate.

They all had heard that a full twelve moons would pass before those third-kafo boys would return to the village — but then as men. Kunta said that someone had told him that the boys in manhood training got beatings daily. A boy named Karamo said they were made to hunt wild animals for food; and Sitafa said they were sent out alone at night into the deep forest, to find their own way back. But the worst thing, which none of them mentioned, although it made Kunta nervous each time he had to relieve himself, was that during the manhood training a part of his foto would be cut off. After a while, the more they talked, the idea of manhood training became so frightening that the boys stopped talking about it, and each one of them tried to conceal his fears within himself, not wanting to show that he wasn't brave.

Kunta and his mates had gotten much

better at goatherding since their first anxious days out in the bush. But they still had much to learn. Their job, they were beginning to discover, was hardest in the mornings, when swarms of biting flies kept the goats bolting this way and that, quivering their skins and switching their stubby tails as the boys and the dogs rushed about trying to herd them together again. But before noon, when the sun grew so hot that even the flies sought cooler places, the tired goats settled down to serious grazing, and the boys could finally enjoy themselves.

By now they were crack shots with their slingshots — and also with the new bows and arrows their fathers had given them on graduating to the second kafo — and they spent an hour or so killing every small creature they could find: hares, ground squirrels, bush rats, lizards, and one day a tricky spurfowl that tried to decoy Kunta away from her nest by dragging a wing as if it had been injured. In the early afternoon, the boys skinned and cleaned the day's game, rubbing the insides with the salt they always carried, and then, building a fire, roasted themselves a feast.

Each day out in the bush seemed to be hotter than the day before. Earlier and earlier, the insects stopped biting the goats to look for shade, and the goats bent down on their knees to get at the short grass that remained green beneath the parched taller grass. But Kunta and his mates hardly noticed the heat. Glistening with sweat, they played as if each day were the most exciting one in their lives. With their bellies tight after the afternoon meal, they wrestled or raced or sometimes just yelled and made faces at one another, taking turns at keeping a wary eye on the grazing goats. Playing at war, the boys clubbed and speared each other with thick-rooted weeds until someone held up a handful of grass as a sign of peace. Then they cooled off their warrior spirits by rubbing their feet with the contents of the stomach of a slaughtered rabbit; they had heard in the grandmothers' stories that real warriors used the stomach of a lamb.

Sometimes Kunta and his mates romped

with their faithful wuolo dogs, which Mandinkas had kept for centuries, for they were known as one of the very finest breeds of hunting and guard dogs in all of Africa. No man could count the goats and cattle that had been saved on dark nights from killer hyenas by the howling of the wuolos. But hyenas weren't the game stalked by Kunta and his mates when they played at being huntsmen. In their imaginations, as they crept about in the tall, sun-baked grass of the savanna, their quarry were rhinoceros, elephant, leopard, and the mighty lion.

Sometimes, as a boy followed his goats around in their search for grass and shade, he would find himself separated from his mates. The first few times it happened to him, Kunta herded up his goats as quickly as he could and headed back to be near Sitafa. But soon he began to like these moments of solitude, for they gave him the chance to stalk some great beast by himself. It was no ordinary antelope, leopard, or even lion that he sought in his daydreaming; it was that most feared and dangerous of all beasts — a maddened buffalo.

The one he tracked had spread so much terror throughout the land that many hunters had been sent to kill the savage animal, but they had managed only to wound it, and one after another, it had gored them with its wicked horns. Even more bloodthirsty than before with its painful wound, the buffalo had then charged and killed several farmers from Juffure who had been working on their fields outside the village. The famed simbon Kunta Kinte had been deep in the forest, smoking out a bee's nest to sustain his energy with rich honey, when he heard the distant drumtalk begging him to save the people of the village of his birth. He could not refuse.

Not even a blade of the dry grass crackled under his feet, so silently did he stalk for signs of the buffalo's trail, using the sixth sense that told master simbons which way animals would travel. And soon he found the tracks he sought; they were larger than any he had ever seen. Now trotting silently, he drew deeply into his nostrils the foul smell that led him to giant, fresh buffalo dung. And maneuvering now with all the craft and skill at his command, simbon Kinte finally spotted the huge bulk of the beast himself — it would have been concealed from ordinary eyes — hiding in the dense, high grass.

Straining back his bow, Kinte took careful aim — and sent the arrow thudding home. The buffalo was badly wounded now, but more dangerous than ever. Springing suddenly from side to side, Kinte evaded the beast's desperate, stricken charge and braced himself as it wheeled to charge again. He fired his second arrow only when he had to leap aside at the last instant — and the huge buffalo crashed down dead.

Kinte's piercing whistle brought from hiding, awed and trembling, those previous hunters who had failed where he had gloriously succeeded. He ordered them to remove the huge hide and horns and to summon still more men to drag the carcass all the way back to Juffure. The joyously shouting people had laid down a pathway of hides within the village gate so that Kinte would not get dust upon his feet. "Simbon Kinte!" the talking drum beat out. "Simbon Kinte!" the children shouted, waving leafy branches above their heads. Everyone was pushing and shoving and trying to touch the mighty hunter so that some of his prowess might rub off on them. Small boys danced around the huge carcass, reenacting the kill with wild cries and long sticks.

And now, walking toward him from amid the crowd, came the strongest, most graceful, and most beautifully black of all the maidens in Juffure — indeed, in all of The Gambia — and kneeling before him, she offered a calabash of cool water; but Kinte, not thirsty, merely wet his fingers, to favor her, whereupon she drank that water with happy tears, thus showing to everyone the fullness of her love.

The clamoring crowd was spreading — making way for aged, wrinkled, gray-headed Omoro and Binta, who came tottering against their canes. The simbon permitted his old mother to embrace him while Omoro looked on, eyes filled with pride. And the people of Juffure chanted "Kinte! Kinte!" Even the dogs were barking their acclaim.

Was that his own wuolo dog barking? "Kinte! Kinte!" Was that Sitafa yelling frantically? Kunta snapped out of it just in time to see his forgotten goats bounding toward someone's farm. Sitafa and his other mates and their dogs helped to herd them up again before any damage was done, but Kunta was so ashamed that a whole moon went by before he drifted off into any more such daydreams.

CHAPTER 14

As hot as the sun already was, the five long moons of the dry season had only begun. The heat devils shimmered, making objects larger in the distance, and the people sweated in their huts almost as much as they did in the fields. Before Kunta left home each morning for his goatherding, Binta saw that he protected his feet well with red palm oil, but each afternoon, when he returned to the village from the open bush, his lips were parched and the soles of his feet were dry and cracked by the baking earth beneath them. Some of the boys came home with bleeding feet, but out they would go again each morning — uncomplaining, like their fathers — into the fierce heat of the dry grazing land, which was even worse than in the village.

By the time the sun reached its zenith, the boys and their dogs and the goats all lay panting in the shade of scrub trees, the boys too tired to hunt and roast the small game that had been their daily sport. Mostly, they just sat and chatted as cheerfully as they could, but somehow by this time the adventure of goatherding had lost some of its excitement.

It didn't seem possible that the sticks they gathered every day would be needed to keep them warm at night, but once the sun set, the air turned as cold as it had been hot. And after their evening meal, the people of Juffure huddled around their crackling fires. Men of Omoro's age sat talking around one fire, and a little distance away was the fire for the elders. Around still another sat the women and the unmarried girls, apart from the old grandmothers, who told their nightly stories to the little first-kafo children around a fourth fire.

Kunta and the other second-kafo boys were too proud to sit with the naked first kafo of Lamin and his mates, so they squatted far enough away not to seem part of that noisy, giggling group — yet near enough to hear the old grandmother's stories, which still thrilled them as much as ever. Sometimes Kunta and his mates eavesdropped on those at other fires; but the conversations were mostly about the heat. Kunta heard the old men recalling times when the sun had killed plants and burned crops; how it had made the well go stale, or dry, of times when the heat had dried the people out like husks. This hot season was bad, they said, but not as bad as many they could remember. It seemed to Kunta that older people always could remember something worse.

Then, abruptly one day, breathing the air was like breathing flames, and that night the people shivered beneath their blankets with the cold creeping into their bones. Again the next morning they were mopping their faces and trying to draw a full breath. That afternoon the harmattan wind began. It wasn't a hard wind, nor even a gusty wind, either of which would have helped. Instead, it blew softly and steadily, dusty and dry, day and night, for nearly half a moon. As it did each time it came, the constant blowing of the harmattan wore away slowly at the nerves of the people of Juffure. And soon parents were yelling more often than usual at their children, and whipping them for no good reason. And though bickering was unusual among the Mandinkas, hardly a daytime hour passed without loud shoutings between some adults, especially between younger husbands and wives like Omoro and Binta. Suddenly then nearby doorways would fill with people watching as the couple's mothers went rushing into that hut. A moment later the shouting would grow louder, and next a rain of sewing baskets, cooking pots, calabashes, stools, and clothes would be hurled out the door. Then, bursting out themselves, the wife and her mother would snatch up the possessions and go storming off to the mother's hut.

After about two moons, just as it had begun, the harmattan suddenly stopped. In less than a day, the air became still, the sky clear. Within one night, a parade of wives slipped back in with their husbands, and their mothers-in-law were exchanging small gifts and patching up arguments all over the village. But the five long moons of the dry season were only half over. Though food was still plentiful in the storehouses, the mothers only cooked small quantities, for no one, not even the usually greedy children, felt like eating much. Everyone was sapped of strength by the sun's heat, and the people talked less and went about doing only the things they had to do.

The hides of the gaunt cattle in the village were broken by lumpy sores where biting flies had laid their eggs. A quietness had come upon the scrawny chickens that normally ran squawking around the village, and they lay in the dust on their sides, with their wings fanned out and their beaks open. Even the monkeys now were seldom seen or heard, for most of them had gone into the forest for more shade. And the goats, Kunta noticed, grazing less and less in the heat, had grown nervous and thin.

For some reason — perhaps it was the heat, or perhaps simply because they were growing older — Kunta and his goatherding mates, who had spent every day together out in the bush for almost six moons, now began to drift off alone with their own small herds. It had happened for several days before Kunta realized that he had never before been completely away from other people for any real length of time. He looked across at other boys and their goats in the distance, scattered across the silence of the sunbaked bush. Beyond them lay the fields where the farmers were chopping the weeds that had grown in the moons since the last harvest. The tall piles of weeds they raked to dry under the sun seemed to wave and shimmer in the heat.

Wiping the sweat from his brow, it seemed to Kunta that his people were always enduring one hardship or another — something uncomfortable or difficult, or frightening, or threatening to life itself. He thought about the burning, hot days and the cold nights that followed them. And he thought about the rains that would come next, turning the village into a mudhole and finally submerging the walking paths until the people had to travel in their canoes from place to place where usually they walked. They needed the rain as they needed the sun, but there always seemed to be too much or too little. Even when the goats were fat and the trees were heavy with fruit and blossoms, he knew that would be the time when the last rain's harvest would run out in the family storehouses and that this would bring the hungry season, with people starving and some even dying, like his own dearly remembered Grandma Yaisa.

The harvest season was a happy one — and after that, the harvest festival — but it was over so soon, and then the long, hot dry season would come again, with its awful harmattan, when Binta kept shouting at him and beating on Lamin — until he almost felt sorry for his pest of a small brother. As he herded his goats back toward the village, Kunta remembered the stories he had heard so many times when he was as young as Lamin, about how the forefathers had always lived through great fears and dangers. As far back as time went, Kunta guessed, the lives of the people had been hard. Perhaps they always would be.

Each evening in the village now, the alimamo led the prayers for Allah to send the rains. And then one day, excitement filled Juffure when some gentle winds stirred up the dust — for those winds meant that the rains were soon to come. And the next morning, the people of the village gathered out in the fields, where the farmers set afire the tall piles of weeds they had raked up, and thick smoke coiled up over the fields. The heat was nearly unbearable, but the sweating people danced and cheered, and the first-kafo children went racing and whooping about, each trying to catch good-luck pieces of drifting, feathery flakes of ashes.

The next day's light winds began to sift the loose ashes over the fields, enriching the soil to grow yet another crop. The farmers now began chopping busily with their hoes, preparing the long rows to receive the seeds — in this seventh planting time through which Kunta had lived in the endless cycle of the seasons.

CHAPTER 15

Two rains had passed, and Binta's belly was big again, and her temper was even shorter than usual. So quick was she to whack both her sons, in fact, that Kunta was grateful each morning when goatherding let him escape her for a few hours, and when he returned in the afternoon, he couldn't help feeling sorry for Lamin, who was only old enough to get into mischief and get beaten but not old enough to get out of the house alone. So one day when he came home and found his little brother in tears, he asked Binta — not without some misgivings — if Lamin could join him on an errand, and she snapped "Yes!" Naked little Lamin could hardly contain his happiness over this amazing act of kindness, but Kunta was so disgusted with his own impulsiveness that he gave him a good kick and a cuffing as soon as they got beyond Binta's earshot. Lamin hollered — and then followed his brother like a puppy.

Every afternoon after that, Kunta found Lamin waiting anxiously at the door in hopes that his big brother would take him out again. Kunta did, nearly every day — but not because he wanted to. Binta would profess such great relief at getting some rest from both of them that Kunta now feared a beating if he didn't take Lamin along. It seemed as if a bad dream had attached his naked little brother to Kunta's back like some giant leech from the bolong. But soon Kunta began to notice that some of the kafo mates also had small brothers tagging along behind them. Though they would play off to one side or dart about nearby, they always kept a sharp eye on their big brothers, who did their best to ignore them. Sometimes the big boys would dash off suddenly, jeering back at the young ones as they scrambled to catch up with them.

When Kunta and his mates climbed trees, their little brothers, trying to follow, usually tumbled back to the ground, and the older boys would laugh loudly at their clumsiness. It began to be fun having them around.

Alone with Lamin, as he sometimes was, Kunta might pay his brother a bit more attention. Pinching a tiny seed between his fingers, he would explain that Juffure's giant silk-cotton tree grew from a thing that small. Catching a honeybee, Kunta would hold it carefully for Lamin to see the stinger; then, turning the bee around, he would explain how bees sucked the sweetness from flowers and used it to make honey in their nests in the tallest trees. And Lamin began to ask Kunta a lot of questions, most of which he would patiently answer. There was something nice about Lamin's feeling that Kunta knew everything. It made Kunta feel older than his eight rains. In spite of himself, he began to regard his little brother as something more than a pest.

Kunta took great pains not to show it, of course, but returning homeward now each afternoon with his goats, he really looked forward to Lamin's eager reception. Once Kunta thought that he even saw Binta smile as he and Lamin left the hut. In fact, Binta would often snap at her younger son, "Have your brother's manners!" The next moment, she might whack Kunta for something, but not as often as she used to. Binta would also tell Lamin that if he didn't act properly, he couldn't go with Kunta, and Lamin would be very good for the rest of the day.

He and Lamin would always leave the hut now walking very politely, hand in hand, but once outside, Kunta went dashing and whooping — with Lamin racing behind him — to join the other second- and first-kafo boys. During one afternoon's romping, when a fellow goatherd of Kunta's happened to run into Lamin, knocking him on his back, Kunta was instantly there, shoving that boy roughly aside and exclaiming hotly, "That's my brother!" The boy protested and they were ready to exchange blows when the others grabbed their arms. Kunta snatched the crying Lamin by the hand

and jerked him away from their staring playmates. Kunta was both deeply embarrassed and astonished at himself for acting as he had toward his own kafo mate — and especially over such a thing as a sniffling little brother. But after that day, Lamin began openly trying to imitate whatever he saw Kunta do, sometimes even with Binta or Omoro looking on. Though he pretended not to like it, Kunta couldn't help feeling just a little proud.

When Lamin fell from a low tree he was trying to climb one afternoon, Kunta showed him how to do it right. At one time or another, he taught his little brother how to wrestle (so that Lamin could win the respect of a boy who had humiliated him in front of his kafo mates); how to whistle through his fingers (though Lamin's best whistle was nowhere near as piercing as Kunta's); and he showed him the kind of berry leaves from which their mother liked to make tea. And he cautioned Lamin to take the big, shiny dung beetles they always saw crawling in the hut and set them gently outside on the ground, for it was very bad luck to harm them. To touch a rooster's spur, he told him, was even worse luck. But however hard he tried, Kunta couldn't make Lamin understand how to tell the time of day by the position of the sun. "You're just too little, but you'll learn." Kunta would still shout at him sometimes, if Lamin seemed too slow in learning something simple; or he would give him a slap if he was too much of a pest. But he would always feel so badly about it that he might even let the naked Lamin wear his dundiko for a while.

As he grew closer to his brother, Kunta began to feel less deeply something that had often bothered him before — the gulf between his eight rains and the older boys and men of Juffure. Indeed, scarcely a day of his life that he could remember had ever passed without something to remind him that he was still of the second kafo — one who yet slept in the hut of his mother. The older boys who were away now at manhood training had always had nothing but sneers and cuffings for those of Kunta's age. And the grown men, such as Omoro and the other fathers, acted as if a second-kafo boy were something merely to be tolerated. As for the mothers, well, often when Kunta was out in the bush, he would think angrily that whenever he got to be a man, he certainly intended to put Binta in her place as a woman — although he did intend to show her kindness and forgiveness, since after all, she was his mother.

Most irritating of all to Kunta and his mates, though, was how the second-kafo girls with whom they had grown up were now so quick to remind them that they were thinking already of becoming wives. It rankled Kunta that girls married at fourteen rains or even younger, while boys didn't get married until they were men of thirty rains or more. In general, being of the second kafo had always been an embarrassment to Kunta and his mates, except for their afternoons off by themselves in the bush, and in Kunta's case, his new relationship with Lamin.

Every time he and his brother would be walking somewhere by themselves, Kunta would imagine that he was taking Lamin on some journey, as men sometimes did with their sons. Now, somehow, Kunta felt a special responsibility to act older, with Lamin looking up to him as a source of knowledge. Walking alongside, Lamin would ply Kunta with a steady stream of questions.

"What's the world like?"

"Well," said Kunta, "no man or canoes ever journeyed so far. And no one knows all there is to know about it."

"What do you learn from the arafang?"

Kunta recited the first verses of the Koran in Arabic and then said, "Now you try." But when Lamin tried, he got badly confused — as Kunta had known he would — and Kunta said paternally, "It takes time."

"Why does no one harm owls?"

"Because all our dead ancestors' spirits are in owls." Then he told Lamin something of their late Grandma Yaisa. "You were just a baby, and cannot remember her."

"What's that bird in the tree?"

"A hawk."

"What does he eat?"

"Mice and other birds and things."

"Oh."

Kunta had never realized how much he knew — but now and then Lamin asked something of which Kunta knew nothing at all.

"Is the sun on fire?" Or: "Why doesn't our father sleep with us?"

At such times, Kunta would usually grunt, then stop talking — as Omoro did when he tired of so many of Kunta's questions. Then Lamin would say no more, since Mandinka home training taught that one never talked to another who did not want to talk. Sometimes Kunta would act as if he had gone into deep private thought. Lamin would sit silently nearby, and when Kunta rose, so would he. And sometimes, when Kunta didn't know the answer to a question, he would quickly do something to change the subject.

Always, at his next chance, Kunta would wait until Lamin was out of the hut and then ask Binta or Omoro the answer he needed for Lamin. He never told them why he asked them both so many questions, but it seemed as if they knew.

In fact, they seemed to act as if they had begun to regard Kunta as an older person, since he had taken on more responsibility with his little brother. Before long, Kunta was speaking sharply to Lamin in Binta's presence about things done wrongly. "You must talk clearly!" he might say with a snap of his fingers. Or he might whack Lamin for not jumping swiftly enough to do anything his mother had ordered him to do. Binta acted as if she neither saw nor heard.

So Lamin made few moves now without either his mother's or his brother's sharp eyes upon him. And Kunta now had only to ask Binta or Omoro any questions of Lamin's and they immediately told him the answer.

"Why is father's bullock's hide mat of that red color? A bullock isn't red."

"I dyed the hide of the bullock with lye and crushed millet," replied Binta.

"Where does Allah live?"

"Allah lives where the sun comes from," said Omoro.

CHAPTER 16

"What are slaves?" Lamin asked Kunta one afternoon. Kunta grunted and fell silent. Walking on, seemingly lost in thought, he was wondering what Lamin had overheard to prompt that question. Kunta knew that those who were taken by toubob became slaves, and he had overheard grown-ups talking about slaves who were owned by people in Juffure. But the fact was that he really didn't know what slaves *were*. As had happened so many other times, Lamin's question embarrassed him into finding out more.

The next day, when Omoro was getting ready to go out after some palm wood to build Binta a new food storehouse, Kunta asked to join his father; he loved to go off anywhere with Omoro. But neither spoke this day until they had almost reached the dark, cool palm grove.

Then Kunta asked abruptly, "Fa, what are slaves?"

Omoro just grunted at first, saying nothing, and for several minutes moved about in the grove, inspecting the trunks of different palms.

"Slaves aren't always easy to tell from those who aren't slaves," he said finally. Between blows of his bush ax against the palm he had selected, he told Kunta that slaves' huts were roofed with nyantang jongo and free people's huts with nyantang foro, which Kunta knew was the best quality of thatching grass.

"But one should never speak of slaves in the presence of slaves," said Omoro, looking very stern. Kunta didn't understand why, but he nodded as if he did.

When the palm tree fell, Omoro began chopping away its thick, tough fronds. As Kunta plucked off for himself some of the ripened fruits, he sensed his father's mood of willingness to talk today. He thought happily how now he would be able to explain to Lamin all about slaves.

"Why are some people slaves and others not?" he asked.

Omoro said that people became slaves in different ways. Some were born of slave mothers — and he named a few of those who lived in Juffure, people whom Kunta knew well. Some of them were the parents of some of his own kafo mates. Others, said Omoro, had once faced starvation during their home villages' hungry season, and they had come to Juffure and begged to become the slaves of someone who agreed to feed and provide for them. Still others — and he named some of Juffure's older people — had once been enemies and been captured as prisoners. "They became slaves, being not brave enough to die rather than be taken," said Omoro.

He had begun chopping the trunk of the palm into sections of a size that a strong man could carry. Though all he had named were slaves, he said, they were all respected people, as Kunta well knew. "Their rights are guaranteed by the laws of our forefathers," said Omoro, and he explained that all masters had to provide their slaves with food, clothing, a house, a farm plot to work on half shares, and also a wife or husband.

"Only those who permit themselves to be are despised," he told Kunta — those who had been made slaves because they were convicted murderers, thieves, or other criminals. These were the only slaves whom the master could beat or otherwise punish, as he felt they deserved.

"Do slaves have to remain slaves always?" asked Kunta.

"No, many slaves buy their freedom with what they save from farming on half share with their masters." Omoro named some in Juffure who had done this. He named others who had won their freedom by marrying into the family that owned them.

To help him carry the heavy sections of palm, Omoro made a stout sling out of green vines, and as he worked, he said that some slaves, in fact, prospered beyond their masters. Some had even taken slaves for themselves, and some had become very famous persons.

"Sundiata was one!" exclaimed Kunta.

Many times, he had heard the grandmothers and the griots speaking of the great forefather slave general whose army had conquered so many enemies.

Omoro grunted and nodded, clearly pleased that Kunta knew this, for Omoro also had learned much of Sundiata when he was Kunta's age. Testing his son, Omoro asked, "And who was Sundiata's mother?"

"Sogolon, the Buffalo Woman!" said Kunta proudly.

Omoro smiled, and hoisting onto his strong shoulders two heavy sections of the palm pole within the vine sling, he began walking. Eating his palm fruits, Kunta followed, and nearly all the way back to the village, Omoro told him how the great Mandinka Empire had been won by the crippled, brilliant slave general whose army had begun with runaway slaves found in swamps and other hiding places.

"You will learn much more of him when you are in manhood training," said Omoro — and the very thought of that time sent a fear through Kunta, but also a thrill of anticipation.

Omoro said that Sundiata had run away from his hated master, as most slaves did who didn't like their masters. He said that except for convicted criminals, no slaves could be sold unless the slaves approved of the intended master.

"Grandmother Nyo Boto also is a slave," said Omoro, and Kunta almost swallowed a mouthful of palm fruit. He couldn't comprehend this. Pictures flashed across his mind of beloved old Nyo Boto squatting before the door of her hut, tending the village's twelve or fifteen naked babies while weaving baskets of twigs, and giving the sharp side of her tongue to any passing adult — even the elders, if she felt like it. "That one is nobody's slave," he thought.

The next afternoon, after he had delivered his goats to their pens, Kunta took Lamin home by a way that avoided their usual playmates, and soon they squatted silently before the hut of Nyo Boto. Within a few moments the old lady appeared in her doorway, having sensed that she had visitors. And with but a glance at Kunta, who had always been one of her very favorite children, she knew that something special was on his mind. Inviting the boys inside her hut, she set about the brewing of some hot herb tea for them.

"How are your papa and mama?" she asked.

"Fine. Thank you for asking," said Kunta politely. "And you are well, Grandmother?"

"I'm quite fine, indeed," she replied.

Kunta's next words didn't come until the tea had been set before him. Then he blurted, "Why are you a slave, Grandmother?"

Nyo Boto looked sharply at Kunta and Lamin. Now it was she who didn't speak for a few moments. "I will tell you," she said finally.

"In my home village one night, very far from here and many rains ago, when I was a young woman and wife," Nyo Boto said, she had awakened in terror as flaming grass roofs came crashing down among her screaming neighbors. Snatching up her own two babies, a boy and a girl, whose father had recently died in a tribal

war, she rushed out among the others —
and awaiting them were armed white slave
raiders with their black slatee helpers. In a
furious battle, all who didn't escape were
roughly herded together, and those who
were too badly injured or too old or too
young to travel were murdered before the
others' eyes, Nyo Boto began to sob, "—
including my own two babies and my aged
mother."

As Lamin and Kunta clutched each
other's hands, she told them how the
terrified prisoners, bound neck-to-neck
with thongs, were beaten and driven
across the hot, hard inland country for
many days. And every day, more and
more of the prisoners fell beneath the
whips that lashed their backs to make
them walk faster. After a few days, yet
more began to fall of hunger and
exhaustion. Some struggled on, but those
who couldn't were left for the wild
animals to get. The long line of prisoners
passed other villages that had been burned
and ruined, where the skulls and bones of
people and animals lay among the burned-
out shells of thatch and mud that had

once been family huts. Fewer than half of those who had begun the trip reached the village of Juffure, four days from the nearest place on the Kamby Bolongo where slaves were sold.

"It was here that one young prisoner was sold for a bag of corn," said the old woman. "That was me. And this was how I came to be called Nyo Boto," which Kunta knew meant "bag of corn." The man who bought her for his own slave died before very long, she said, "and I have lived here ever since."

Lamin was wriggling in excitement at the story, and Kunta felt somehow even greater love and appreciation than he had felt before for old Nyo Boto, who now sat smiling tenderly at the two boys, whose father and mother, like them, she had once dandled on her knee.

"Omoro, your papa, was of the first kafo when I came to Juffure," said Nyo Boto, looking directly at Kunta. "Yaisa, his mother, who was your grandmother, was my very good friend. Do you remember her?" Kunta said that he did and added proudly that he had told his little brother all about their grandma.

"That is good!" said Nyo Boto. "Now I must get back to work. Run along, now."

Thanking her for the tea, Kunta and Lamin left and walked slowly back to Binta's hut, each deep in his own private thoughts.

The next afternoon, when Kunta returned from his goatherding, he found Lamin filled with questions about Nyo Boto's story. Had any such fire ever burned in Juffure? he wanted to know. Well, he had never heard of any, said Kunta, and the village showed no signs of it. Had Kunta ever seen one of those white people? "Of course not!" he exclaimed. But he said that their father had spoken of a time when he and his brothers had seen the toubob and their ships at a point along the river.

Kunta quickly changed the subject, for he knew very little about toubob, and he wanted to think about them for himself. He wished that he could *see* one of them — from a safe distance, of course, since everything he'd ever heard about them made it plain that people were better off who never got too close to them.

Only recently a girl out gathering herbs — and before her two grown men out hunting — had disappeared, and everyone was certain that toubob had stolen them away. He remembered, of course, how when drums of other villages warned that toubob had either taken somebody or was known to be near, the men would arm themselves and mount a double guard while the frightened women quickly gathered all of the children and hid in the bush far from the village — sometimes for several days — until the toubob was felt to be gone.

Kunta recalled once when he was out with his goats in the quiet of the bush, sitting under his favorite shade tree. He had happened to look upward and there, to his astonishment, in the tree overhead, were twenty or thirty monkeys huddled along the thickly leaved branches as still as statues, with their long tails hanging down. Kunta had always thought of monkeys rushing noisily about, and he couldn't forget how quietly they had been watching his every move. He wished that now *he* might sit in a tree and watch some toubob on the ground below him.

The goats were being driven homeward the afternoon after Lamin had asked him about toubob when Kunta raised the subject among his fellow goatherds — and in no time they were telling about the things they had heard. One boy, Demba Conteh, said that a very brave uncle had once gone close enough to *smell* some toubob, and they had a peculiar stink. All of the boys had heard that toubob took people away to eat them. But some had heard that the toubob claimed the stolen people were not eaten, only put to work on huge farms. Sitafa Silla spat out his grandfather's answer to that: "White man's lie!"

The next chance he had, Kunta asked Omoro, "Papa, will you tell me how you and your brothers saw the toubob at the river?" Quickly, he added, "The matter needs to be told correctly to Lamin." It seemed to Kunta that his father nearly smiled, but Omoro only grunted, evidently not feeling like talking at that moment.

But a few days later, Omoro casually invited both Kunta and Lamin to go with him out beyond the village to collect some roots he needed. It was the naked Lamin's first walk anywhere with his father, and he was overjoyed. Knowing that Kunta's influence had brought this about, he held tightly onto the tail of his big brother's dundiko.

Omoro told his sons that after their manhood training, his two older brothers Janneh and Saloum had left Juffure, and the passing of time brought news of them as well-known travelers in strange and distant places. Their first return home came when drumtalk all the way from Juffure told them of the birth of Omoro's first son. They spent sleepless days and nights on the trail to attend the naming ceremony. And gone from home so long, the brothers joyously embraced some of their kafo mates of boyhood. But those few sadly told of others gone and lost — in burned villages, some killed by fearsome firesticks, some kidnaped, some missing while farming, hunting, or traveling — and all because of toubob.

Omoro said that his brothers had then angrily asked him to join them on a trip to see what the toubob were doing, to see what might be done. So the three brothers trekked for three days along the banks of the Kamby Bolongo, keeping carefully concealed in the bush, until they found what they were looking for. About twenty great toubob canoes were moored in the river, each big enough that its insides might hold all the people of Juffure, each with a huge white cloth tied by ropes to a treelike pole as tall as ten men. Nearby was an island, and on the island was a fortress.

Many toubob were moving about, and black helpers were with them, both on the fortress and in small canoes. The small canoes were taking such things as dried indigo, cotton, beeswax, and hides to the big canoes. More terrible than he could describe, however, said Omoro, were the beatings and other cruelties they saw being dealt out to those who had been captured for the toubob to take away.

For several moments, Omoro was quiet, and Kunta sensed that he was pondering something else to tell him. Finally he spoke: "Not as many of our people are being taken away now as then." When Kunta was a baby, he said, the King of Barra, who ruled this part of The Gambia, had ordered that there would be no more burning of villages with the capturing or killing of all their people. And soon it did stop, after the soldiers of some angry kings had burned the big canoes down to the water, killing all the toubob on board.

"Now," said Omoro, "nineteen guns are fired in salute to the King of Barra by every toubob canoe entering the Kamby Bolongo." He said that the King's personal agents now supplied most of the people whom the toubob took away — usually criminals or debtors, or anyone convicted for suspicion of plotting against the king — often for little more than whispering. More people seemed to get convicted of crimes, said Omoro, whenever toubob ships sailed in the Kamby Bolongo looking for slaves to buy.

"But even our king cannot stop the stealings of some people from their villages," Omoro continued. "You have known some of those lost from our village, three from among us just within the past few moons, as you know, and you have heard the drumtalk from other villages." He looked hard at his sons, and spoke slowly. "The things I'm going to tell you now, you must hear with more than your ears — for not to do what I say can mean your being stolen away forever!" Kunta and Lamin listened with rising fright. "Never be alone when you can help it," said Omoro. "Never be out at night when you can help it. And day or night, when you're alone, keep away from any high weeds or bush if you can avoid it."

For the rest of their lives, "even when you have come to be men," said their father, they must be on guard for toubob. "He often shoots his firesticks, which can be heard far off. And wherever you see much smoke away from any villages, it is probably his cooking fires, which are too big. You should closely inspect his signs to learn which way the toubob went. Having much heavier footsteps than we do, he leaves signs you will recognize as not ours:

He breaks twigs and grasses. And when you get close where he has been, you will find that his scent remains there. It's like a wet chicken smells. And many say a toubob sends forth a nervousness that we can feel. If you feel that, become quiet, for often he can be detected at some distance."

But it's not enough to know the toubob, said Omoro. "Many of our own people work for him. They are slatee traitors. But without knowing them, there is no way to recognize them. In the bush, therefore, trust *no* one you don't know."

Kunta and Lamin sat frozen with fear. "You cannot be told these things strongly enough," said their father. "You must know what your uncles and I saw happening to those who had been stolen. It is the difference between slaves among ourselves and those whom toubob takes away to be slaves for him." He said that they saw stolen people chained inside long, stout, heavily guarded bamboo pens along the shore of the river. When small canoes brought important-acting toubob from the big canoes, the stolen people were dragged outside their pens onto the sand.

"Their heads had been shaved, and they had been greased until they shined all over. First they were made to squat and jump up and down," said Omoro. "And then, when the toubob had seen enough of that, they ordered the stolen people's mouths forced open for their teeth and their throats to be looked at."

Swiftly, Omoro's finger touched Kunta's crotch, and as Kunta jumped, Omoro said, "Then the men's foto was pulled and looked at. Even the women's private parts were inspected." And the toubob finally made the people squat again and stuck burning hot irons against their backs and shoulders. Then, screaming and struggling, the people were shipped toward the water, where small canoes waited to take them out to the big canoes.

"My brothers and I watched many fall onto their bellies, clawing and eating the sand, as if to get one last hold and bite of their own home," said Omoro. "But they were dragged and beaten on." Even in the small canoes out in the water, he told

Kunta and Lamin, some kept fighting against the whips and the clubs until they jumped into the water among terribly long fish with gray backs and white bellies and curved mouths full of thrashing teeth that reddened the water with their blood.

Kunta and Lamin had huddled close to each other, each gripping the other's hands. "It's better that you know these things than that your mother and I kill the white cock one day for you." Omoro looked at his sons. "Do you know what that means?"

Kunta managed to nod, and found his voice. "When someone is missing, Fa?" He had seen families frantically chanting to Allah as they squatted around a white cock bleeding and flapping with its throat slit.

"Yes," said Omoro. "If the white cock dies on its breast, hope remains. But when a white cock flaps to death on its back, then *no* hope remains, and the whole village joins the family in crying to Allah."

"Fa —" Lamin's voice, squeaky with fear, startled Kunta, "where do the big canoes take the stolen people?''

"The elders say to Jong Sang Doo," said Omoro, "a land where slaves are sold to huge cannibals called toubabo koomi, who eat us. No man knows any more about it.''

CHAPTER 17

So frightened was Lamin by his father's talk of slave-taking and white cannibals that he awakened Kunta several times that night with his bad dreams. And the next day, when Kunta returned from goatherding, he decided to turn his little brother's mind — and his own — from such thoughts by telling him about their distinguished uncles.

"Our father's brothers are also the sons of Kairaba Kunta Kinte, for whom I am named," said Kunta proudly. "But our uncles Janneh and Saloum were born of Sireng," he said. Lamin looked puzzled, but Kunta kept on explaining. "Sireng was our grandfather's first wife, who died before he married our Grandma Yaisa." Kunta arranged twigs on the ground to show the Kinte family's different individuals. But he could see that Lamin still didn't understand. With a sigh, he began to talk instead of their uncles' adventures, which Kunta himself had thrilled to so often when his father had told of them.

"Our uncles have never taken wives for themselves because their love of traveling is go great," said Kunta. "For moons on end, they travel under the sun and sleep under the stars. Our father says they have been where the sun burns upon endless sand, a land where there is never any rain." In another place their uncles had visited, said Kunta, the trees were so thick that the forests were dark as night even in the daytime. The people of this place were no taller than Lamin, and like Lamin, always went naked — even after they grew up. And they killed huge elephants with tiny, poisoned darts. In still another place, a land of giants, Janneh and Saloum had seen warriors who could throw their hunting spears twice as far as the mightiest Mandinka, and dancers who could leap higher than their own heads, which were six hands higher than the tallest man in Juffure.

Before bedtime, as Lamin watched with wide eyes, Kunta acted out his favorite of all the stories — springing suddenly about with an imaginary sword slashing up and down, as if Lamin were one of the bandits whom their uncles and others had fought off every day on a journey of many moons, heavily laden with elephants' teeth, precious stones, and gold, to the great black city of Zimbabwe.

Lamin begged for more stories, but Kunta told him to go to sleep. Whenever Kunta had been made to go to bed after his father told him such tales, he would lie on his mat — as his little brother now would — with his mind making the uncles' stories into pictures. And sometimes Kunta would even dream that he was traveling *with* his uncles to all the strange places, that he was talking with the people who looked and acted and lived so differently from the Mandinkas. He had only to hear the names of his uncles and his heart would quicken.

A few days later, it happened that their

names reached Juffure in a manner so exciting that Kunta could hardly contain himself. It was a hot, quiet afternoon, and just about everyone in the village was sitting outside his hut's doorway or in the shade of the baobab — when suddenly there came a sharp burst of drumtalk from the next village. Like the grown-ups, Kunta and Lamin cocked their heads intently to read what the drum was saying. Lamin gasped aloud when he heard his own father's name. He wasn't old enough to understand the rest, so Kunta whispered the news it brought: Five days of walking in the way the sun rose, Janneh and Saloum Kinte were building a new village. And their brother Omoro was expected for the ceremonial blessing of the village on the second next new moon.

The drumtalk stopped; Lamin was full of questions. "Those are *our* uncles? Where is that place? Will our *fa* go there?" Kunta didn't reply. Indeed, as Kunta dashed off across the village toward the hut of the jaliba, he barely heard his brother. Other people were already gathering there — and then came Omoro,

144

with the big-bellied Binta behind him. Everyone watched as Omoro and the jaliba spoke briefly, and Omoro gave him a gift. The talking drum lay near the small fire, where its goatskin head was heating to extreme tautness. Soon the crowd looked on as the jaliba's hands pounded out Omoro's reply that, Allah willing, he would be in his brothers' new village before the second next new moon. Omoro went nowhere during the next days without other villagers pressing upon him their congratulations and their blessings for the new village, which history would record as founded by the Kinte clan.

It wasn't many days before Omoro was to depart when an idea that was almost too big to think about seized upon Kunta. Was it remotely possible that his papa might let him share the journey? Kunta could think of nothing else. Noticing his unusual quietness, Kunta's fellow goatherds, even Sitafa, left him alone. And toward his adoring little brother, he became so short-tempered that even Lamin drew away, hurt and puzzled. Kunta knew how he was acting and felt badly, but he couldn't help himself.

He knew that now and then some lucky boy was allowed to share a journey with his father, uncle, or grown-up brother. But he also knew that such boys had never been so young as his eight rains, except for some fatherless boys, who got special privileges under the forefathers' laws. Such a boy could start following closely behind any man, and the man would never object to sharing whatever he had — even if he was on a journey lasting for moons — so long as the boy followed him at exactly two paces, did everything he was told, never complained, and never spoke unless spoken to.

Kunta knew not to let anyone, especially his mother, even suspect what he dreamed of. He felt certain that not only would Binta disapprove, but she would also probably forbid his ever mentioning it again, and that would mean Omoro would never know how desperately Kunta hoped he could go. So Kunta knew that his only hope lay in asking Fa himself — if he could ever catch him alone.

There were soon but three days before

Omoro was to leave, and the watchful, almost despairing Kunta was herding his goats after breakfast when he saw his father leaving Binta's hut. Instantly he began maneuvering his goats into milling back and forth, going nowhere, until Omoro had gone on in a direction and to a distance that Binta surely wouldn't see. Then, leaving his goats alone, because he had to take the chance, Kunta ran like a hare and came to a breathless stop and looked up pleadingly at his father's startled face. Gulping, Kunta couldn't remember a single thing he had meant to say.

Omoro looked down at his son for a long moment, and then he spoke. "I have just told your mother," he said — and walked on.

It took Kunta a few seconds to realize what his father meant. "Aieee!" Kunta shouted, not even aware that he had shouted. Dropping onto his belly, he sprang froglike into the air — and bolting back to his goats, sent them racing toward the bush.

When he collected himself enough to tell

his fellow goatherds what had happened, they were so jealous that they went off by themselves. But by midday they could no longer resist the chance to share with him the excitement of such wonderful luck. By that time he had fallen silent with the realization that ever since the drumtalk message had come, his father had been thinking about his son.

Late that afternoon, when Kunta raced happily home and into his mother's hut, Binta grabbed him without a word and began to cuff him so hard that Kunta fled, not daring to ask what he had done. And her manner changed suddenly toward Omoro in a way that shocked Kunta almost as much. Even Lamin knew that a woman was absolutely never allowed to disrespect a man, but with Omoro standing where he could plainly hear her, Binta loudly muttered her disapproval of his and Kunta's traveling in the bush when the drums of different villages were reporting regularly of new people missing. Fixing the breakfast couscous, she pounded the pestle into the mortar so furiously that the sound was like drums.

As Kunta was hurrying out of the hut the next day — to avoid another whacking — Binta commanded Lamin to stay behind and began to kiss and pat and hug him as she hadn't done since he was a baby. Lamin's eyes told Kunta his embarrassment, but there was nothing either of them could do about it.

When Kunta was outside the hut away from his mother, practically every adult who saw him offered congratulations upon his being Juffure's youngest boy ever given the honor of sharing an elder's long journey, Kunta said, "Thank you," reflecting his proper home-training — but once out in the bush beyond the sight of grown-ups, he pranced under an extra-large headbundle he had brought along to show his mates how well he balanced it — and would balance it the next morning when he strutted past the travelers' tree behind his father. It fell to the ground three times before he took as many steps.

On his way homeward, with many things he wanted to do around the village before leaving, Kunta felt a strange pull to visit old Nyo Boto before doing anything else. After delivering his goats, he escaped from Binta's hut as quickly as he could and went to squat before Nyo Boto's. Shortly she appeared in her doorway. "I have expected you," she said, inviting him inside. As usual, whenever Kunta visited her alone, the two of them just sat quietly for a while. He had always liked and looked forward to that feeling. Although he was very young and she was very old, they still felt very close to each other, just sitting there in the dim hut, each of them thinking private thoughts.

"I have something for you," said Nyo Boto finally. Moving to the dark pouch of cured bullock's hide that hung from the wall by her bed, she withdrew a dark saphie charm of the kind that encircled one's upper arm. "Your grandfather blessed this charm when your father went to manhood training," said Nyo Boto. "It was blessed for the manhood training of Omoro's first son — yourself. Your Grandma Yaisa left it with me for when your manhood training would start. And that is really this journey with your *fa*."

Kunta looked with love at the dear old grandmother, but he couldn't think of a right way to say how the saphie charm would make him feel that she was with him no matter how far away he went.

The next morning, returning from prayers at the mosque, Omoro stood waiting impatiently as Binta took her time completing the adjustment of Kunta's headload. When Kunta had laid awake too filled with excitement to sleep through the night, he had heard her sobbing. Then suddenly she was hugging Kunta so hard that he could feel her body trembling, and he knew, more than ever before in his life, how much his mother really loved him.

With his friend Sitafa, Kunta had carefully reviewed and practiced what he and his father now did: First Omoro and then Kunta made two steps out into the dust beyond the doorway of his hut. Then, stopping and turning and bending down, they scraped up the dust of their first footprints and put it into their hunters' bags, thus insuring that their footprints would return to that place.

Binta watched, weeping, from her hut's

doorway, pressing Lamin against her big belly, as Omoro and Kunta walked away. Kunta started to turn for a last look — but seeing that his father didn't, kept his eyes front and marched on, remembering that it wasn't proper for a man to show his emotions. As they walked through the village, the people they passed spoke to them and smiled, and Kunta waved at his kafo mates, who had delayed their rounding up of the goats in order to see him off. He knew they understood that he didn't return their spoken greetings because any talking now was taboo for him. Reaching the travelers' tree, they stopped, and Omoro added two more narrow strips to the weather-tattered hundreds already hanging from the lower limbs, each strip representing the prayer of the traveler that his journey would be safe and blessed.

Kunta couldn't believe it was really happening. It was the first time in his life he would spend a night away from his mother's hut, the first time he would ever go farther from the gates of Juffure than one of his goats had strayed, the first

152

time — for so many things. While Kunta was thus preoccupied, Omoro had turned and without a word or a backward glance, started walking very fast down the path into the forest. Almost dropping his headload, Kunta raced to catch up with him.

CHAPTER 18

Kunta found himself nearly trotting to keep the proper two paces behind Omoro. He saw that almost two of his quick, short steps were necessary for each long, smooth stride of his father. After about an hour of this, Kunta's excitement had waned almost as much as his pace. His headbundle began to feel heavier and heavier, and he had a terrible thought: Suppose he grew so tired he couldn't keep up? Fiercely, he told himself he would drop in his tracks before that would happen.

Here and there, as they passed, snuffling wild pigs would go rushing into the underbush, and partridges would whir up, and rabbits would bound for cover. But Kunta wouldn't have paid an elephant much attention in his determination to keep up with Omoro. The muscles below Kunta's knees were beginning to ache a little. His face was sweating, and so was his head; he could tell by the way his bundle began sliding off balance, a little bit one way or the other, and he kept having to put both his hands up there to readjust it.

Ahead, after a while, Kunta saw that they were approaching the travelers' tree of some small village. He wondered what village it was; he was sure he would know its name if his father said it, but Omoro had neither spoken nor looked back ever since they left Juffure. A few minutes later, Kunta saw dashing out to meet them — as he himself had once done — some naked children of the first kafo. They were waving and hallooing, and when they got closer, he could see their eyes widen at the sight of one so young traveling with his father.

"Where are you going?" they chattered, scampering on either side of Kunta. "Is he your *fa?*" "Are you Mandinka?" "What's your village?" Weary as he was,

Kunta felt very mature and important, ignoring them just as his father was doing.

Near every travelers' tree, the trail would fork, one leading on into the village and the other past it, so that a person with no business there could pass on by without being considered rude. As Omoro and Kunta took the fork that passed by this village, the little children exclaimed unhappily, but the grown-ups seated under the village baobab only threw glances at the travelers, for holding everyone's attention was a griot whom Kunta could hear loudly orating about the greatness of Mandinkas. There would be many griots, praise singers, and musicians at the blessing of his uncles' new village, Kunta thought.

The sweat began to run into Kunta's eyes, making him blink to stop the stinging. Since they had begun walking, the sun had crossed only half the sky, but his legs already hurt so badly, and his headload had become so heavy, that he began to think he wasn't going to make it. A feeling of panic was rising in him when Omoro suddenly stopped and swung his

156

headload to the ground alongside a clear pool at the side of the trail. Kunta stood for a moment trying to control his unsteady legs. He clutched his headbundle to take it down, but it slipped from his fingers and fell with a bump. Mortified, he knew his father had heard — but Omoro was on his knees drinking from the spring, without a sign that his son was even there.

Kunta hadn't realized how thirsty he was. Hobbling over to the water's edge, he kneeled down to drink — but his legs refused the position. After trying again in vain, he finally lay down on his stomach, braced himself on his elbows, and managed to lower his mouth to the water.

"Just a little." It was the first time his father had spoken since they left Juffure, and it shocked Kunta. "Swallow a little, wait, then a little more." For some reason, he felt angry toward his father. "Yes, Fa," he intended to say, but no sound came. He sipped some cool water and swallowed it. Making himself wait, he wanted to collapse. After sipping a little more, he sat up and rested beside the pool. The thought passed through his mind that manhood training must be something like this. And then, sitting upright, he drifted off to sleep.

When he awakened with a start — how long had it been? — Omoro was nowhere to be seen. Jumping up, Kunta saw the big headload under a nearby tree; so his father wouldn't be far away. As he began to look around, he realized how sore he was. He shook himself and stretched. The muscles hurt, but he felt much better than he had. Kneeling for a few more gulps of water from the spring, Kunta noticed his reflection in the still surface of the pool — a narrow black face with wide eyes and mouth. Kunta smiled at himself, then grinned with all his teeth showing. He couldn't help laughing, and as he looked up — there was Omoro standing at his side. Kunta sprang up, embarrassed but his father's attention seemed to be on other things.

In the shade of some trees, neither of them speaking a word, as the monkeys chattered and the parrots screeched above their heads, they ate some of the bread from their headloads, along with the four plump wood pigeons Omoro had shot with his bow and roasted while Kunta slept. As they ate, Kunta told himself that the first time there was any chance, he was going to show his father how well he too could kill and cook food, the way he and his kafo mates did out in the bush.

When they finished eating, the sun was three fourths across the sky, so it wasn't as hot when the headloads were retied and readjusted on their heads and they set out on the trail once again.

"Toubob brings his canoes one day of walking from here," said Omoro when they had gone a good distance. "Now is daytime when we can see, but we must avoid high bush and grass, which can hide surprises." Omoro's finger touched his knife sheath and his bow and arrows. "Tonight we must sleep in a village."

With his father, he need not fear, of course, but Kunta felt a flash of fright after a lifetime of hearing people and drums tell of disappearances and stealings. As they walked on — a little faster now — Kunta noticed hyena dung on the trail, its color lily-white because hyenas with their strong jaws cracked and ate so many bones. And beside the path, their approach caused a herd of antelope to stop eating and stand like statues, watching until the humans had passed by.

"Elephants!" said Omoro, a little later, and Kunta saw the surrounding trampled bush, the young saplings stripped to bare bark and limbs, and some half-uprooted trees the elephants had leaned on to push the topmost tender leaves downward where they could reach them with their trunks. Since elephants never grazed near villages and people, Kunta had seen only a few of them in his life, and then only from a great distance. They had been among the thousands of forest animals that ran together, sounding like thunder, ahead of frightening black smoke clouds when a great fire had swept across the brushland once when Kunta was very young; but Allah's rain had put it out before it harmed Juffure or any other nearby villages.

As they trudged along the seemingly endless trail, it occurred to Kunta that just as people's walking feet made trails, so did spiders spin the long, thin threads they traveled on. Kunta wondered if Allah willed matters for the insects and the animals as He did for people; it surprised him to realize he never had thought about that before. He wished he could ask Omoro about it right now. He was even more surprised that Lamin hadn't asked him about it, for Lamin had asked him about even smaller matters than insects. Well, he would have much to tell his little brother when he returned to Juffure — enough to fill days out in the bush with his fellow goatherds for moons to come.

It seemed to Kunta that he and Omoro were entering a different kind of country than the one where they lived. The sinking sun shone down on heavier grasses than he had ever seen before, and among the familiar trees were large growths of palm and cactus. Apart from the biting flies, the only flying things he saw here were not pretty parrots and birds such as those that squawked and sang around Juffure, but circling hawks in search of prey and vultures hunting for food already dead.

The orange ball of the sun was nearing the earth when Omoro and Kunta sighted a thick trail of smoke from a village up ahead. As they reached the travelers' tree, even Kunta could tell that something wasn't right. Very few prayer strips hung from the limbs, showing that few of those who lived here ever left their village and that most travelers from other villages had taken the trail that passed it by. Alas, no children came running out to meet them.

As they passed by the village baobab, Kunta saw that it was partly burned. Over half of the mud huts he could see were empty; trash was in the yards; rabbits were hopping about; and birds were bathing in the dust. The people of the village — most of them leaning or lying about in the doorways of their huts — were almost all old or sick, and a few crying babies seemed to be the only children. Kunta saw not a person of his age — or even as young as Omoro.

Several wrinkled old men weakly received the travelers. The eldest among them, rapping his walking stick, ordered a toothless old woman to bring the travelers water and couscous; maybe she's a slave, thought Kunta. Then the old men began interrupting each other in their haste to explain what had happened to the village. Slave takers one night had stolen or killed all of their younger people, "from your rains to his!" One old man pointed at Omoro, then at Kunta. "We old they spared. We ran away into the forest."

Their abandoned village had begun going to pieces before they could bring themselves to return. They had no crops yet, and not much food or strength. "We will die out without our young people," said one of the old men. Omoro had listened closely as they talked, and his words were slow as he spoke: "My brother's village, which is four days distant, will welcome you, grandfathers."

But all of them began shaking their heads as the oldest said: "This is our village. No other well has such sweet water. No other trees' shade is as pleasant. No other kitchens smell of the cooking of our women."

The old men apologized that they had no hospitality hut to offer. Omoro assured them that he and his son enjoyed sleeping under the stars. And that night, after a simple meal of bread from their headloads, which they shared with the villagers, Kunta lay on his pallet of green, springy boughs, and thought about all he had heard. Suppose it had been Juffure, with everybody he knew dead or taken away — Omoro, Binta, Lamin, and himself too, and the baobab burned, and the yards filled with trash. Kunta made himself think about something else.

Then suddenly, in the darkness, he heard the shrieks of some forest creature caught by some ferocious animal, and he thought about people catching other people. In the distance he could also hear the howling of hyenas — but rainy season or dry, hungry or harvest, every night of his life, he had heard hyenas howling somewhere. Tonight he found their familiar cry almost comforting as he finally drifted off to sleep.

CHAPTER 19

In the first light of dawn, Kunta came awake, springing onto his feet. Standing beside his pallet was a queer old woman demanding in a high, cracked voice to know what had happened to the food she had sent him for two moons ago. Behind Kunta, Omoro spoke softly: "We wish we could tell you, Grandmother."

As they hurried on beyond the village after washing and eating, Kunta remembered an old woman in Juffure who would totter about, peering closely into anyone's face and telling him happily, "My daughter arrives tomorrow!" Her daughter had disappeared many rains before, everyone knew, and the white cock had died on its back, but all those she stopped would gently agree, "Yes, Grandmother

— tomorrow."

Before the sun was very high, they saw ahead a lone figure walking toward them on the trail. They had passed two or three other travelers the day before — exchanging smiles and greetings — but this old man, drawing near, made it clear that he wanted to talk. Pointing from the direction he had come, he said, "You may see a toubob." Behind Omoro, Kunta nearly stopped breathing. "He has many people carrying his headloads." The old man said the toubob had seen him and stopped him, but only sought help in finding out where the river began. "I told him the river begins farthest from where it ends."

"He meant you no harm?" asked Omoro.

"He acted very friendly," said the old man, "but the cat always eats the mouse it plays with."

"That's the truth!" said Omoro.

Kunta wanted to ask his father about this strange toubob who came looking for rivers rather than for people; but Omoro had bade farewell to the old man and was walking off down the footpath — as usual, without a glance to see if Kunta was behind him. This time Kunta was glad, for Omoro would have seen his son holding onto his headload with both hands while he ran painfully to catch up. Kunta's feet had begun to bleed, but he knew it would be unmanly to take notice of it, let alone mention it to his father.

For the same reason, Kunta swallowed his terror when, later that day, they rounded a turn and came upon a family of lions — a big male, a beautiful female, and two half-grown cubs — lounging in a meadow very near the path. To Kunta, lions were fearsome, slinking animals that would tear apart a goat that a boy permitted to stray too far in its grazing.

Omoro slowed his pace, and without taking his eyes from the lions, said quietly, as if sensing his son's fear, "They don't hunt or eat at this time of the day unless they're hungry. These are fat." But he kept one hand on his bow and the other by his quiver of arrows as they passed by. Kunta held his breath but kept walking, and he and the lions watched each other until they were out of sight.

He would have continued to think about them, and about the toubob, also somewhere in the area, but his aching legs wouldn't let him. By that night, he would have ignored twenty lions if they had been feeding at the place Omoro chose for them to spend the night. Kunta had barely lain down on his bed of soft branches before he was into a deep sleep — and it seemed only minutes before his father was shaking him awake in the early dawn. Though he felt as if he hadn't slept at all, Kunta watched with unconcealed admiration how swiftly Omoro skinned, cleaned, and roasted their morning meal of two hares, which he had caught in night snares. As Kunta squatted and ate the tasty meat, he thought how he and his goatherding mates used up hours of catching and cooking game, and he wondered how his father and other men ever found time to ever learn so much — about everything there was to know, it seemed.

His blistered feet, and his legs, and his back, and his neck all began to hurt again this third day on the trail — in fact, his

whole body seemed to be one dull ache —
but he pretended that manhood training
had already begun and that he would be
the last boy in his kafo to betray his pain.
When he stepped on a sharp thorn just
before midday, Kunta bravely bit his lip to
avoid crying out, but he began to limp
and fall so far behind that Omoro decided
to let him rest for a few minutes beside
the path while they ate their afternoon
meal. The soothing paste his father rubbed
into the wound made it feel better, but
soon after they began walking again, it
began to hurt — and bleed — in earnest.
Before long, however, the wound was
filled with dirt, so the bleeding stopped,
and the constant walking numbed the pain
enough to let him keep up with his father.
Kunta couldn't be sure, but it seemed to
him that Omoro had slowed down a tiny
bit. The area around the wound was ugly
and swollen by the time they stopped that
night, but his father applied another
poultice, and in the morning it looked and
felt good enough to bear his weight
without too much pain.

Kunta noticed with relief, as they set

out the next day, that they had left behind the thorn and cactus land they had been traveling through and were moving into bush country more like Juffure's, with even more trees and thickly flowering plants, and more chattering monkeys and multicolored landbirds than he had ever seen before. Breathing in the fragrant air made Kunta remember times when he had taken his little brother to catch crabs down along the banks of the bolong, where he and Lamin would wait to wave at their mother and the other women rowing homeward after work in their rice fields.

Omoro took the bypass fork at every travelers' tree, but each village's first-kafo children always raced out to meet them and to tell the strangers whatever happened to be the most exciting of the local news. In one such village, the little couriers rushed out yelling, "Mumbo jumbo! Mumbo jumbo!," and considering their job done, fled back inside the village gate. The bypassing trail went near enough for Omoro and Kunta to see the townspeople watching a masked and costumed figure brandishing a rod over the bare back of a screaming woman whom several other women held. All of the women spectators were shrieking with each blow of the rod. From discussions with his fellow goatherds, Kunta knew how a husband, if enough annoyed by a quarrelsome, troublemaking wife, could go quietly to another village and hire a mumbo jumbo to come to his village and shout fearsomely at intervals from concealment, then appear and publicly discipline that wife, after which all of the village's women were apt to act better for a time.

At one travelers' tree, no children came out to meet the Kintes. In fact, there was no one to be seen at all, and not a sound was to be heard in the silent village, except for the birds and monkeys. Kunta wondered if slave takers had come here, too. He waited in vain for Omoro to explain the mystery, but it was the chattering children of the next village who did so. Pointing back down the trail, they said that village's chief had kept on doing things his people disliked until one night not long ago, as he slept, everyone had quietly gone away with all their possessions to the homes of friends and families in other places — leaving behind an "empty chief," the children said, who was now going about promising to act better if only his people would return.

Since nighttime was near, Omoro decided to enter this village, and the crowd under the baobab was abuzz with this exciting gossip. Most felt certain that their new neighbors would return home after they had taught their chief his lesson for a few more days. While Kunta stuffed his stomach with groundnut stew over steamed rice, Omoro went to the village jaliba and arranged for a talking-drum message to his brothers. He told them to expect him by the next sundown and that traveling with him was his first son.

Kunta had sometimes daydreamed about hearing his name drum-sounding across the land, and now it had happened. It wouldn't leave his ears. Later, on the hospitality hut's bamboo bed, bone-weary as he was, Kunta thought of the other jalibas hunched over their drums pounding out his name in every village along their route to the village of Janneh and Saloum.

At every travelers' tree now, since the drums had spoken, were not only the usual naked children but also some elders and musicians. And Omoro couldn't refuse a senior elder's request to grant his village the honor of at least a brief visit. As the Kintes freshened themselves in each hospitality hut and then sat down to share food and drink in the shade of the baobab and silk-cotton trees, the adults gathered eagerly to hear Omoro's answers to their questions, and the first, second, and third kafos clustered about Kunta.

While the first kafo stared at him in silent awe, those of Kunta's rains and older, painfully jealous, asked him respectful questions about his home village and his destination. He answered them gravely with, he hoped, the same dignity as his father did their fathers' questions. By the time they left, he was sure the villagers felt they had seen a young man who had spent most of his life traveling with his father along The Gambia's long trails.

CHAPTER 20

They had tarried so long at the last village that they would have to walk faster and harder to reach their destination by sundown, as Omoro had promised his brothers. Though he sweated and ached, Kunta found it easier than before to keep his headload balanced, and he felt a new spurt of strength with each of the drumtalk messages that now filled the air with word of the arrival of griots, jalibas, senior elders, and other important people in the town ahead, each representing such distant home villages as Karantaba, Kootacunda, Pisania, and Jonkakonda, most of which Kunta had never heard of. A griot from the Kingdom of Wooli was there, said the drums, and even a prince sent by his father, the King of Barra. As

174

Kunta's cracked feet padded quickly along the hot, dusty trail, he was amazed at how famous and popular his uncles were. Soon he was all but running, not only to keep close behind the ever more rapidly striding Omoro, but also because these past few hours seemed to be taking forever.

Finally, just as the sun began to turn crimson on the western horizon, Kunta spotted smoke rising from a village not far ahead. The wide, circular pattern of the smoke told Kunta that dried baobab hulls were being burned to drive away mosquitoes. That means the village was entertaining important visitors. He felt like cheering. They had arrived! Soon he began to hear the thunder of a big ceremonial tobalo drum — being pounded, he guessed, as each new personage entered between the village gates. Intermingling was the throb of smaller tan-tang drums and the shriekings of dancers. Then the trail made a turn, and there under the rising smoke was the village. And alongside a bushy growth they saw a man who caught sight of them at the same instant and began to point and wave as if he had been posted there to await an oncoming man with a boy. Omoro waved back at the man, who immediately squatted over his drum and announced on it: "Omoro Kinte and first son —"

Kunta's feet scarcely felt the ground. The travelers' tree, soon in sight, was festooned with cloth strips, and the original single-file trail had already been widened by many feet — evidence of an already popular and busy village. The pounding of the tan-tangs grew louder and louder, and suddenly the dancers appeared, grunting and shouting in their leaf-and-bark costumes, leaping and whirling and stamping out through the village gate ahead of everyone else, all of them rushing to meet the distinguished visitors. The village's deep-voiced tobalo began to boom as two figures came running through the crowd. Ahead of Kunta, Omoro's headbundle dropped suddenly to the ground, and Omoro was running toward them. Before he knew it, Kunta's own headbundle had dropped and he was running too.

The two men and his father were hugging and pounding each other. "And this is our nephew?" Both men yanked Kunta off his feet and embraced him amid exclamations of joy. Sweeping them on to the village, the huge welcoming party cried out their greetings all around them, but Kunta saw and heard no one but his uncles. They certainly resembled Omoro, but he noticed that they were both somewhat shorter, stockier, and more muscular than his father. The older uncle Janneh's eyes had a squinting way of seeming to look a long distance, and both men moved with an almost animal quickness. They also talked much more rapidly than his father as they plied him with questions about Juffure and about Binta.

Finally, Saloum thumped his fist on Kunta's head. "Not since he got his name have we been together. And now look at him! How many rains have you, Kunta?"

"Eight, sir," he answered politely.

"Nearly ready for manhood training!" exclaimed his uncle.

All around the village's tall bamboo

fence, dry thornbushes were piled up, and concealed among them were sharp-pointed stakes to cripple any marauding animal or human. But Kunta wasn't noticing such things, and the few others of around his age who were there he saw only out of the corners of his eyes. He scarcely heard the racket of the parrots and monkeys above their heads, or the barking of the wuolo dogs underfoot, as the uncles took them on a tour of their beautiful new village. Every hut had its own private yard, said Saloum, and every woman's dry-foods storehouse was mounted directly over her cooking fire, so the smoke would keep her rice, couscous, and millet free of bugs.

Kunta almost got dizzy jerking his head toward this or that exciting sight, smell, or sound. It was both fascinating and confusing to overhear people speaking in Mandinka dialects that he couldn't understand beyond an occasional word. Like the rest of the Mandinkas — except for those as learned as the arafang — Kunta knew next to nothing of the languages of other tribes, even of those who lived nearby. But he had spent enough time around the travelers' tree to know which tribes were which. The Fulas had oval faces, longer hair, thinner lips, and sharper features, with vertical scars on their temples. The Wolof were extremely black and very reserved, the Serahuli lighter-skinned and small in stature. And the Jolas — there was no mistaking *them* — scarred their entire bodies, and their faces always seemed to wear a ferocious expression.

Kunta recognized people from all of these tribes here in the new village, but there were even more he didn't recognize. Some were haggling loudly with traders as they hawked their wares. Older women clamored over tanned hides, and younger women bargained for hairpieces made from sisal and baobab. The cry "Kola! Fine purple kola!" drew a cluster of those whose few remaining teeth were already orange-stained from chewing the nuts.

Amid friendly elbowing and pushing, Omoro was introduced to an endless stream of villagers and important persons from exciting places. Kunta marveled at his uncles' fluent talking in the strange tongues they spoke. Letting himself drift into the shifting throng, knowing that he could find his father and uncles whenever he wanted to, Kunta soon found himself among the musicians who were playing for all who felt like dancing. Next he sampled the roast antelope and beef and the groundnut stew that the village women kept bountifully supplied on tables in the baobabs' shade for anyone who wanted it. It was all right as food went, Kunta thought, but not as tasty as the succulent harvest-festival dishes prepared by the mothers of Juffure.

Seeing some women over by the well talking excitedly about something, Kunta sidled over, his ears as wide as his eyes, and heard that a very great marabout was reported to be only about half a day's travel away on the trail, journeying with his party to honor the new village, since it had been founded by sons of the late holy man Kairaba Kunta Kinte. Kunta was thrilled anew to hear his own grandfather spoken of so reverently. Unrecognized by any of the women, he heard them chatter next about his uncles. It was time they traveled less and settled down to have wives and sons, one woman said. "The only trouble they will have," said another, "is so many maidens eager to be their wives."

It was almost dark when Kunta, feeling very awkward, finally approached some boys of around his own age. But they didn't seem to mind that he had hung around the grown-ups until now. Mostly, they seemed anxious to tell Kunta how their new village had come to be. "All of our families became your uncles' friends somewhere during their travels," said one boy. All of them had been dissatisfied with their lives where they were, for one reason or another. "My grandfather didn't have enough space for all his family and his children's family to be close to him," a boy said. "Our bolong wouldn't grow good rice," said another.

His uncles, Kunta heard, began telling friends they knew an ideal place where they were thinking of building a village. And the families of Janneh and Saloum's friends were soon on the trail with their goats, chickens, pets, prayer rugs, and other possessions.

Soon it was dark and Kunta watched as the fires of the new village were lit with the sticks and branches that his new friends had collected earlier in the day. Because it was a time of celebration, they told him all the villagers and visitors would sit together around several fires, instead of the usual custom, which dictated that the men and the women and children would sit at separate fires. The alimamo would bless the gathering, they said, and then Janneh and Saloum would walk inside the circle to tell stories about their travels and adventures. In the circle with them would be the oldest visitor to the village, a senior elder from the distant upper-river of Fulladu. It was whispered that he had over a hundred rains, and would share his wisdom with all who had ears to hear.

Kunta ran to join his father at the fireside just in time to hear the alimamo's prayer. After it, no one said anything for a few minutes. Crickets rasped loudly, and the smoky fires cast dancing shadows upon the wide circle of faces. Finally, the leathery old elder spoke: "Hundreds of rains before even my earliest memories, talk reached across the big waters of an African mountain of gold. This is what first brought toubob to Africa!'' There was no gold mountain, he said, but gold beyond description had been found in streams and mined from deep shafts first in northern Guinea, then later in the forests of Ghana. "Toubob was never told where gold came from," said the old man, "for what one toubob knows, soon they all know."

Then Janneh spoke. Nearly as precious as gold in many places, he said, was salt. He and Saloum had personally seen salt and gold exchanged in equal weights. Salt was found in thick slabs under certain distant sands, and certain waters elsewhere would dry into a salty mush, which was shaped into blocks after sitting in the sun.

"There was once a *city* of salt," said the old man. "The city of Taghaza, whose people built their houses and mosques of blocks of salt."

"Tell of the strange humpbacked animals you have spoken of before now," demanded an ancient-looking old woman, daring to interrupt. She reminded Kunta of Grandmother Nyo Boto.

A hyena howled somewhere in the night as people leaned forward in the flickering light. It was Saloum's turn to speak. "Those animals that are called camels live in a place of endless sand. They find their way across it from the sun, the stars, and the wind. Janneh and I have ridden these animals for as long as three moons with few stops for water."

"But many stops to fight off the bandits!" said Janneh.

"Once we were part of a caravan of twelve thousand camels," Saloum continued. "Actually, it was many smaller caravans traveling together to protect ourselves against bandits."

Kunta saw that as Saloum spoke, Janneh was unrolling a large piece of tanned hide. The elder made an impatient gesture to two young men who sprang to throw onto the fire some dry branches. In the flaring light, Kunta and the others could follow Janneh's finger as it moved across a strange-looking drawing. "This is Africa," he said. The finger traced what he told them was "the big water" to the west, and then "the great sand desert," a place larger by many times than all of The Gambia — which he pointed out in the lower left of the drawing.

"To the north coast of Africa, the toubob ships bring porcelain, spices, cloth, horses, and countless things made by men," said Saloum. "Then, camels, and donkeys bear those goods inland to places like Sijilmasa, Ghadames, and Marrakech." The moving finger of Janneh showed where those cities were. "And as we sit here tonight," said Saloum, "there are many men with heavy headloads crossing deep forests taking our own African goods — ivory, skins, olives, dates, kola nuts, cotton, copper, precious stones — back to the toubob's ships."

Kunta's mind reeled at what he heard, and he vowed silently that someday he too would venture to such exciting places.

"The marabout!" From far out on the trail, the lookout drummer beat out the news. Quickly a formal greeting party was lined up — Janneh and Saloum as the village's founders; then the Council of

Elders, the alimamo, the arafang; then the honored representatives of other villages, including Omoro; and Kunta was placed with those of his height among the village's young ones. Musicians led them all out toward the travelers' tree, timing their approach to meet the holy man as he arrived. Kunta stared hard at the white-bearded, very black old man at the head of his long and tired party. Men, women, and children were heavily loaded with large headbundles, except for a few men herding cattle and, Kunta judged, more than a hundred goats.

With quick gestures, the holy man blessed the welcoming party and bade them rise from their knees. Then Janneh and Saloum were specially blessed, and Omoro was introduced by Janneh, and Saloum beckoned to Kunta, who went dashing up alongside them. "This is my first son," said Omoro, "who bears his holy grandfather's name."

Kunta heard the marabout speak words in Arabic over him — which he couldn't understand, except for his grandfather's name — and he felt the holy man's fingers touching his head as lightly as a butterfly's wing, and then he went dashing back among those of his own age as the marabout went to meet the others in the welcoming party, conversing with them as if he were an ordinary man. The young ones in Kunta's group began to trail away and stare at the long line of wives, children, students, and slaves who brought up the rear of the procession.

The marabout's wives and children quickly retired into guest huts. The students, taking seats on the ground and opening their headbundles, withdrew books and manuscripts — the property of their teacher, the holy man — and began reading aloud to those who gathered around each of them to listen. The slaves, Kunta noticed, didn't enter the village with the others. Remaining outside the fence, the slaves squatted down near where they had tethered the cattle and penned the goats. They were the first slaves Kunta had ever seen who kept away from other people.

The holy man could scarcely move for all the people on their knees around him.

Villagers and distinguished visitors alike pressed their foreheads to the dirt and wailed for him to hear their plaints, some of the nearest presuming to touch his garment. Some begged him to visit their villages and conduct long-neglected religious services. Some asked for legal decisions, since law and religion were companions under Islam. Fathers asked to be given meaningful names for new babies. People from villages without an arafang asked if their children might be taught by one of the holy man's students.

These students were now busily selling small squares of cured goathide, which many hands then thrust toward the holy man for him to make his mark on. A holy-marked piece of goatskin, sewn into a treasured saphie charm such as Kunta wore around his upper arm, would insure the wearer's constant nearness to Allah. For the two cowrie shells he had brought with him from Juffure, Kunta purchased a square of goathide and joined the jostling crowd that pressed in upon the marabout.

It ran through Kunta's mind that his grandfather must have been like this holy

188

man, who had the power, through Allah, to bring the rain to save a starving village, as Kairaba Kunte Kinte had once saved Juffure. So his beloved grandmas Yaisa and Nyo Boto had told him since he was old enough to understand. But only now, for the first time, did he truly understand the greatness of his grandfather — and of Islam. Only one person, thought Kunta, was going to be told why he had decided to spend his precious two cowries and now stood holding his own small square of cured goatskin waiting his turn for a holy mark. He was going to take the blessed goatskin back home and turn it over to Nyo Boto, and ask her to keep it for him until the time came to sew it into a precious saphie charm for the arm of his own first son.

CHAPTER 21

Kunta's kafo, galled with envy of his trip, and expecting that he would return to Juffure all puffed up with himself, had decided — without any of them actually saying so — to show no interest whatever in him or his travels when he returned. And so they did, thinking nothing of how heartsick it made Kunta feel to arrive home and find his lifelong mates not only acting as if he hadn't been away, but actually ending conversations if he came near, his dearest friend Sitafa acting even colder than the others. Kunta was so upset that he hardly even thought about his new infant brother, Suwadu, who had been born while he was away with Omoro.

One noon, as the goats grazed, Kunta finally decided to overlook his mates' unkindness and try to patch things up. Walking over to the other boys, who were sitting apart from him eating their lunches, he sat down among them and simply began talking. "I wish you could have been with me," he said quietly, and without waiting for their reaction, began to tell them about the trip.

He told how hard the days of walking had been, how his muscles had ached, about his fright in passing the lions. And he described the different villages he had passed through and the people who lived there. While he spoke, one of the boys jumped up to regroup his goats, and when he returned — without seeming to notice — sat down closer to Kunta. Soon Kunta's words were being accompanied by grunts and exclamations from the others, and before they knew it, just at that point in his story when he reached his uncles' new village, the time had come to drive the goats homeward.

The next morning in the schoolyard, all of the boys had to strain not to let the arafang suspect their impatience to leave. Finally out again with their goats, they huddled around Kunta, and he began to tell them about the different tribes and languages all intermingled in his uncles' village. He was in the middle of one of the tales of faraway places that Janneh and Saloum had told around the campfire — the boys hanging raptly on every word — when the stillness of the fields was broken by the ferocious barking of the wuolo dog and the shrill, terrified bleating of a goat.

Springing upright, they saw over the edge of the tall grass a great, tawny panther dropping a goat from his jaws and lunging at two of their wuolo dogs. The boys were still standing there, too shocked and scared to move, when one of the dogs was flung aside by the panther's sweeping paw — as the other dog leaped wildly back and forth, the panther crouched to spring, their horrible snarlings drowning out the frantic barking of the other dogs and the cries of the other goats, which were bounding off in all directions.

Then the boys fanned out, shouting and running, most trying to head off the goats. But Kunta bolted blindly toward his father's fallen goat. "Stop, Kunta! *No!*" screamed

192

Sitafa as he tried to stop him from running between the dogs and the panther. He couldn't catch him; but when the panther saw the two yelling boys rushing at him he backed off a few feet, then turned and raced back toward the forest with the enraged dogs at his heels.

The panther stink and the mangled nanny goat made Kunta sick — blood was running darkly down her twisted neck; her tongue lolled out; her eyes were rolled back up in her head and — most horribly — her belly was ripped wide open and Kunta could see her unborn kid inside, still slowly pulsing. Nearby was the first wuolo dog, whining in pain from its gashed side and trying to crawl toward Kunta. Vomiting where he stood, Kunta turned, ashen, and looked at Sitafa's anguished face.

Dimly, through his tears, Kunta sensed some of the other boys around him, staring at the hurt dog and the dead goat. Then slowly they all drew back — all but Sitafa, who put his arms around Kunta. None of them spoke, but the question hung in the air: How is he going to tell his father? Somehow Kunta found his voice. "Can you care for my goats?" he asked Sitafa. "I must take this hide to my father."

Sitafa went over and talked with the other boys, and two of them quickly picked up and carried off the whimpering dog. Kunta then motioned Sitafa to go away with the others. Kneeling by the dead nanny goat with his knife, Kunta cut and pulled, and cut again, as he had seen his father do it, until finally he rose with the wet hide in his hands. Pulling weeds, he covered over the nanny's carcass and the unborn kid, and started back toward the village. Once before he had forgotten his goats while herding, and he had vowed never to let it happen again. But it *had* happened again, and this time a nanny goat had been killed.

Desperately, he hoped it was a nightmare and that he'd awaken now, but the wet hide was in his hands. He wished death upon himself, but he knew his disgrace would be taken among the ancestors. Allah must be punishing him for boasting, Kunta thought with shame. He stopped to kneel toward the way the sun rose and prayed for forgiveness.

Rising, he saw that his kafo had all the

goats herded back together and were getting ready to leave the grazing area, lifting their headloads of firewood. One boy was carrying the injured dog, and two of the other dogs were limping badly. Sitafa, seeing Kunta looking toward them, put his headload down and started toward Kunta, but quickly Kunta waved him away again to go on with the rest.

Each footstep along the worn goat trail seemed to take Kunta closer to the end — the end of everything. Guilt and terror and numbness washed over him in waves. He would be sent away. He would miss Binta, Lamin, and old Nyo Boto. He would even miss the arafang's class. He thought of his late Grandma Yaisa, of his holy man grandfather whose name he bore, now disgraced; of his famous traveling uncles, who had built a village. He remembered that he had no headload of firewood. He thought of the nanny goat, whom he remembered well, always skittish and given to trotting off from the rest. And he thought of the kid not yet born. And while he thought of all these things, he could think of nothing but what he most feared to think of: his father.

His mind lurched, and he stopped, rooted, not breathing, staring ahead of him down the path. It was Omoro, running toward him. No boy would have dared tell him; how had he known?

"Are you all right?" his father asked.

Kunta's tongue seemed cleaved to the roof of his mouth. "Yes, Fa," he said finally. But by then Omoro's hand was exploring Kunta's belly, discovering that the blood soaking his dundiko wasn't Kunta's.

Straightening, Omoro took the hide and laid it on the grass. "Sit down!" he ordered, and Kunta did, trembling as Omoro sat across from him.

"There is something you need to know," said Omoro. "All men make mistakes. I lost a goat to a lion when I was of your rains."

Pulling at his tunic, Omoro bared his left hip. The pale, deeply scarred place there shocked Kunta. "I learned, and you must learn. *Never* run toward any dangerous animal!" His eyes searched Kunta's face. "Do you *hear* me?"

"Yes, Fa."

Omoro got up, took the goat's hide,

and flung it far off into the brush. "Then that is all that needs to be said."

Kunta's head reeled as he walked back to the village behind Omoro. Greater even than his guilt, and his relief, was the love he felt for his father at this moment.

CHAPTER 22

Kunta had reached his tenth rain, and the second-kafo boys his age were about to complete the schooling they had received twice daily since they were five rains old. When the day of graduation came, the parents of Kunta and his mates seated themselves in the arafang's schoolyard beaming with pride in the very front rows, even ahead of the village elders. While Kunta and the others squatted before the arafang, the village alimamo prayed. Then the arafang stood and began looking around at his pupils as they waved their hands to be asked a question. Kunta was the first boy he chose.

"What was the profession of your forefathers, Kunta Kinte?" he asked.

"Hundreds of rains ago in the land of

Mali," Kunta confidently replied, "the Kinte men were blacksmiths, and their women were makers of pots and weavers of cloth." With each pupil's correct answer, all those assembled made loud sounds of pleasure.

When the arafang asked a mathematical question: "If a baboon has seven wives, each wife has seven children, and each child eats seven groundnuts for seven days, how many nuts did the baboon steal from some man's farm?" After much frantic figuring with grass-quill pens on their cottonwood slates, the first to yelp out the right answer was Sitafa Silla, and the crowd's shouting of praise drowned out the groans of the other boys.

Next the boys wrote their names in Arabic, as they had been taught. And one by one, the arafang held up the slates for all the parents and other spectators to see for themselves what education had achieved. Like the other boys, Kunta had found the marks that talk even harder to read than they were to write. Many mornings and evenings, with the arafang rapping their knuckles, they had all wished that writing was as easy to understand as the talking drum, which even those of Lamin's age could read as if someone standing beyond sight were calling out the words.

One by one now, the arafang asked each graduate to stand. Finally came Kunta's turn. "Kunta Kinte!" With all eyes upon him, Kunta felt the great pride of his family in the front row, even of his ancestors in the burying ground beyond the village — most especially of his beloved Grandma Yaisa. Standing up, he read aloud a verse from the Koran's last page; finishing, he pressed it to his forehead and said, "Amen!" When the readings were done, the teacher shook each boy's hand and announced loudly that as their education was complete, these boys were now of the third kafo, and everyone broke out into a loud cheering. Binta and the other mothers quickly removed the covers from the bowls and calabashes they had brought, heaped with delicious foods, and the graduation ceremony ended in a feast that soon emptied both.

Omoro was waiting the next morning when Kunta came to take the family's goats out for the day's grazing. Pointing to a fine young male and female, Omoro said, "These two are your school-finishing present." Almost before Kunta could stammer out his thanks, Omoro walked away without another word — as if he gave away a pair of goats every day — and Kunta tried very hard not to seem excited. But the moment his father was out of sight, Kunta whooped so loud that his new charges jumped and started running — with all the others in hot pursuit. By the time he caught up with them and herded them out to the fields, the rest of his mates were already there — showing off their *own* new goats. Treating them like sacred animals, the boys steered their charges to only the most tender grasses, already picturing the strong young kids they would soon produce, and the kids would have soon after, until each boy had a herd as large and valuable as his father's.

Before the next new moon appeared, Omoro and Binta were among the parents who gave away a third goat — this one to the arafang as an expression of gratitude for their son's education. If they had been more prosperous, they would have been glad to give even a cow, but they knew he understood that this was beyond their means, as it was beyond the means of everyone in Juffure, which was a humble village. Indeed, some parents — new slaves with nothing saved — had little to offer but their own backs, and their grateful gift of a moon's farm work for the arafang was graciously accepted.

The passing moons soon flowed into seasons until yet another rain had passed and Kunta's kafo had taught Lamin's kafo how to be goatherds. A time long awaited now drew steadily nearer. Not a day passed that Kunta and his mates didn't feel both anxiety and joy at the approach of the next harvest festival, which would end with the taking away of the third kafo — those boys between ten and fifteen rains of age — to a place far away from Juffure, to which they would return, after four moons, as men.

Kunta and the others tried to act as if none of them were really giving the matter any particular thought or concern. But they thought of little else, and they watched and listened for the slightest sign or word from a grown-up that had anything at all to do with manhood training. And early in the dry season, after several of their fathers quietly left Juffure for two or three days and just as quietly returned, the boys whispered tensely among themselves, especially after Kalilu Conteh overheard his uncle say that much-needed repairs had been made on the jujuo, the manhood-training village that had gone unused and exposed to weather and animals for almost five rains since the last training had been completed there. Even more excited whispering followed talk among their fathers about which elder might be selected by the Council of Elders to be the kintango, the man in charge of manhood training. Kunta and all of his mates had many times heard their fathers, uncles, and older brothers speaking reverently of the kintangos who had supervised their own manhood training many rains before.

It was just before the harvest season when all of the third-kafo boys reported to one another in a fever of excitement how their mothers had silently measured each of them with a sewing tape around his head and down to his shoulders. Kunta did his best to hide the vivid memory of that morning five rains before when, as brand-new little goatherds, he and his mates had been scared nearly out of their wits as they watched screaming boys under white hoods being kicked and jeered from the village by a band of terrifyingly masked, shrieking, spear-carrying kankurang dancers.

The tobalo soon boomed out the beginning of the new harvest, and Kunta joined the rest of the villagers in the fields. He welcomed the long days of hard work, for they kept him too busy and too tired to give much thought to what lay ahead. But when the harvesting was done and the festival began, he found himself unable to enjoy the music and the dancing and the feasting as the others did — as he himself had done for as long as he could remember. The louder the merriment, in fact, the unhappier he became until finally he spent most of the last two days of the festival sitting by himself on the banks of the bolong skipping stones across the water.

On the night before the last day of the festival, Kunta was in Binta's hut silently finishing his evening meal of groundnut stew with rice when Omoro walked in behind him. From the corner of his eye, Kunta glimpsed his father raising something white, and before he had a chance to turn around, Omoro had pulled a long hood down firmly over his head. The terror that shot through Kunta all but numbed him. He felt his father's hand gripping his upper arm and urging him to stand up, then to move backward until he was pushed down onto a low stool. Kunta was grateful to sit, for his legs felt like water and his head felt light. He listened to himself breathing in short gasps, knowing that if he tried to move, he would fall off the stool. So he sat very still, trying to accustom himself to the darkness. Terrified as he was, it seemed almost a double darkness. As his upper lip felt the moist warmth of his breath inside the hood, it flashed through Kunta's mind that surely once such a hood had been thrust in the same way over his father's head. Could Omoro have been so frightened? Kunta couldn't even imagine that, and he felt ashamed to be such a disgrace to the Kinte clan.

It was very quiet in the hut. Wrestling the fear that knotted the pit of his stomach, Kunta closed his eyes and focused his very pores on trying to hear something, anything at all. He thought he heard Binta moving about, but he couldn't be sure. He wondered where Lamin was, and Suwadu, who surely would be making noise. He knew only one thing for sure: Neither Binta nor anyone else was going to speak to him, let alone lift that hood off his head. And then Kunta thought how awful it would be if his hood *did* get lifted, for everyone would see how scared he really was, and perhaps therefore a boy unworthy of joining his kafo mates in manhood training.

Even boys the size of Lamin knew — since Kunta had told him — what would happen to anyone who showed himself too weak or cowardly to endure the training that turned boys into hunters, into warriors, into men — all within a period of twelve moons. Suppose he should fail?

He began gulping down his fear, remembering how he had been told that any boy who failed the manhood training would be treated as a child for the rest of his life, even though he might look like a grown man. He would be avoided, and his village would never permit him to marry, lest he father others like himself. These sad cases, Kunta had heard, usually slipped away from their villages sooner or later, never to return, and even their own fathers, mothers, brothers, and sisters would never mention them again. Kunta saw himself slinking away from Juffure like some mangy hyena, scorned by everyone; it was too horrible to think of.

After a time, Kunta realized that he was faintly hearing the drumbeats and the shouting of dancers in the distance. More time passed. What hour was it, he wondered. He guessed it must be near the sutoba hour, halfway between dusk and dawn, but after a few moments he heard the alimamo's high-pitched wailing for the village's safo prayer, two hours before midnight. The music ceased and Kunta knew that the villagers had stopped their celebrating and the men were hastening to the mosque.

Kunta sat until he knew the prayers must have been over, but the music didn't resume. He listened hard, but could hear only silence. Finally he nodded off, awakening with a start only a few moments later. It was still quiet — and darker under the hood than a moonless night. Finally, faintly, he was certain that he could hear the early yippings of hyenas. He knew that hyenas always yipped for a while before settling down to steady howling, which they would continue until early daybreak, sounding eerily far away.

During the harvest festival week, at the first streaks of daybreak, Kunta knew the tobalo would boom. He sat waiting for that to happen — for *anything* to happen. He felt his anger building, expecting the tobalo to sound at any moment — but nothing happened. He grated his teeth and waited some more. And then, at last, after jerking awake a few times, he dozed off into a fitful sleep. He all but leaped from his skin when the tobalo finally did boom. Under the hood, his cheeks were hot with embarrassment that he had fallen asleep.

Having become accustomed to the hood's darkness, Kunta could all but see the morning's activities from the sounds his ears picked up — the crowing of the cocks, the barking of the wuolo dogs, the wailing of the alimamo, the bumping of the women's pestles as they beat the breakfast couscous. This morning's prayer to Allah, he knew, would be for the success of the manhood training that was about to begin. He heard movement in the hut, and he sensed that it was Binta. It was strange how he couldn't see her, but he knew it was his mother. Kunta wondered about Sitafa and his other mates. It surprised him to realize that throughout the night, he hadn't once thought about them until now. He told himself that they must surely have had as long a night as he had.

When the music of koras and balafons began playing outside the hut, Kunta heard the sound of people walking and talking, louder and louder. Then drums joined the din, their rhythm sharp and cutting. A moment later, his heart seemed to stop as he sensed the sudden movement of someone rushing into the hut. Before he could even brace himself, his wrists were grabbed, and roughly he was snatched up from the stool and jerked out through the hut door into the all but deafening noise of staccato drums and screeching people.

Hands knocked him and feet kicked him. Kunta thought desperately of bolting away somehow, but just as he was about to try, a firm yet gentle hand grasped one of his. Breathing hoarsely under his hood, Kunta realized that he was no longer being hit and kicked and that the screaming of the crowd was suddenly no longer nearby. The people, he guessed, had moved along to some other boy's hut, and the guiding hand that held his must belong to the slave Omoro would have hired, as every father did, to lead his hooded son to the jujuo.

The crowd's shouting rose to a frenzied pitch every time another boy was dragged from a hut, and Kunta was glad he couldn't see the kankurang dancers, who were making bloodcurdling whoops as they sprang high into the air brandishing their spears. Big drums and small drums — every drum in the village, it seemed — were pounding as the slave guided Kunta faster and faster between rows of people shouting on either side of him, crying out things like "Four moons!" and "They will become men!" Kunta wanted to burst into tears. He wished wildly that he could reach out and touch Omoro, Binta, Lamin — even the sniveling Suwadu — for it felt too much to bear that four long moons were going to pass before he would see again those he loved even more than he had ever realized until now. Kunta's ears told him that he and his guide had joined a moving line of marchers, all stepping to the swift rhythm of the drums. As they passed through the village gates — he could tell because the noise of the crowd began to fade — he felt hot tears well up and run down his cheeks. He closed his eyes tight, as if to hide the tears even from himself.

As he had felt Binta's presence in the hut, now he felt, almost as if it were a smell, the fear of his kafo mates ahead and behind him in the line, and he knew that theirs was as great as his. Somehow that made him feel less ashamed. As he trudged on in the white blindness of his hood, he knew that he was leaving behind more than his father and his mother and his brothers and the village of his birth, and this filled him with sadness as much as terror. But he knew it must be done, as it had been done by his father before him and would some day be done by his son. He would return, but only as a man.

CHAPTER 23

They must be approaching — within a stone's throw, Kunta sensed — a recently cut bamboo grove. Through his hood, he could smell the rich fragrance of bamboo freshly chopped. They marched closer; the smell became stronger and stronger; they were at the barrier, then through it; but they were still outdoors. Of course — it was a bamboo fence. Suddenly the drums stopped and the marchers halted. For several minutes, Kunta and the others stood still and silent. He listened for the slightest sound that might tell him when they had stopped or where they were, but all he could hear was the screeching of parrots and the scolding of monkeys overhead.

Then, suddenly, Kunta's hood was

lifted. He stood blinking in the bright sun of midafternoon, trying to adjust his eyes to the light. He was afraid even to turn his head enough to see his kafo mates, for directly before them stood stern, wrinkled senior elder Silla Ba Dibba. Like all the other boys, Kunta knew him and his family well. But Silla Ba Dibba acted as if he had never seen any of them before — indeed, as if he would rather not see them now; his eyes scanned their faces as he would have looked at crawling maggots. Kunta knew that this surely was their kintango. Standing on either side of him were two younger men, Ali Sise and Soru Tura, whom Kunta also knew well; Soru was a special friend of Omoro's. Kunta was grateful that neither of them *was* Omoro, to see his son so scared.

As they had been taught, the entire kafo — all twenty-three boys — crossed their palms over their hearts and greeted their elders in the traditional way: "Peace!" "Peace only!" replied the old kintango and his assistants. Widening his gaze for a moment — careful not to move his head — Kunta saw that they stood in a compound dotted with several small, mud-walled, thatch-roofed huts and surrounded by the tall new bamboo fence. He could see where the huts had been patched, undoubtedly by the fathers who had disappeared from Juffure for a few days. All this he saw without moving a muscle. But the next moment he nearly jumped out of his skin.

"Children left Juffure village," said the kintango suddenly in a loud voice. "If men are to return, your fears must be erased, for a fearful person is a weak person, and a weak person is a danger to his family, to his village, and to his tribe." He glared at them as if he had never seen such a sorry lot, and then turned away. As he did so, his two assistants sprang forward and began to lay about among the boys with limber sticks, pummeling their shoulders and backsides smartly as they herded them like so many goats, a few boys apiece, into the small mud huts.

Huddled in their bare hut, Kunta and his four mates were too terrified to feel the lingering sting of the blows they had received, and too ashamed to raise their heads even enough to look at one another. After a few minutes, when it seemed that they would be spared from further abuse for a little while, Kunta began to sneak looks at his companions. He wished that he and Sitafa were in the same hut. He knew these others, of course, but none as well as his yayo brother, and his heart sank. But perhaps that's no accident, he reasoned. They probably don't want us to have even that small comfort. Maybe they're not even going to feed us, he began to think, when his stomach started to growl with hunger.

Just after sunset, the kintango's assistants burst into the hut. *"Move!"* A stick caught him sharply across the shoulders, and the scrambling boys were hissed at as they rushed outside into the dusk, bumping into boys from other huts, and under the flying sticks were herded with gruff orders into a ragged line, each boy grasping the hand of the boy ahead. When they were all in place, the kintango fixed them with a dark scowl and announced that they were about to undertake a night journey deep into the surrounding forest.

At the order to march, the long line of boys set out along the path in clumsy disarray, and the sticks fell steadily among them. "You walk like buffalo!" Kunta heard close to his ear. A boy cried out as he was hit, and both assistants shouted loudly in the darkness, "Who was that?," and their sticks rained down even harder. After that no boy uttered a sound.

Kunta's legs soon began to hurt — but not as soon or as badly as they would have done if he hadn't learned the manner of loose striding taught him by his father on their trip to the village of Janneh and Saloum. It pleased him to think that the other boys' legs were surely hurting worse than his, for they wouldn't yet know how to walk. But nothing he had learned did anything to help Kunta's hunger and thirst. His stomach felt tied in knots, and he was starting to feel light-headed when at last a stop was called near a small stream. The reflection of the bright moon in its surface was soon set to rippling as the boys fell to their knees and began to scoop up and gulp down handfuls of water. A moment later the kintango's assistants commanded them away from the stream with orders not to drink too much at once, then opened their headpacks and passed out some chunks of dried meat. The boys tore away at the morsels like hyenas; Kunta chewed and swallowed so fast that he barely tasted the four bites he managed to wrest away for himself.

Every boy's feet had big, raw blisters on them, Kunta's as bad as any of the rest; but it felt so good to have food and water in his stomach that he hardly noticed. As they sat by the stream, he and his kafo mates began to look around in the moonlight at one another, this time too tired rather than too afraid to speak. Kunta and Sitafa exchanged long glances, but neither could tell in the dim light if his friend looked as miserable as he felt himself.

Kunta hardly had a chance to cool his burning feet in the stream before the kintango's assistants ordered them back into formation for the long walk back to the jujuo. His legs and head were numb when they finally came within sight of the bamboo gates shortly before dawn. Feeling ready to die, he trudged to his hut, bumped into another boy already inside, lost his footing, stumbled to the dirt floor — and fell deep asleep right where he lay.

On every night for the next six nights came another march, each one longer than the last. The pain of his blistered feet was terrible, but Kunta found by the fourth night that he somehow didn't *mind* the pain as much, and he began to feel a welcome new emotion: pride. By the sixth march, he and the other boys discovered that though the night was very dark, they no longer needed to hold the next boy's hand in order to maintain a straight marching line.

On the seventh night came the kintango's first personal lesson for the boys: showing them how men deep in the forest used the stars to guide them, so that they would never be lost. Within the first half moon, every boy of the kafo had learned how to lead the marching line by the stars, back toward the jujuo. One night when Kunta was the leader, he almost stepped on a bush rat before it noticed him and scurried for cover. Kunta was almost as proud as he was startled, for this meant that the marchers had been walking too silently to be heard even by an animal.

But animals, the kintango told them, were the best teachers of the art of hunting, which was one of the most important things for any Mandinka to learn. When the kintango was satisfied that they had mastered the techniques of marching, he took the kafo, for the next half moon, deep into the bush far from the jujuo, where they built lean-to shelters to sleep in between countless lessons in the secrets of becoming a simbon. Kunta's eyes never seemed to have been closed before one of the kintango's assistants was shouting them awake for some training session.

The kintango's assistants pointed out where lions had recently crouched in wait, then sprung out to kill passing antelope; then where the lions had gone after their meal and laid down to sleep for the rest of the night. The tracks of the antelope herd were followed backward until they almost painted a picture for the boys of what those antelope had done through the day before they met the lions. The kafo inspected the wide cracks in rocks where wolves and hyenas hid. And they began to learn many tricks of hunting that they had never dreamed about. They had never realized, for example, that the first secret of the master simbon was never moving abruptly. The old kintango himself told the boys a story about a foolish hunter who finally starved to death in an area thick with game, because he was so clumsy and made so much noise, darting here and there, that all about him animals of every sort swiftly and silently slipped away without his even realizing that any had been near.

The boys felt like that clumsy hunter during their lessons in imitating the sounds of animals and birds. The air was rent with their grunts and whistles, yet no birds or animals came near. Then they would be told to lie very quietly in hiding places while the kintango and his assistants made what seemed to them the same sounds, and soon animals and birds would come into sight, cocking their heads and looking for the others who had called to them.

When the boys were practicing bird calls one afternoon, suddenly a large-bodied, heavy-beaked bird landed with a great squawking in a nearby bush. "Look!" one boy shouted with a loud laugh — and every other boy's heart leaped into his throat, knowing that once again that boy's big mouth was going to get them all punished together. No few times before had he shown his habit of acting before thinking — but now the kintango surprised them. He walked over to the boy and said to him very sternly, "Bring that bird to me — alive!" Kunta and his mates held their breaths as they watched the boy hunch down and creep toward the bush where the heavy bird sat stupidly, turning its head this way and that. But when the boy sprang, the bird managed to escape his clutching hands, frantically beating its stubby wings just enough to raise its big body over the brushtops — and the boy went leaping after it in hot pursuit, soon disappearing from sight.

Kunta and the others were thunderstruck.

There was clearly no limit to what the kintango might order them to do. For the next three days and two nights, as the boys went about their training sessions, they cast long glances at each other and then the nearby bush, all of them wondering and worrying about what had befallen their missing mate. As much as he had annoyed them before by getting them all beaten for things he'd done, he seemed never more one of them now that he was gone.

The boys were just getting up on the morning of the fourth day when the jujuo lookout signaled that someone was approaching the village. A moment later came the drum message: It was he. They rushed out to meet him, whooping as if their own brother had returned from a trek to Marrakech. Thin and dirty and covered with cuts and bruises, he swayed slightly as they ran up and slapped him on the back. But he managed a weak smile — and well he should: under his arm, its wings and feet and beak bound with a length of vine, he held the bird. It looked even worse than he did, but it was still alive.

The kintango came out, and though

speaking to that boy, he made it clear that he was really speaking to them all: "This taught you two important things — to do as you are told, and to keep your mouth shut. These are among the makings of men." Then Kunta and his mates saw that boy receive the first clearly approving look cast upon anyone by the old kintango, who had known that the boy would sooner or later be able to catch a bird so heavy that it could make only short, low hops through the bush.

The big bird was quickly roasted and eaten with great relish by everyone except his captor, who was so tired that he couldn't stay awake long enough for it to cook. He was permitted to sleep through the day and also through the night, which Kunta and the others had to spend out in the bush on a hunting lesson. The next day, during the first rest period, the boy told his hushed mates what a torturous chase he had led, until finally, after two days and a night, he had laid a trap that the bird walked into. After trussing it up — including the snapping beak — he had somehow kept himself awake for another day and night, and by following the stars as they had been taught, had found his way back to the jujuo. For a while after that, the other boys had very little to say to him. Kunta told himself that he wasn't really jealous; it was just that the boy seemed to think that his exploit — and the kintango's approval of it — had made him more important than his kafo mates. And the very next time the kintango's assistants ordered an afternoon of wrestling practice, Kunta seized the chance to grab that boy and throw him roughly to the ground.

By the second moon of manhood training, Kunta's kafo had become almost as skilled at survival in the forest as they would have been in their own village. They could now both detect and follow the all but invisible signs of animals, and now they were learning the secret rituals and prayers of the forefathers that could make a very great simbon himself invisible to animals. Every bite of meat they ate now was either trapped by the boys or shot by their slings and arrows. They could skin an animal twice as fast as they could before, and cook the meat over the nearly smokeless fires they had learned to build by striking flint close to dry moss under light, dry sticks. Their meals of roasted game — sometimes small bush rats — were usually topped off with insects toasted crispy in the coals.

Some of the most valuable lessons they learned weren't even planned. One day, during a rest period, when a boy was testing his bow and one careless arrow happened to strike a nest of kurburungo bees high in a tree, a cloud of angry bees swarmed down — and once again all of the boys suffered for the mistake of one. Not even the fastest runner among them escaped the painful stings.

"The simbon never shoots an arrow without knowing what it will hit," the kintango told them later. Ordering the boys to rub one another's puffed and hurting places with shea tree butter, he said, "Tonight, you will deal with those bees in the proper manner." By nightfall, the boys had piled dry moss beneath the tree that held the nest. After one of the kintango's assistants set it afire, the other one threw into the flames a quantity of leaves from a certain bush. Thick, choking smoke rose into the tree's upper limbs, and soon dead bees were dropping around the boys by the thousands, as harmlessly as rain. In the morning, Kunta and his kafo were shown how to melt down the honeycombs — skimming off the rest of the dead bees — so that they could eat their fill of honey. Kunta could almost feel himself tingle with that extra strength it was said honey would give to great hunters when they were in need of quick nourishment deep in the forest.

But no matter what they went through, no matter how much they added to their knowledge and abilities, the old kintango was never satisfied. His demands and his discipline remained so strict that the boys were torn between fear and anger most of the time — when they weren't too weary to feel either. Any command to one boy that wasn't instantly and perfectly performed still brought a beating to the entire kafo. And when they weren't being beaten, it seemed to Kunta, they were being wakened roughly in the middle of the night for a long march — always as a punishment for some boy's wrongdoing.

The only thing that kept Kunta and the others from giving that boy a beating of their own was the certain knowledge that they would be beaten for fighting; among the first lessons they had learned in life — long before coming to the jujuo — having been that Mandinkas must never fight among themselves. Finally the boys began to understand that the welfare of the group depended on each of them — just as the welfare of their *tribe* would depend on each of them one day. Violations of the rules slowly dwindled to an occasional lapse, and with the decline in beatings, the fear that they felt for the kintango was slowly replaced by a respect they had felt before only for their fathers.

But still hardly a day would pass without something new to make Kunta and his mates feel awkward and ignorant all over again. It amazed them to learn, for example, that a rag folded and hung in certain ways near a man's hut would inform other Mandinka men when he planned to return, or that sandals crossed in certain ways outside a hut told many things that only other men would understand. But the secret Kunta found the most remarkable of all was sira kango, a kind of men's talk in which sounds of Mandinka words were changed in such a way that no women or children or non-Mandinkas were permitted to learn. Kunta remembered times when he had heard his father say something very rapidly to another man that Kunta had not understood nor dared to ask explained. Now that he had learned it himself, he and his mates soon spoke nearly everything they said in the secret talk of men.

In every hut as each moon went by, the boys added a new rock to a bowl to mark how long they had been gone from Juffure. Within days after the third rock was dropped in the bowl, the boys were wrestling in the compound one afternoon when suddenly they looked toward the gate of the jujuo, and there stood a group of twenty-five or thirty men. A loud gasp rose from the boys as they recognized their fathers, uncles, and older brothers. Kunta sprang up, unable to believe his eyes, as a bolt of joy shot through him at the first sight of Omoro for three moons. But it was as if some unseen hand held him back and stifled a cry of gladness — even before he saw in his father's face no sign that he recognized his son.

Only one boy rushed forward, calling out his father's name, and without a word that father reached for the stick of the nearest kintango's assistant and beat his son with it, shouting at him harshly for betraying his emotions, for showing that he was still a boy. He added, unnecessarily, as he gave him the last licks, that his son should expect no favors from his father. Then the kintango himself barked a command for the entire kafo to lie on their bellies in a row, and all of the visiting men walked along the row and flailed the upturned backsides with their walking sticks. Kunta's emotions were in a turmoil; the blows he didn't mind at all, knowing them to be merely another of the rigors of manhood training, but it pained him not to be able to hug his father or even hear his voice, and it shamed him to know that it wasn't manly even to wish for such indulgences.

The beating over, the kintango ordered the boys to race, to jump, to dance, to wrestle, to pray as they had been taught, and the fathers, uncles, and older brothers watched it all silently, and then departed with warm compliments to the kintango and his assistants, but not so much as a backward look at the boys, who stood with downcast faces. Within the hour, they got another beating for sulking about the preparation of their evening meal. It hurt all the more because the kintango and his assistants acted as if the visitors had never even been there. But early that night, while the boys were wrestling before bedtime — only halfheartedly now — one of the kintango's assistants passed by Kunta and said brusquely to him, under his breath, "You have a new brother, and he is named Madi."

Four of us now, thought Kunta, lying awake later that night. Four brothers — four sons for his mother and father. He thought how that would sound in the Kinte family history when it was told by griots for hundreds of rains in the future. After Omoro, thought Kunta, he would be the first man of the family when he returned to Juffure. Not only was he learning to be a man, but he was also learning many, many things he would be able to teach Lamin, as already he had taught him so many of the things of boyhood. At least he would teach him that which was permissible for boys to know; and then Lamin would teach Suwadu, and Suwadu would teach this new one whom Kunta had not even seen, whose name was Madi. And some day, Kunta thought as he drifted off to sleep, when he was as old as Omoro, he would have sons of his own, and it would all begin again.

CHAPTER 24

"You are ceasing to be children. You are experiencing rebirth as men," the kintango said one morning to the assembled kafo. This was the first time the kintango had used the word "men" except to tell them what they weren't. After moons of learning together, working together, being beaten together, he told them, each of them was finally beginning to discover that he had two selves — one within him, and the other, larger self in all those whose blood and lives he shared. Not until they learned that lesson could they undertake the next phase of manhood training: how to be warriors. "You know already that Mandinkas fight only if others are warlike," said the kintango. "But we are the finest warriors if driven to fight."

For the next half moon, Kunta and his mates learned how to make war. Famous Mandinka battle strategies were drawn in the dust by the kintango or his assistants, and then the boys were told to re-enact the strategies in mock battles. "Never completely encircle your enemy," counseled the kintango. "Leave him some escape, for he will fight even more desperately if trapped." The boys learned also that battles should start in late afternoon, so that any enemy, seeing defeat, could save face by retreating in the darkness. And they were taught that during any wars, neither enemy should ever do harm to any traveling marabouts, griots, or blacksmiths, for an angered marabout could bring down the displeasure of Allah; an angered griot could use his eloquent tongue to stir the enemy army to greater savagery; and an angered blacksmith could make or repair weapons for the enemy.

Under the direction of the kintango's assistants, Kunta and the others carved out barbed spears and made barbed arrows of the kind used only in battle, and practiced with them on smaller and smaller targets. When a boy could hit a bamboo cane twenty-five steps away, he was cheered and praised. Tramping into the woods, the boys found some koona shrub, whose leaves they picked to be boiled back at the jujuo. Into the resulting thick, black juice they would dip a cotton thread, and they were shown how that thread, wound around an arrow's barbs, would seep a deadly poison into whatever wound the arrow made.

At the end of the war-training period, the kintango told them more than they had ever known before — and told them more excitingly than they had ever heard it — about that greatest of all Mandinka wars and warriors — the time when the army of the fabled ex-slave general Sundiata, son of Sogolon, the Buffalo Woman, conquered the forces of the Boure country's King Soumaoro, a king so cruel that he wore human-skin robes and adorned his palace walls with enemy's bleached skulls.

Kunta and his mates held their breaths,

hearing how both armies suffered thousands of wounded or dead. But the archers of the Mandinkas closed in on Soumaoro's forces like a giant trap, raining down arrows from both sides and moving in steadily until Soumaoro's terrified army finally fled in rout. For days and nights, said the kintango — and it was the first time the boys ever had seen him smile — the talking drums of every village followed the marching progress of the victorious Mandinka forces, laden with enemy booty and driving thousands of captives before them. In every village, happy crowds jeered and kicked the prisoners, whose shaved heads were bowed and whose hands were tied behind their backs. Finally General Sundiata called a huge meeting of the people, and he brought before them the chiefs of all the villages he had defeated and gave them back their spears of chiefhood's rank, and then he established among those chiefs the bonds of peace, which would last among them for the next one hundred rains. Kunta and his mates went dreamily to their beds, never prouder to be Mandinkas.

As the next moon of training began, drumtalk reached the jujuo telling of new visitors to be expected within the next two days. The excitement with which the news of *any* visitors would have been received, after so long since the fathers and brothers had come to see them, was doubled when the boys learned that the sender of the message was the drummer of Juffure's champion wrestling team, which was coming to conduct special lessons for the trainees.

Late in the afternoon of the next day, the drums announced their arrival even earlier than expected. But the boys' pleasure at seeing all the familiar faces again was forgotten when, without a word, the wrestlers grabbed them and began to flip them onto the ground harder than they had ever been thrown in their lives. And every boy was bruised and hurting when the wrestlers divided them into smaller groups to grapple one another, as the champions supervised. Kunta had never imagined there were so many wrestling holds, nor how effectively they could work if used correctly. And the champions kept drumming into the boys' ears that it was knowledge and expertness and not strength that made the difference between being an ordinary wrestler and a champion. Still, as they demonstrated the holds for their pupils, the boys couldn't help admiring their bulging muscles as much as their skill in using them. Around the fire that night, the drummer from Juffure chanted the names and the feats of great Mandinka wrestling champions of even a hundred rains in the past, and when it was the boys' time for bed, the wrestlers left the jujuo to return to Juffure.

Two days later came news of another visitor. This time the message was brought by a runner from Juffure — a young man of the fourth kafo whom Kunta and his mates knew well, though in his own new manhood, he acted as if he never had seen these third-kafo children. Without so much as a glance at them, he ran up to the kintango and announced, between deep breaths, that Kujali N'jai, a griot well known throughout The Gambia, would soon spend one full day at the jujuo.

In three days he arrived, accompanied by

several young men of his family. He was much older than any of the griots Kunta had seen before — so old, in fact, that he made the kintango seem young. After gesturing for the boys to squat in a semicircle about him, the old man began to talk of how he became what he was. He told them how, over years of study from young manhood, every griot had buried deep in his mind the records of the ancestors. "How else could you know of the great deeds of the ancient kings, holy men, hunters, and warriors who came hundreds of rains before us? Have you met them?" asked the old man. "No! The history of our people is carried to the future in here." And he tapped his gray head.

The question in the mind of every boy was answered by the old griot: Only the sons of griots could become griots. Indeed, it was their solemn *duty* to become griots. Upon finishing their manhood training, these boys — like those grandsons of his own who sat beside him here today — would begin studying and traveling with selected elders, hearing over and again the historical names and stories as they had been passed down. And in due time, each young man would know that special part of the forefathers' history in the finest and fullest detail, just as it had been told to his father and his father's father. And the day would come when that boy would become a man and have sons to whom *he* would tell those stories, so that the events of the distant past would forever live.

When the awed boys had wolfed down their evening meal and rushed back to gather again around the old griot, he thrilled them until late into the night with stories his own father had passed down to him — about the great black empires that had ruled Africa hundreds of rains before.

"Long before toubob ever put his foot in Africa," the old griot said, there was the Empire of Benin, ruled by an all-powerful King called the Oba, whose every wish was obeyed instantly. But the actual governing of Benin was done by trusted counselors of the Oba, whose full time was needed just for making the necessary sacrifices to appease the forces of evil and for his proper attentions to a harem of more than a hundred wives. But even before Benin was a yet richer kingdom called Songhai, said the griot. Songhai's capital city was Gao, filled with fine houses for black princes and rich merchants who lavishly entertained traveling tradesmen who brought much gold to buy goods.

"Nor was that the richest kingdom," said the old man. And he told the boys of ancestral Ghana, in which an entire town was populated with only the King's court. And King Kanissaai had a thousand houses, each of which had three servants and its own urinal made of copper. Kunta could hardly believe his ears. "And each evening," said the griot, "when King Kanissaai would emerge from his palace, a thousand fires would be lit, lighting up all between the heavens and the earth. And the servants of the great King would bring forth food enough to serve the ten thousand people who gathered there each evening."

Here he paused, and exclamations of wonder could not be restrained by the boys, who knew well that no sound should be made as a griot talked, but neither he nor even the kintango himself seemed to notice their rudeness. Putting into his mouth half of a kola nut and offering the other half to the kintango, who accepted it with pleasure, the griot drew the skirt of his robe closer about his legs against the chill of the early night and resumed his stories.

"But even Ghana was not the richest black kingdom!" he exclaimed. "The very richest, the very oldest of them all was the kingdom of ancient Mali!" Like the other empires, Mali had its cities, its farmers, its artisans, its blacksmiths, tanners, dyers, and weavers, said the old griot. But Mali's enormous wealth came from its far-flung trade routes in salt and gold and copper. "Altogether Mali was four months of travel long and four months of travel wide," said the griot, "and the greatest of all its cities was the fabled Timbuktu!" The major center of learning in all Africa, it was populated by thousands of scholars, made even more numerous by a steady parade of visiting wise men seeking to increase their knowledge — so many that some of the biggest merchants sold nothing but parchments and books. "There is not a marabout, not a teacher in the smallest village, whose knowledge has not come at least in part from Timbuktu," said the griot.

When finally the kintango stood up and thanked the griot for the generosity with which he had shared with them the treasures of his mind, Kunta and the others — for the first time since they came to the jujuo — actually dared to voice their displeasure, for the time had come for them to go to bed. The kintango chose to ignore this impertinence, at least for the time being, and sternly commanded them to their huts — but not before they had a chance to beg him to urge the griot to come back and visit them again.

They were still thinking and talking of the wondrous tales the griot had told them when — six days later — word came that a famous moro would soon be visiting the camp. The moro was the highest grade of teacher in The Gambia; indeed, there were only a few of them, and so wise were they — after many rains of study — that their job was to teach not schoolboys but other teachers, such as the arafang of Juffure.

Even the kintango showed unusual concern about this visitor, ordering the entire jujuo to be thoroughly cleaned, with the dirt raked and then brushed with leafy branches to a smoothness that would capture the honor of the fresh footprints of the moro when he arrived. Then the kintango assembled the boys in the compound and told them, "The advice and the blessings of this man who will be with us is sought not only by ordinary people but also by village chiefs and even by kings."

When the moro arrived the next morning, five of his students were with him, each carrying headbundles that Kunta knew would contain treasured Arabic books and parchment manuscripts such as those from ancient Timbuktu. As the old man passed through the gate, Kunta and his mates joined the kintango and his assistants on their knees, with their foreheads touching the ground. When the moro had blessed them and their jujuo, they rose and seated themselves respectfully around him as he

244

opened his books and began to read — first from the Koran, then from such unheard-of books as the Taureta La Musa, the Zabora Dawidi and the Lingeeli la Isa, which he said were known to "Christians" as The Pentateuch of Moses, The Psalms of David and The Book of Isaiah. Each time the moro would open or close a book, roll or unroll a manuscript, he would press it to his forehead and mutter "Amen!"

When he had finished reading, the old man put his books aside and spoke to them of great events and people from the Christian Koran, which was known as the Holy Bible. He spoke of Adam and Eve, of Joseph and his brethren; of Moses, David, and Solomon; of the death of Abel. And he spoke to them of great men of more recent history, such as Djoulou Kara Naini, known to the toubob as Alexander the Great, a mighty King of gold and silver whose sun had shown over half of the world.

Before the moro finally rose to leave that night, he reviewed what they already knew of the five daily prayers to Allah, and he instructed them thoroughly in how to conduct themselves inside the sacred mosque of their village, which they would enter for their first time when they returned home as men. Then he and his students had to hurry in order to reach the next place on his busy schedule, and the boys honored him — as the kintango had instructed them — by singing one of the men's songs they had learned from the jalli kea: "One generation passes on. . . . Another generation comes and goes. . . . But Allah abides forever."

In his hut after the moro had gone that night, Kunta lay awake thinking how so many things — indeed, nearly everything they had learned — all tied together. The past seemed with the present, the present with the future; the dead with the living and those yet to be born; he himself with his family, his mates, his village, his tribe, his Africa; the world of man with the world of animals and growing things — they all lived with Allah. Kunta felt very small, yet very large. Perhaps, he thought, this is what it means to become a man.

CHAPTER 25

The time had come for that which made
Kunta and every other boy shudder to
think of: the kasas boyo operation, which
would purify a boy and prepare him to
become a father of many sons. They knew
it was coming, but when it came it was
without warning. One day as the sun
reached the noontime position, one of the
kintango's assistants gave what seemed to
be only a routine order for the kafo to
line up in the compound, which the boys
did as quickly as usual. But Kunta felt a
twinge of fear when the kintango himself
came from his hut, as he rarely did at
midday, and walked before them.

"Hold out your fotos," he commanded.
They hesitated, not believing — or
wanting to believe — what they had

heard. "Now!" he shouted. Slowly and shyly, they obeyed, each keeping his eyes on the ground as he reached inside his loincloth.

Working their way from either end of the line, the kintango's assistants wrapped around the head of each boy's foto a short length of cloth spread with a green paste made of a pounded leaf. "Soon your fotos will have no feeling," the kintango said, ordering them back into their huts.

Huddled inside, ashamed and afraid of what would happen next, the boys waited in silence until about midafternoon, when again they were ordered outside, where they stood watching as a number of men from Juffure — the fathers, brothers, and uncles who had come before, and others — filed in through the gate. Omoro was among them, but this time Kunta pretended that he didn't see his father. The men formed themselves into a line facing the boys and chanted together: "This thing to be done . . . also has been done to us . . . as to the forefathers before us . . . so that you also will become

. . . all of us men together." Then the kintango ordered the boys back into their huts once again.

Night was falling when they heard many drums suddenly begin to pound just outside the jujuo. Ordered out of their huts, they saw bursting through the gate about a dozen leaping, shouting kankurang dancers. In leafy branch costumes and bark masks, they sprang about brandishing their spears among the terrified boys, and then — just as abruptly as they had appeared — were gone. Almost numb with fear, the boys now heard and followed dumbly the kintango's order to seat themselves close together with their backs against the jujuo's bamboo fence.

The fathers, uncles, and older brothers stood nearby, this time chanting, "You soon will return to home . . . and to your farms . . . and in time you will marry . . . and life everlasting will spring from your loins." One of the kintango's assistants called out one boy's name. As he got up, the assistant motioned him behind a long screen of woven bamboo.

Kunta couldn't see or hear what happened after that, but a few moments later, the boy reappeared — with a bloodstained cloth between his legs. Staggering slightly, he was half carried by the other assistant back to his place along the bamboo fence. Another boy's name was called; then another, and another, and finally:

"Kunta Kinte!"

Kunta was petrified. But he made himself get up and walk behind the screen. Inside were four men, one of whom ordered him to lie down on his back. He did so; his shaking legs wouldn't have supported him any longer anyway. The men then leaned down, grasped him firmly, and lifted his thighs upward. Just before closing his eyes, Kunta saw the kintango bending over him with something in his hands. Then he felt the cutting pain. It was even worse than he thought it would be, though not as bad as it would have been without the numbing paste. In a moment he was bandaged tightly, and an assistant helped him back outside, where he sat, weak and dazed, alongside the others who had already been behind the screen. They didn't dare to look at one another. But the thing they had feared above all else had now been done.

As the fotos of the kafo began healing, a general air of jubilation rose within the jujuo, for gone forever was the indignity of being mere boys in body as well as in mind. Now they were very nearly men — and they were boundless in their gratitude and reverence for the kintango. And he, in turn, began to see Kunta's kafo with different eyes. The old, wrinkled, gray-haired elder whom they had slowly come to love was sometimes seen even to smile now. And very casually, when talking to the kafo, he or his assistants would say, "You men —" and to Kunta and his mates, it seemed as unbelievable as it was beautiful to hear.

Soon afterward the fourth new moon arrived, and two or three members of Kunta's kafo, at the kintango's personal order, began to leave the jujuo each night and trot all the way to the sleeping village of Juffure, where they would slip like shadows into their own mothers' storehouses, steal as much couscous, dried meats, and millet as they could carry, and then race back with it to the jujuo, where it was gleefully cooked the next day — "to prove yourselves smarter than all women, even your mother," the kintango had told them. But the next day, of course, those boys' mothers would boast to their friends how they had heard their sons prowling and had lain awake listening with pride.

There was a new feeling now in the evenings at the jujuo. Nearly always, Kunta's kafo would squat in a semicircle around the kintango. Most of the time he remained as stern in manner as before, but now he talked to them not as bumbling little boys but as young men of his own village. Sometimes he spoke to them about the qualities of manhood — chief among which, after fearlessness, was total honesty in all things. And sometimes he spoke to them about the forefathers. Worshipful regard was a duty owed by the living to those who dwelled with Allah, he told them. He asked each boy to name the ancestor he remembered the best; Kunta named his Grandma Yaisa, and the kintango said that each of the ancestors the boys had named — as was the way of ancestors — was petitioning Allah in the best interests of the living.

Another evening, the kintango told them how in one's village, every person who lived there was equally important to that village; from the newest baby to the oldest elder. As new men, they must therefore learn to treat everyone with the same respect, and — as the foremost of their manhood duties — to protect the welfare of every man, woman, and child in Juffure as they would their own.

"When you return home," said the kintango, "you will begin to serve Juffure as its eyes and ears. You will be expected to stand guard over the village — beyond the gates as lookouts for toubob and other savages, and in the fields as sentries to keep the crops safe from scavengers. You will also be charged with the responsibility of inspecting the women's cooking pots — including those of your own mothers — to make sure they are kept clean, and you will be expected to reprimand them most severely if any dirt or insects are found inside." The boys could hardly wait to begin their duties.

Though all but the oldest of them were still too young to dream of the responsibilities they would assume when they reached the fourth kafo, they knew that some day, as men of fifteen to nineteen rains, they would be appointed to the important job of carrying messages — like the young man who had brought them word of the moro's visit — between Juffure and other villages. It would have been hard for Kunta's kafo to imagine such a thing, but those old enough to be messengers longed for nothing more than to *stop* being messengers; when they reached the fifth kafo at twenty rains, they would graduate to *really* important work — assisting the village elders as emissaries and negotiators in all dealings with other villages. Men of Omoro's age — over thirty — rose gradually in rank and responsibility with each passing rain until they themselves acquired the honored status of elders. Kunta had often proudly watched Omoro sitting on the edges of the Council of Elders, and looked forward to the day when his father would enter the inner circle of those who would inherit the mantle of office from such revered leaders as the kintango when they were called to Allah.

It was no longer easy for Kunta and the others to pay attention as they should to everything the kintango said. It seemed impossible to them that so much could have happened in the past four moons and that they were really about to become *men*. The past few days seemed to last longer than the moons that preceded them, but finally — with the fourth moon high and full in the heavens — the kintango's assistants ordered the kafo to line up shortly after the evening meal.

Was this the moment for which they had waited? Kunta looked around for their fathers and brothers, who would surely be there for the ceremony. They were nowhere to be seen. And where was the kintango? His eyes searched the compound and found him — standing at the gate of the jujuo — just as he swung it open wide, turned to them, and called out: "Men of Juffure, return to your village!"

For the moment they stood rooted; then they rushed up whooping and grabbed and hugged their kintango and his assistants, who pretended to be offended by such impertinence. Four moons before, as the hood was being lifted from his head in this very compound, Kunta would have found it difficult to believe that he would be sorry to leave this place, or that he would come to love the stern old man who stood before them on that day; but he felt both emotions now. Then his thoughts turned homeward and he was racing and shouting with the others out the gate and down the path to Juffure. They hadn't gone very far before, as if upon some unspoken signal, their voices were stilled and their pace slowed by the thoughts they all shared, each in his own way — of what they were leaving behind, and of what lay ahead of them. This time they didn't need the stars to find their way.

CHAPTER 26

"Aiee! Aiee!" The women's happy shrieks rang out, and the people were rushing from their huts, laughing, dancing, and clapping their hands as Kunta's kafo — and those who had turned fifteen and become fourth kafo while they were away at the jujuo — strode in through the village gate at the break of dawn. The new men walked slowly, with what they hoped was dignity, and they didn't speak or smile — at first. When he saw his mother running toward him, Kunta felt like dashing to meet her, and he couldn't stop his face from lighting up, but he made himself continue walking at the same measured pace. Then Binta was upon him — arms around his neck, hands caressing his cheeks, tears welling in her eyes, murmuring his name. Kunta permitted this only briefly before he drew away, being now a man; but he made it seem as if he did so only to get a better look at the yowling bundle cradled snugly in the sling across her back. Reaching inside, he lifted the baby out with both hands.

"So this is my brother Madi!" he shouted happily, holding him high in the air.

Binta beamed at his side as he walked toward her hut with the baby in his arms — making faces and cooing and squeezing the plump little cheeks. But Kunta wasn't so taken with his little brother that he failed to notice the herd of naked children that followed close behind them with eyes as wide as their mouths. Two or three were at his knees, and others darted in and out among Binta and the other women, who were all exclaiming over how strong and healthy Kunta looked, how manly he'd become. He pretended not to hear, but it was music to his ears.

Kunta wondered where Omoro was, and where Lamin was — remembering abruptly that his little brother would be away grazing the goats. He had sat down inside Binta's hut before he noticed that one of the bigger first-kafo children had followed them inside and now stood staring at him and clinging to Binta's skirt. "Hello, Kunta," said the little boy. It was Suwadu! Kunta couldn't believe it. When he had left for manhood training, Suwadu was just something underfoot, too small to take notice of except when he was annoying Kunta with his eternal whining. Now, within the space of four moons, he seemed to have grown taller, and he was beginning to talk; he had become a *person*. Giving the baby back to Binta, he picked up Suwadu and swung him high up to the roof of Binta's hut, until his little brother yelped with delight.

When he finished visiting with Suwadu, who ran outside to see some of the other new men, the hut fell silent. Brimming over with joy and pride, Binta felt no need to speak. Kunta did. He wanted to tell her how much he had missed her and how it gladdened him to be home. But he couldn't find the words. And he knew it wasn't the sort of thing a man should say to a woman — even to his mother.

"Where is my father?" he asked finally.

"He's cutting thatch grass for your hut," said Binta. In his excitement, Kunta had nearly forgotten that, as a man, he would now have his own private hut. He walked outside and hurried to the place where his father had always told him one could cut the best quality of roofing thatch.

Omoro saw him coming, and Kunta's heart raced as he saw his father begin walking to meet him. They shook hands in the manner of men, each looking deeply into the other's eyes, seeing the other for the first time as man to man. Kunta felt almost weak with emotion, and they were silent for a moment. Then Omoro said, as if he were commenting on the weather, that he had acquired for Kunta a hut whose previous owner had married and built a new house. Would he like to inspect the hut now? Kunta said softly that he would, and they walked along together, with Omoro doing most of the talking, since Kunta was still having trouble finding words.

The hut's mud walls needed as many repairs as the thatching. But Kunta hardly noticed or cared, for this was his own private hut, and it was all the way across the village from his mother's. He didn't allow himself to show his satisfaction, of course, let alone to speak of it. Instead, he told Omoro only that he would make the repairs himself. Kunta could fix the walls, said Omoro, but he would like to finish the roof repairs he had already begun. Without another word, he turned and headed back to the thatch-grass field — leaving Kunta standing there, grateful for the everyday manner with which his father had begun their new relationship as men.

Kunta spent most of the afternoon covering every corner of Juffure, filling his eyes with the sight of all the dearly remembered faces, familiar huts and haunts — the village well, the schoolyard, the baobab and silk-cotton trees. He hadn't realized how homesick he had been until he began to bask in the greetings of everyone he passed. He wished it was time for Lamin to return with the goats, and found himself missing one other very special person, even if she was a woman. Finally — not caring whether it was something a man should properly do — he headed for the small, weathered hut of old Nyo Boto.

"Grandmother!" he called at the door.

"Who is it?" came the reply in a high, cracked, irritable tone.

"Guess, Grandmother!" said Kunta, and he went inside the hut.

It took his eyes a few moments to see her better in the dim light. Squatting beside a bucket and plucking long fibers from a slab of baobab bark that she had been soaking with water from the bucket, she peered sharply at him for a while before speaking. "Kunta!"

"It's so good to see you, Grandmother!" he exclaimed.

Nyo Boto returned to her plucking of fibers. "Is your mother well?" she asked, and Kunta assured her that Binta was.

He was a little taken aback, for her manner was almost as if he hadn't even been away anywhere, as if she hadn't noticed that he had become a man.

"I thought of you often while I was

away — each time I touched the saphie charm you put on my arm."

She only grunted, not even looking up from her work.

He apologized for interrupting her and quickly left, deeply hurt and terribly confused. He wouldn't understand until much later that her rebuff had hurt Nyo Boto even more than it did him; she had acted as she knew a woman must toward one who could no longer seek comfort at her skirts.

Still troubled, Kunta was walking slowly back toward his new hut when he heard a familiar commotion: bleating goats, barking dogs, and shouting boys. It was the second kafo returning from their afternoon's work in the bush. Lamin would be among them. Kunta began to search their faces anxiously as the boys approached. Then Lamin saw him, shouted his name, and came dashing, wreathed in smiles. But he stopped short a few feet away when he saw his brother's cool expression, and they stood looking at each other. It was finally Kunta who spoke.

"Hello."

"Hello, Kunta."

Then they looked at each other some more. Pride shone in Lamin's eyes, but Kunta saw also the same hurt he had just felt in the hut of Nyo Boto, and uncertainty about just what to make of his new big brother. Kunta was thinking that the way they were both acting wasn't as he would have had it be, but it was necessary that a man be regarded with a certain amount of respect, even by his own brother.

Lamin was the first to speak again: "Your two goats are both big with kids." Kunta was delighted; that meant he would soon own four, maybe five goats, if one of those nannies was big with twins. But he didn't smile or act surprised. "That's good news," he said, with even less enthusiasm than he wanted to show. Not knowing what else to say, Lamin dashed away without another word, hollering for his wuolo dogs to reassemble his goats, which had begun to wander.

Binta's face kept a set, tight expression as she assisted Kunta in moving to his own hut. His old clothes were all outgrown, she said, and with her tone properly respectful, added that whenever he had time for her to measure him between the important things he had to do, she would sew him some new clothes. Since he owned not much more than his bow and arrows and his slingshot, Binta kept murmuring, "You'll need this" and "You'll need that," until she had provided him with such household essentials as a pallet, some bowls, a stool, and a prayer rug she had woven while he was away. With each new thing, as he had always heard his father do, Kunta would grunt, as if he could think of no objection to having it in his house. When she noticed him scratching his head, she offered to inspect his scalp for ticks, and he bluntly told her "No!," ignoring the grumbling sounds she made afterward.

It was nearly midnight when Kunta finally slept, for much was on his mind. And it seemed to him that his eyes had hardly closed before the crowing cocks had waked him, and then came the singsong call of the alimamo to the mosque, for what would be the first morning prayer that he and his mates would be allowed to attend with the other men of Juffure. Dressing quickly, Kunta took his new prayer rug and fell in among his kafo as, with heads bowed and rolled prayer rugs under their arms — as if they had done it all their lives — they entered the sacred mosque behind the other men of the village. Inside, Kunta and the others watched and copied every act and utterance of the older men, being especially careful to be neither too soft nor too loud in their reciting of the prayers.

After prayers, Binta brought breakfast to her new man's hut. Setting the bowl of steaming couscous before Kunta — who just grunted again, not letting his face say anything — Binta left quickly, and Kunta ate without pleasure, irritated by a suspicion that she had seemed to be suppressing something like mirth.

After breakfast, he joined his mates in undertaking their duties as the eyes and ears of the village with a diligence their elders found equally amusing. The women could hardly turn around without finding one of the new men demanding to inspect their cooking pots for insects. And rummaging around outside peoples' huts and all around the village fence, they found hundreds of spots where the state of repair failed to measure up to their exacting standards. Fully a dozen of them drew up buckets of well water, tasting carefully from the gourd dipper in hopes of detecting a saltiness or a muddiness or something else unhealthy. They were disappointed, but the fish and turtle that were kept in the well to eat insects were removed anyway and replaced with fresh ones.

The new men, in short, were everywhere. "They are thick as fleas!" old Nyo Boto snorted as Kunta approached a stream where she was pounding laundry on a rock, and he all but sprinted off in another direction. He also took special care to stay clear of any known place where Binta might be, telling himself that although she was his mother, he would show her no special favors; that, indeed, he would deal firmly with her if she ever made it necessary. After all, she was a woman.

CHAPTER 27

Juffure was so small, and its kafo of diligent new men so numerous, it soon seemed to Kunta, that nearly every roof, wall, calabash, and cooking pot in the village had been inspected, cleaned, repaired, or replaced moments before he got to it. But he was more pleased than disappointed, for it gave him more time to spend farming the small plot assigned to his use by the Council of Elders. All new men grew their own couscous or groundnuts, some to live on and the rest to trade — with those who grew too little to feed their families — for things they needed more than food. A young man who tended his crops well, made good trades, and managed his goats wisely — perhaps swapping a dozen goats for a female calf that would grow up and have other calves — could move ahead in the world and become a man of substance by the time he reached twenty-five or thirty rains and begin to think about taking a wife and raising sons of his own.

Within a few moons after his return, Kunta had grown so much more than he could eat himself, and made such shrewd trades for this or that household possession to adorn his hut, that Binta began to grumble about it within his hearing. He had so many stools, wicker mats, food bowls, gourds, and sundry other objects in his hut, she would mutter, that there was hardly any room left inside for Kunta. But he charitably chose to ignore her impertinence, since he slept now upon a fine bed of woven reeds over a springy bamboo mattress that she had spent half a moon making for him.

In his hut, along with several saphies he had acquired in exchange for crops from his farm plot, he kept a number of other potent spiritual safeguards: the perfumed extracts of certain plants and barks which, like every other Mandinka man, Kunta rubbed onto his forehead, upper arms, and thighs each night before going to bed. It was believed that this magical essence would protect a man from possession by evil spirits while he slept. It would also make him smell good — a thing that, along with his appearance, Kunta had begun to think about.

He and the rest of his kafo were becoming increasingly exasperated about a matter that had been rankling their manly pride for many moons. When they went off to manhood training, they had left behind a group of skinny, giggling, silly little girls who played almost as hard as the boys. Then, after only four moons away, they had returned — as new men — to find these same girls, with whom they had grown up, flouncing about wherever one looked, poking out their mango-sized breasts, tossing their heads and arms, showing off their jangly new earrings, beads, and bracelets. What irritated Kunta and the others wasn't so much that the girls were behaving so absurdly, but that they seemed to be doing so exclusively for the benefit of men at least ten rains older than themselves. For new men like Kunta, these maidens of marriageable age — fourteen and fifteen — had scarcely a glance except to sneer or laugh. He and his mates finally grew so disgusted with these airs and antics that they resolved to pay no further attention either to the girls or to the all-too-willing older men they sought to entice with such fluttery coyness.

But Kunta's foto would be as hard as his thumb some mornings when he waked. Of course, it had been hard many times before, even when he was Lamin's age; but now it was much different in the feeling, very deep and strong. And Kunta couldn't help putting his hand down under his bedcover and tightly squeezing it. He also couldn't help thinking about things he and his mates had overheard — about fotos being put into women.

One night dreaming — for ever since he was a small boy, Kunta had dreamed a great deal, even when he was awake, Binta liked to say — he found himself watching a harvest-festival seoruba, when the loveliest, longest-necked, sootiestblack maiden there chose to fling down her headwrap for him to pick up. When he did so, she rushed home shouting, "Kunta likes me!," and after careful consideration, her parents gave permission for them to marry. Omoro and Binta also agreed, and both fathers bargained for the bride price. "She is beautiful," said Omoro, "but my concerns are of her true value as my son's wife. Is she a strong, hard worker? Is she of pleasant disposition in the home? Can she cook well and care for children? And above all, is she guaranteed a virgin?" The answers were all yes, so a price was decided and a date set for the wedding.

Kunta built a fine new mud house, and both mothers cooked bountiful delicacies, to give guests the best impression. And on the wedding day, the adults, children, goats, chickens, dogs, parrots, and monkeys all but drowned out the musicians they had hired. When the bride's party arrived, the praise singer shouted of the fine families being joined together. Yet louder shouts rose when the bride's best girlfriends roughly shoved her inside

272

Kunta's new house. Grinning and waving to everyone, Kunta followed her and drew the curtain across the door. When she had seated herself on his bed, he sang to her a famous ancestral song of love: "Mandumbe, your long neck is very beautiful. . . ." Then they lay down on soft cured hides and she kissed him tenderly, and they clung together very tightly. And then the thing happened, as Kunta had come to imagine it from the ways it had been described to him. It was even greater than he had been told, and the feeling grew and grew — until finally he *burst*.

Jerking suddenly awake, Kunta lay very still for a long moment, trying to figure out what had happened. Then, moving his hand down between his legs, he felt the warm wetness on himself — and on his bed. Frightened and alarmed, he leaped up, felt for a cloth, and wiped himself off, and the bed, too. Then, sitting there in the darkness, his fear was slowly overtaken by embarrassment, his embarrassment by shame, his shame by pleasure, and his pleasure, finally, by a kind of pride. Had this ever happened to any of his mates? he wondered. Though he hoped it had, he also hoped it hadn't, for perhaps this is what happens when one really becomes a man, he thought; and he wanted to be the first. But Kunta knew that he would never know, for this experience and even these thoughts weren't the kind he could ever share with anyone. Finally, exhausted and exhilarated, he lay down again and soon fell into a mercifully dreamless sleep.

CHAPTER 28

Kunta knew every man, woman, child, dog, and goat in Juffure, he told himself one afternoon while he sat eating lunch beside his plot of groundnuts, and in the course of his new duties, he either saw or spoke with almost all of them nearly every day. Why then, did he feel so alone? Was he an orphan? Did he not have a father who treated him as one man should another? Did he not have a mother who tended dutifully to his needs? Did he not have brothers to look to him? As a new man, was he not their idol? Did he not have the friendship of those with whom he had played in the mud as children, herded goats as boys, returned to Juffure as men? Had he not earned the respect of his elders — and the envy of his kafo mates — for husbanding his farm plot into seven goats, three chickens, and a splendidly furnished hut before reaching his sixteenth birthday? He couldn't deny it.

And yet he was lonely. Omoro was too busy to spend even as much time with Kunta as he had when he had only one son and fewer responsibilities in the village. Binta was busy too, taking care of Kunta's younger brothers, but his mother and he had little to say to one another anyway. Even he and Lamin were no longer close; while he had been away at the jujuo, Suwadu had become Lamin's adoring shadow as Lamin had once been Kunta's, and Kunta watched with mixed emotions while Lamin's attitude toward his little brother warmed from irritation to toleration to affection. Soon they were inseparable, and this had left as little room for Kunta as it had for Madi, who was too young yet to join them but old enough to whine because they wouldn't let him. On days when the two older boys couldn't get out of their mother's hut fast enough, of course, Binta would often order them to take Madi along, so that she could get him out from underfoot, and Kunta would have to smile in spite of himself at the sight of his three brothers marching around the village, one behind the other, in the order of their births, with the two in front staring glumly ahead while the little one, smiling happily, brought up the rear, almost running to keep up.

No one walked behind Kunta any longer, and not often did anyone choose to walk beside him either, for his kafo mates were occupied almost every waking hour with their new duties and — perhaps like him — with their own broodings about what had so far proved to be the dubious rewards of manhood. True, they had been given their own farm plots and were beginning to collect goats and other possessions. But the plots were small, the work hard, and their possessions were embarrassingly few in comparison to those of older men. They had also been made the eyes and ears of the village, but the cooking pots were kept clean without their supervision, and nothing ever trespassed in the fields except occasional baboon families or dense flocks of birds. Their elders, it soon became clear, got to do all the really important jobs, and as if to rub it in, gave the new men only what they felt was the appearance of respect, as they had been given only the appearance of responsibility. Indeed, when they paid any attention at all to the younger men, the elders seemed to have as much difficulty as the young girls of the village in restraining themselves from laughter, even when one of them performed the most challenging task without a mistake. Well, someday he would be one of those older men, Kunta told himself, and he would wear the mantle of manhood not only with more dignity but also with more compassion and understanding toward younger men than he and his mates received now.

Feeling restless — and a little sorry for himself — that evening, Kunta left his hut to take a solitary walk. Though he had no destination in mind, his feet drew him toward the circle of rapt children's faces glowing in the light of the campfire around which the old grandmothers were telling their nightly stories to the first kafo of the village. Stopping close enough to listen — but not close enough to be noticed listening — Kunta squatted down on his haunches and pretended to be inspecting a rock at his feet while one of the wrinkled old women waved her skinny arms and jumped around the clearing in front of the children as she acted out her story of the four thousand brave warriors of the King of Kasoon who had been driven into battle by the thunder of five hundred great war drums and the trumpeting of five hundred elephant-tusk horns. It was a story he had heard many times around the fires as a child, and as he looked at the wide-eyed faces of his Madi in the front row, and Suwadu in the back row, it somehow made him feel sad to hear it again.

With a sigh, he rose and walked slowly away — his departure as unnoticed as his arrival had been. At the fire where Lamin sat with other boys his age chanting their Koranic verses, and the fire where Binta sat with other mothers gossiping about husbands, households, children, cooking, sewing, makeup, and hairdos, he felt equally unwelcome. Passing them by, he found himself finally beneath the spreading branches of the baobab where the men of Juffure sat around the fourth fire discussing village business and other matters of gravity. As he had felt too old to be wanted around the first fire, he felt too young to be wanted around this one. But he had no place else to go, so Kunta seated himself among those in the outer circle — beyond those of Omoro's age, who sat closer to the fire, and those of the kintango's age, who sat closest, among the Council of Elders. As he did so, he heard one of them ask:

"Can anyone say how many of us are getting stolen?"

They were discussing slave taking, which had been the main subject around the men's fire for the more than one hundred rains that toubob had been stealing people and shipping them in chains to the kingdom of white cannibals across the sea.

There was silence for a little while, and then the alimamo said, "We can only thank Allah that it's less now than it was."

"There are fewer of us left to steal!"

said an angry elder.

"I listen to the drums and count the lost," said the kintango. "Fifty to sixty each new moon just from along our part of the bolong would be my guess." No one said anything to that, and he added, "There is no way, of course, to count the losses farther inland, and farther up the river."

"Why do we count only those *taken away* by the toubob?" asked the arafang. "We must count also the burned baobabs where villages once stood. He has killed more in fires and in fighting him than he has ever taken away!"

The men stared at the fire for a long time, and then another elder broke the silence: "Toubob could never do this without help from our own people. Mandinkas, Fulas, Wolofs, Jolas — none of The Gambia's tribes is without its slatee traitors. As a child I saw these slatees beating those like themselves to walk faster for the toubob!"

"For toubob money, we turn against our own kind," said Juffure's senior elder. "Greed and treason — these are the things toubob has given us in exchange for those he has stolen away.

No one talked again for a while, and the fire sputtered quietly. Then the kintango spoke again: "Even worse than toubob's money is that he lies for nothing and he cheats with method, as naturally as he breathes. That's what gives him the advantage over us."

A few moments passed, and then a young man of the kafo ahead of Kunta's asked, "Will toubob never change?"

"That will be," said one of the elders, "when the river flows backward!"

Soon the fire was a pile of smoking embers, and the men began to get up, stretch themselves, wish one another good night, and head home to their huts. But five young men of the third kafo stayed behind — one to cover with dust the warm ashes of all the fires, and the rest, including Kunta, to take the late shift as village lookouts beyond each corner of Juffure's high bamboo fence. After such alarming talk around the fire, Kunta knew he would have no trouble staying awake, but he didn't look forward to spending this particular night beyond the safety of the village.

Ambling through Juffure and out the gate with what he hoped was nonchalance, Kunta waved to his fellow guards and made his way along the outside of the fence — past the sharp-thorned bushes piled thickly against it, and the pointed stakes concealed beneath them — to a leafy hiding place that afforded him a silvery view of the surrounding countryside on this moonlit night. Getting as comfortable as he could, he slung his spear across his lap, drew up his knees, clasped his arms around them for warmth, and settled in for the night. Scanning the bush with straining eyes for any sign of movement, he listened to the shrilling of crickets, the eerie whistling of nightbirds, the distant howling of hyenas, and the shrieks of unwary animals taken by surprise, and he thought about the things the men had said around the fire. When dawn came without an incident, he was almost as surprised that he hadn't been set upon by slave stealers as he was to realize that for the first time in a moon, he hadn't spent a moment worrying about his personal problems.

CHAPTER 29

Nearly every day, it seemed to Kunta, Binta would irritate him about something. It wasn't anything she would do or say, but in other ways — little looks, certain tones of voice — Kunta could tell she disapproved of something about him. It was worst when Kunta added to his possessions new things that Binta hadn't obtained for him herself. One morning, arriving to serve his breakfast, Binta nearly dropped the steaming couscous upon Kunta when she saw he was wearing his first dundiko not sewn with her own hands. Feeling guilty for having traded a cured hyena hide to get it, Kunta angrily offered her no explanation, though he could feel that his mother was deeply hurt.

From that morning on, he knew that

Binta never brought his meals without her eyes raking every item in his hut to see if there was anything else — a stool, a mat, a bucket, a plate, or a pot — that she'd had nothing to do with. If something new had appeared, Binta's sharp eyes would never miss it. Kunta would sit there fuming while she put on that look of not caring and not noticing that he had seen her wear so many times around Omoro, who knew as well as Kunta did that Binta could hardly wait to get to the village well among her women friends so that she could loudly bemoan her troubles — which was what all Mandinka women did when they disagreed with their husbands.

One day, before his mother arrived with the morning meal, Kunta picked up a beautifully woven basket that Jinna M'Baki, one of Juffure's several widows, had given him as a gift and he set it just inside the door of his hut, where his mother would be sure to all but stumble over it. The widow was actually a little younger than Binta, it occurred to him. While Kunta was still a second-kafo goatherd, her husband had gone away to hunt and never returned. She lived near Nyo Boto, whom Kunta often visited, and that was how he and the widow had seen each other and come to speak to each other as Kunta had grown older. It had annoyed Kunta when the widow's gift caused some of Kunta's friends to tease him about her reason for giving him a valuable bamboo basket. When Binta arrived at his hut and saw it — recognizing the widow's style of weaving — she flinched as if the basket were a scorpion before managing to compose herself.

She didn't say a word about it, of course, but Kinta knew he had made his point. He was no longer a boy, and it was time for her to stop acting like his mother. He felt it was his own responsibility to change her in that regard. It wasn't something to speak to Omoro about, for Kunta knew he couldn't put himself into the ridiculous position of asking Omoro's advice on how to make Binta respect her son the same as she did her husband. Kunta thought about discussing his problem with Nyo Boto, but changed his mind when he recalled how peculiarly she had acted toward him upon his return from manhood training.

So Kunta kept his own counsel, and before long he decided not to go any more into Binta's hut, where he had lived most of his life. And when Binta brought his meals, he would sit stiffly silent while she set his food on the mat before him and left without speaking or even looking at him. Kunta finally began thinking seriously of seeking out some new eating arrangement. Most of the other new young men still ate from their mothers' kitchens, but some were cooked for by an older sister or sister-in-law. If Binta got any worse, Kunta told himself, he was going to find some other woman to cook for him — perhaps the widow who had given him the woven basket. He knew without asking that she would gladly cook for him — and yet Kunta didn't want to let her know that he was even considering such a thing. In the meantime, he and his mother continued to meet at mealtimes — and to act as if they didn't even see each other.

Early one morning, returning from a night of sentry duty out in the groundnut fields, Kunta saw hurrying along the trail some distance ahead of him three young men whom he could tell were about his own age, and whom he knew had to be travelers from somewhere else. Shouting until they turned around, he went running to meet and greet them. They told Kunta they were from the village of Barra, a day and a night of walking from Juffure, and they were on their way to hunt for gold. They were of the Feloop tribe, which was a branch of Mandinka, but he had to listen carefully to understand them, as they did to understand him. It made Kunta remember his visit with his father to his uncles' new village, where he couldn't understand what some people were saying, although they lived only two or three days away from Juffure.

Kunta was intrigued by the trip the young men were taking. He thought it might also interest some of his friends, so he asked the young men to stop in his village for a day of hospitality before they went on. But they graciously refused the invitation, saying that they had to reach the place where the gold could be panned by the third afternoon of travel. "But why don't you come along with us?" one of the young men asked Kunta.

Never having dreamed of such a thing, Kunta was so taken aback that he found himself saying no, telling them that as much as he appreciated the offer, he had much work to do on his farm, as well as other duties. And the three young men expressed their regret. "If you should change your mind, please join us," one said. And they got down on their knees and drew in the dust to show Kunta where the gold-hunting place was located — about two days and nights of travel beyond Juffure. The father of one of the boys, a traveling musician, had told them where it was.

Kunta walked along talking with his newfound friends until they came to where the travelers' trail forked. After the three men took the fork that led on past Juffure — and turned to wave back at him — Kunta walked slowly home. He was thinking hard as he entered his hut and lay down on his bed, and though he had been awake all night, he still couldn't seem to fall asleep. Perhaps he might go to hunt gold after all if he could find a friend to tend his farm plot. And he knew that someone of his mates would take over his sentry duties if they were only asked — as he would gladly do if they asked him.

Kunta's next thought hit him so hard it made him leap right up out of bed: As a man now, he could take Lamin along, as his father had once taken *him*. For the next hour Kunta paced the dirt floor of his hut, his mind wrestling with the questions raised by this exciting thought. First of all, would Omoro permit such a trip for Lamin, who was yet a boy and thus required his father's approval? It galled Kunta enough, as a man, to have to ask permission for anything; but suppose Omoro said *no?* And how would his three new friends feel about it if he showed up with his little brother?

Come to think of it, Kunta wondered why he was pacing the floor, and risking serious embarrassment, just to do a favor for Lamin. After all, ever since he had returned from manhood training, Lamin hadn't even been that close to him any more. But Kunta knew that this wasn't something that either of them wanted. They had really enjoyed each other before Kunta went away. But now Lamin's time was taken up by Suwadu, who was always hanging around his bigger brother in the same way that Lamin used to hang around Kunta, full of pride and admiration. But Kunta felt that Lamin had never quit feeling that way about him. If anything, he felt that Lamin admired his big brother even more than before. It was just that some kind of distance had come between them because of his having become a man. Men simply spent no great deal of time with boys; and even if that wasn't as he and Lamin wanted it, there just seemed no way for either of them to crack through it — until Kunta thought of taking Lamin along on his gold-hunting trip.

"Lamin is a good boy. He displays his home training well. And he takes good care of my goats," was Kunta's opening comment to Omoro, for Kunta knew that men almost never began conversations directly with what they meant to discuss. Omoro, of course, knew this, too. He nodded slowly and replied: "Yes, I would say that is true." As calmly as he could, Kunta then told his father of meeting his three new friends and of their invitation to join them in hunting for gold. Taking a deep breath, Kunta finally said, "I've been thinking that Lamin might enjoy the trip."

Omoro's face showed not a flicker of expression. A long moment passed before he spoke. "For a boy to travel is good," he said — and Kunta knew that his father was at least not going to say no absolutely. In some way, Kunta could feel his father's trust in him, but also his concern, which he knew Omoro didn't want to express any more strongly than he had to. "It has been rains since I've had any travel in that area. I seem not to remember that trail's route very well," said Omoro, as casually as if they were merely discussing the weather. Kunta knew that his father — whom Kunta had never known to forget anything — was trying to find out if he knew the route to the gold-hunting place.

Dropping onto his knees in the dust, Kunta drew the trail with a stick as if he had known it for years. He drew circles to show the villages that were both near the trail and at some distance from it along the way. Omoro got down onto his knees as well, and when Kunta had finished drawing the trail, said, "I would go so as to pass close by the most villages. It will take a little longer, but it will be the safest."

Kunta nodded, hoping that he appeared more confident than he suddenly felt. The thought hit him that though the three friends he had met, traveling together, could catch each other's mistakes — if they made any — he, traveling with a younger brother for whom he would be responsible, would have no one to help if something went wrong.

Then Kunta saw Omoro's finger circling the last third of the trail. "In this area, few speak Mandinka," Omoro said. Kunta remembered the lessons of his manhood training and looked into his father's eyes. "The sun and the stars will tell me the way," he said.

A long moment passed, and then Omoro spoke again. "I think I'll go by your mother's house." Kunta's heart leaped. He knew it was his father's way of saying that his permission was given, and he felt it best that he personally make his decision known to Binta.

Omoro wasn't long in Binta's hut. He had hardly left to return to his own when she burst out her door, hands pressed tightly to her shaking head. "Madi! Suwadu!" she shrieked, and they came rushing to her from among the other children.

Now other mothers came from their huts, and unmarried girls, all rushing behind Binta as she began hollering and pulling the two boys alongside her toward the well. Once there, all of the women crowded about her as she wept and moaned that now she had only two children left, that her others certainly would soon be lost to toubob.

A second-kafo girl, unable to contain the news of Kunta's trip with Lamin, raced all the way out to where the boys of her kafo were grazing the goats. A short time later, back in the village, heads jerked around with smiles on their faces as a deliriously joyful boy came whooping into the village in a manner fit to wake the ancestors. Catching up with his mother just outside her hut, Lamin — though still a hand's span shorter than her — bearhugged Binta, planted big kisses on her forehead and swept her whirling up off her feet as she shouted to be put down. Once back on the ground, she ran to pick up a nearby piece of wood and struck Lamin with it. She would have done it again, but he dashed away — feeling no pain — toward Kunta's hut. He didn't even knock as he burst inside. It was an unthinkable intrusion into a man's house — but after a glimpse at his brother's face, Kunta had to overlook it. Lamin just stood there, looking up into the face of his big brother. The boy's mouth was trying to say something; indeed, his whole body was trembling, and Kunta had to catch himself to keep from grabbing and hugging Lamin in the rush of love he felt passing between them in that moment.

Kunta heard himself speaking, his tone almost gruff. "I see you've already heard. We'll leave tomorrow after first prayer."

Man or not, Kunta took care to walk nowhere near Binta as he made several quick calls to see friends about caring for his farm and filling in for him on sentry duty. Kunta could tell where Binta was from the sound of her wailing as she marched around the village holding Madi and Suwadu by the hand. "These two only I have left!" she cried, as loudly as she could. But like everyone else in Juffure, she knew that no matter what she felt or said or did, Omoro had spoken.

CHAPTER 30

At the travelers' tree, Kunta prayed for their journey to be a safe one. So that it would be a properous one as well, he tied the chicken he had brought along to a lower branch by one of its legs, leaving it flapping and squawking there as he and Lamin set forth on the trail. Though he didn't turn back to look, Kunta knew Lamin was trying very hard to keep pace with him, and to keep his headload balanced — and to keep Kunta from noticing either.

After an hour, the trail took them by a low, spreading tree strung thickly with beads. Kunta wanted to explain to Lamin how such a tree meant that living nearby were some of the few Mandinkas who were kafirs, pagan unbelievers who used snuff and smoked tobacco in pipes made of wood with earthen bowls, and also drank a beer they made of mead. But more important than that knowledge was for Lamin to learn the discipline of silent marching. By noontime, Kunta knew that Lamin's feet and legs would be hurting him badly, and also his neck under the heavy headload. But it was only by keeping on despite pain that a boy could toughen his body and his spirit. At the same time, Kunta knew that Lamin must stop for rest before he collapsed, which would hurt his pride.

Taking the bypass trail to miss the first village they passed, they soon shook off the naked little first-kafo children who raced out to inspect them. Kunta still didn't look back, but he knew that Lamin would have quickened his pace and straightened his back for the children's benefit. But as they left the children and the village behind, Kunta's mind drifted off Lamin to other things. He thought again of the drum he was going to make for himself — making it first in his mind, as the men did who carved out masks and figures. For the drum's head, he had a young goat's skin already scraped and curing in his hut, and he knew just the place — only a short trot beyond the women's rice fields — where he could find the tough wood he needed for a strong drumframe. Kunta could almost hear how his drum was going to sound.

As the trail took them into a grove of trees close by the path, Kunta tightened his grip on the spear he carried, as he had been taught to do. Cautiously, he continued walking — then stopped and listened very quietly. Lamin stood wide-eyed behind him, afraid to breathe. A moment later, however, his big brother relaxed and began walking again, toward what Kunta recognized — with relief — as the sound of several men singing a working song. Soon he and Lamin came into a clearing and saw twelve men dragging a dugout canoe with ropes. They had felled a tree and burned and chopped it out, and now they were starting to move it the long way to the river. After each haul on the ropes, they sang the next line of the song, each one ending "All together!," then again, straining hard, as they moved the dugout about another arm's length. Waving to the men, who waved back, Kunta passed them and made a mental note to tell Lamin later who these men were and why they had made the canoe from a tree that grew here in the forest rather than near the riverbank: They were from the village of Kerewan, where they made the best Mandinka dugouts; and they knew that only forest trees would float.

Kunta thought with a rush of warmth about the three young men from Barra whom they were traveling to meet. It was strange that though they never had seen each other before, they seemed as brothers. Perhaps it was because they too were Mandinkas. They said things differently than he did, but they weren't different *inside*. Like them, he had decided to leave his village to seek his fortune — and a little excitement — before returning to their homes ahead of the next big rains.

When the time neared for the alansaro prayer in midafternoon, Kunta stepped off the trail where a small stream ran among trees. Not looking at Lamin, he slipped off his headload, flexed himself, and bent to scoop up handfuls of water in order to splash his face. He drank sparingly, then, in the midst of his prayer, he heard Lamin's headload thud to the earth. Springing up at the end of the prayer intending to rebuke him, he saw how painfully his brother was crawling toward the water. But Kunta still made his voice hard: "Sip a little at a time!" As Lamin drank, Kunta decided that an hour's resting here would be long enough. After eating a few bites of food, he thought, Lamin should be able to keep walking until time for the fitiro prayer, at about dusk, when a fuller meal and a night's rest would be welcomed by them both.

But Lamin was too tired even to eat. He lay where he had drunk from the stream, face down with his arms flung out, palms up. Kunta stepped over quietly to look at the soles of his feet; they weren't bleeding yet. Then Kunta himself catnapped, and when he got up he took from his headload enough dried meat for two. Shaking

Lamin awake, he gave him his meat and ate his own. Soon they were back on the trail, which made all the turns and passed all the landmarks the young men from Barra had drawn for Kunta. Near one village, they saw two old grandmothers and two young girls with some first-kafo children busily catching crabs, darting their hands into a little stream and snatching out their prey.

Near dusk, as Lamin began to grab more and more often at his headload, Kunta saw ahead a flock of large bushfowl circling down to land. Abruptly he stopped, concealing himself, as Lamin sank onto his knees behind a bush nearby. Kunta pursed his lips, making the male bushfowl mating call, and shortly several fat, fine hens came flapping and waddling over. They were cocking their heads and looking around when Kunta's arrow went straight through one. Jerking its head off, he let the blood drain out, and while the bird roasted he built a rough bush shelter, then prayed. He also roasted some ears of wild corn that he had plucked along the way before awakening Lamin, who had fallen asleep again the moment they put their headloads down. Hardly had Lamin wolfed down his meal before he flopped back down onto the soft moss under a slanting roof of leafy boughs and went back to sleep without a murmur.

Kunta sat hugging his knees in the night's still air. Not far away, hyenas began yipping. For some time, he diverted himself by identifying the other sounds of the forest. Then three times he faintly heard a melodious horn. He knew it was the next village's final prayer call, blown by their alimamo through a hollowed elephant's tooth. He wished that Lamin had been awake to hear its haunting cry, which was almost like a human voice, but then he smiled, for his brother was beyond caring what anything sounded like. Then himself praying, Kunta also slept.

Soon after sunrise, they were passing that village and hearing the drumming rhythm of the women's pestles pounding couscous for breakfast porridge. Kunta could almost taste it; but they didn't stop. Not far beyond, down the trail, was another village, and as they went by, the men were leaving their mosque and the women were bustling around their cooking fires. Still farther on, Kunta saw ahead of them an old man sitting beside the trail. He was bent nearly double over a number of cowrie shells, which he was shuffling and reshuffling on a plaited bamboo mat while mumbling to himself. Not to interrupt him, Kunta was about to pass by when the old man looked up and hailed them over to where he sat.

"I come from the village of Kootacunda, which is in the kingdom of Wooli, where the sun rises over the Simbani forest," he said in a high, cracking voice. "And where may you be from?" Kunta told him the village of Juffure, and the old man nodded. "I have heard of it." He was consulting his cowries, he said, to learn their next message about his journey to the city of Tumbuktu, "which I want to see before I die," and he wondered if the travelers would care to be of any help to him. "We are poor, but happy to share whatever we have with you, Grandfather," said Kunta, easing off his headload, reaching within it and withdrawing some dried meat, which he gave the old man, who thanked him and put the food in his lap.

Peering at them both, he asked, "You are brothers traveling?"

"We are, Grandfather," Kunta replied.

"That is good!" the old man said, and picked up two of his cowries. "Add this to those on your hunting bag, and it will bring you a fine profit," he said to Kunta, handing him one of the cowries. "And you, young man," he said to Lamin, giving him the other, "keep this for when you become a man with a bag of your own." They both thanked him, and he wished them Allah's blessings.

They had walked on for quite a while when Kunta decided that the time was ripe to break the silence with Lamin. Without stopping or turning, he began to speak: "There is a legend, little brother, that it was traveling Mandinkas who named the place where the old man is bound. They found there a kind of insect they had never seen before and named the place 'Tumbo Kutu,' which means 'new insect.'" When there was no response from Lamin, Kunta turned his head; Lamin was well behind, bent down over his headload — which had fallen open on the ground — and struggling to tie it back together. As Kunta trotted back, he realized that Lamin's grabbing at his headload had finally caused it to work its bindings loose and that he had somehow eased it off his head without making any noise, not wanting to break the rule of silence by asking Kunta to stop. While Kunta was retying the headload, he saw that Lamin's feet were bleeding; but this was to be expected, so he said nothing of it. The tears shone in Lamin's eyes as he got the load back on his head, and they went on. Kunta upbraided himself that he hadn't missed Lamin's presence and might have left him behind.

They hadn't walked much farther when Lamin let out a choked scream. Thinking he had stepped on a thorn, Kunta turned — and saw his brother staring upward at a big panther flattened on the limb they would have walked under in another moment. The panther went *sssss,* then seemed to flow almost lazily into the branches of a tree and was gone from sight. Shaken, Kunta resumed walking, alarmed and angry and embarrassed at himself. Why had he not seen that panther? The odds were that it was only wishing to remain unseen and wouldn't have sprung down upon them, for unless the big cats were extremely hungry, they rarely attacked even their animal prey during the daylight, and humans seldom at any time, unless they were cornered, provoked, or wounded. Still, a picture flashed through Kunta's memory of the panther-mangled nanny goat from his goat-herding days. He could almost hear the kintango's stern warning: "The hunter's senses must be fine. He must hear what others cannot, smell what others cannot. He must see through the darkness." But while he had been walking along with his own thoughts wandering, it was Lamin who had seen the panther. Most of his bad troubles had come from that habit, which he absolutely must correct, he thought. Bending quickly without breaking pace, Kunta picked up a small stone, spit on it three times, and hurled it far back down the trail, the stone having thus carried behind them the spirits of misfortune.

They walked on with the sun burning down upon them as the country gradually changed from green forest to oil palms and muddy, dozing creeks, taking them past hot, dusty villages where — just as in Juffure — first-kafo children ran and screamed around in packs, where men lounged under the boabab and women gossiped beside the well. But Kunta wondered why they let their goats wander around these villages, along with the dogs and chickens, rather than keeping them either out grazing or penned up, as in Juffure. He decided that they must be an odd, different kind of people.

They pushed on over grassless, sandy soil sprinkled with the burst dry fruit of weirdly shaped baobabs. When the time came to pray, they rested and ate lightly, and Kunta would check Lamin's headbundle and his feet, whose bleeding was not so bad any more. And the crossroads kept unfolding like a picture, until finally there was the huge old shell of a baobab that the young men from Barra had described. It must have been hundreds of rains old to be dying at last, he thought, and he told Lamin what one of the young men had told him: "A griot rests inside there," adding from his own knowledge that griots were always buried not as other people were but within the shells of ancient baobabs, since both the trees and the histories in the heads of griots were timeless. "We're close now," Kunta said, and he wished he had the drum he was going to make, so that he could signal ahead to his friends. With the sinking of the sun, they finally reached the clay pits — and there were the three young men.

"We felt you would come!" they shouted, happy to see him. They merely ignored Lamin as if he were their own second-kafo brother. Amid brisk talk, the three young men proudly showed the tiny grains of gold they had collected. By the next morning's first light, Kunta and Lamin had joined in, chopping up chunks of sticky clay, which they dropped into large calabashes of water. After whirling the calabash, then slowly pouring off most of the muddy water, they carefully felt with their fingers to see if any gold grains had sunk to the bottom. Now and then there was a grain as tiny as a millet seed, or maybe a little larger.

They worked so feverishly that there was no time for talk. Lamin seemed even to forget his aching muscles in the search for gold. And each precious grain went carefully into the hollow of the largest quills from bush pigeons' wings, stoppered with a bit of cotton. Kunta and Lamin had six quills full when the three young men said they'd collected enough. Now, they said, they'd like to go farther up the trail, deeper into the interior of the country, to hunt elephants' teeth. They said they had been told where old elephants sometimes broke off their teeth in trying to uproot small trees and thick brush while feeding. They had heard also that if one could ever find the secret graveyards of the elephants, a fortune in teeth would be there. Would Kunta join them? He was sorely tempted; this sounded even more exciting than hunting for gold. But he couldn't go — not with Lamin. Sadly he thanked them for the invitation and said he must return home with his brother. So warm farewells were exchanged, but not before Kunta had made the young men accept his invitation to stop for hospitality in Juffure on their way home to Barra.

The trip back seemed shorter to Kunta. Lamin's feet bled worse, but he walked faster when Kunta handed him the quills to carry, saying "Your mother should enjoy these." Lamin's happiness was no greater than his own at having taken his brother traveling, just as their father had done for him — just as Lamin would one day take Suwadu, and Suwadu would take Madi. They were approaching Juffure's travelers' tree when Kunta heard Lamin's headload fall off again. Kunta whirled angrily, but then he saw his brother's pleading expression. "All right, get it later!" he snapped. Without a word, his aching muscles and his bleeding feet forgotten, Lamin bolted past Kunta for the village, his thin legs racing faster than they'd ever taken him.

By the time Kunta entered the village gate, excited women and children were clustered around Binta, who was sticking the six quills of gold into her hair, clearly bursting with relief and happiness. A moment later, Binta's and Kunta's faces exchanged a look of tenderness and warmth far beyond the usual greetings that passed between mother and her grown-up son home from traveling. The women's clacking tongues soon let everyone in Juffure know what the two oldest Kinte sons had brought home with them. "There's a cow on Binta's head!" shouted an old grandmother — there was enough gold in the quills to buy a cow — and the rest of the women took up that cry.

"You did well," said Omoro simply when Kunta met him. But the feeling they shared without further words was even greater than with Binta. In the days that followed, elders seeing Kunta around the village began to speak to him and smile in a special way, and he solemnly replied with his respects. Even Suwadu's little second-kafo mates greeted Kunta as a grown-up, saying "Peace!" and then standing with palms folded over their chests until he passed by. Kunta even chanced to overhear Binta one day gossiping about "the two men I feed," and he was filled with pride that his mother had finally realized he was a man.

It was all right with Kunta now not only for Binta to feed him, but even to do such things as searching on Kunta's head for ticks, as she had been resenting not doing. And Kunta felt it all right now also to visit her hut again now and then. As for Binta, she bustled about all smiles, even humming to herself as she cooked. In an offhand manner, Kunta would ask if she needed him to do anything; she would say so if she did, and he did whatever it was as soon as he could. If he but glanced at Lamin or Suwadu, when they were playing too loudly, for example, they were instantly still and quiet. And Kunta liked tossing Madi into the air, catching him as he fell, and Madi liked it even more. As for Lamin, he clearly regarded his man-brother as ranking second only to Allah. He cared for Kunta's seven goats — which were multiplying well — as if they were goats of gold, and he eagerly helped Kunta to raise his small farm plot of couscous and groundnuts.

Whenever Binta needed to get some work done around the hut, Kunta would take all three children off her hands, and she would stand smiling in her doorway as he marched off with Madi on his shoulder, Lamin following — strutting like a rooster — and Suwadu jealously tagging along behind. It was nice, thought Kunta — so nice that he caught himself wishing that he might have a family of his own like this someday. But not until the time comes, of course, he told himself; and that's a long way off.

CHAPTER 31

As new men were permitted to do
whenever there was no conflict with their
duties, Kunta and the others of his kafo
would sit at the outermost edges of the
formal sessions of the Council of Elders,
which were held once each moon under
Juffure's ancient baobab. Sitting beneath
it on cured hides very close together, the
six senior elders seemed almost as old as
the tree, Kunta thought, and to have been
carved from the same wood, except that
they were as black as ebony against the
white of their long robes and round
skullcaps. Seated facing them were those
with troubles or disputes to be resolved.
Behind the petitioners, in rows, according
to their ages, sat junior elders such as
Omoro, and behind them sat the new men

of Kunta's kafo. And behind *them* the village women could sit, though they rarely attended except when someone in their immediate family was involved in a matter to be heard. Once in a long while, *all* the women would be present — but only if a case held the promise of some juicy gossip.

No women at all attended when the Council met to discuss purely administrative affairs, such as Juffure's relationship with other villages. On the day for matters of the people, however, the audience was large and noisy — but all settled quickly into silence when the most senior of the elders raised his stick, sewn with bright-colored beads, to strike out on the talking drum before him the name of the first person to be heard. This was done according to their ages, to serve the needs of the oldest first. Whoever it was would stand, stating his case, the senior elders all staring at the ground, listening until he finished and sat down. At this point, any of the elders might ask him questions.

If the matter involved a dispute, the

second person now presented his side, followed by more questions, whereupon the elders turned around to present their backs as they huddled to discuss the matter, which could take a long time. One or more might turn with further questions. But all finally turned back around toward the front, one motioning the person or persons being heard to stand again, and the senior elder then spoke their decision, after which the next name was drumtalked.

Even for new men like Kunta, most of these hearings were routine matters. People with babies recently born asked for a bigger farm plot for the husband and an additional rice plot for the wife — requests that were almost always quickly granted, as were the first farming-land requests of unmarried men like Kunta and his mates. During man-training, the kintango had directed them never to miss any Council of Elders sessions unless they had to, as the witnessing of its decisions would broaden a man's knowledge as his own rains increased until he too would be a senior elder. Attending his first session,

Kunta had looked at Omoro seated ahead of him, wondering how many hundreds of decisions his father must have in his head, though he wasn't even a senior elder yet.

At his first session, Kunta witnessed a land matter involving a dispute. Two men both claimed the fruit of some trees originally planted by the first man on land to which the second man now had the farming rights, since the first man's family had decreased. The Council of Elders awarded the fruit to the first man, saying, "If he hadn't planted the trees, that fruit wouldn't be there."

At later sessions, Kunta saw people frequently charged with breaking or losing something borrowed from an irate lender who claimed that the articles had been both valuable and brand-new. Unless the borrower had witnesses to disprove that, he was usually ordered to pay for or replace the article at the value of a new one. Kunta also saw furious people accusing others of inflicting bad fortune on them through evil magic. One man testified that another had touched him with a cock's spur, making him violently ill. A young wife declared that her new mother-in-law had hidden some bourein shrub in the wife's kitchen, causing whatever was cooked there to turn out badly. And a widow claimed that an old man whose advances she had spurned had sprinkled powdered eggshells in her path, making her walk into a long succession of troubles, which she proceeded to describe. If presented with enough impressive evidence of evil magic's motives and results, the Council would command immediate corrective magic to be done by the nearest traveling magic man, whom a drumtalk message would summon to Juffure at the expense of the evildoer.

Kunta saw debtors ordered to pay up, even if they had to sell their possessions; or with nothing to sell, to work off the amount as the lender's slave. He saw slaves charging their masters with cruelty, or with providing unsuitable food or lodgings, or with taking more than their half share of what the slaves' work had produced. Masters, in turn, accused slaves of cheating by hiding some of their produce, or of insufficient work, or of deliberately breaking farm tools. Kunta saw the Council weigh carefully the evidence in these cases, along with each person's past record in the village, and it was not uncommon for some slaves' reputations to be better than their masters'!

But sometimes there was no dispute between a master and his slave. Indeed, Kunta saw them coming together asking permission for the slave to marry into the master's family. But any couple intending to marry, first had to obtain the Council's permission. Couples judged by the Council to be too close of kinship were refused out of hand, but for those not thus disqualified, there was a waiting period of one moon between the request and the reply, during which the villagers were expected to pay quiet visits to any senior elder and reveal any private information, either good or bad, about the couple in question. Since childhood, had each of them always demonstrated a good home training? Had either of them ever caused undue trouble to anyone, including their own families? Had either of them ever displayed any undesirable tendencies of any kind, such as cheating or telling less than the full truth? Was the girl known for being irritable and argumentative? Was the man known for beating goats unmercifully? If so, the marriage was refused, for it was believed that such a person might pass these traits along to his or her children. But as Kunta knew even before he began attending the Council sessions, most couples won approval for marriage, because both sets of parents involved had already learned the answers to these questions, and found them satisfactory, before granting their own permission.

At the Council sessions, however, Kunta learned that sometimes parents hadn't been told things that people did tell the senior elders. Kunta saw one marriage permission flatly refused when a witness came forth to testify that the young man of the planned marriage, as a young goatherd, had once stolen a basket from him, thinking he hadn't been seen. The crime hadn't been reported then, out of compassion for the fact that he was still a boy; if it *had* been reported, the law would have dictated that his right hand be cut off. Kunta sat riveted as the young thief, exposed at last, burst into tears, blurting out his guilt before his horrified parents and the girl he was asking to marry, who began screaming. Soon afterward, he disappeared from Juffure and was never seen or heard of again.

After attending Council sessions for a number of moons, Kunta guessed that most problems for the senior elders came from married people — especially from men with two, three, or four wives. Adultery was the most frequent charge by such men, and unpleasant things happened to an offending man if a husband's accusation was backed up with convincing outside testimony or other strong evidence. If a wronged husband was poor and the offending man well off, the Council might order the offender to deliver his possessions to the husband, one at a time, until the husband said "I have enough," which might not be until the adulterer had only his bare hut left. But with both men poor, which was usually the case, the Council might order the offender to work as the husband's slave for a period of time considered worth the wrongful use of his wife. And Kunta flinched for one repeated offender when the elders set a date and time for him to receive a public flogging of thirty-nine lashes across his bare back by his most recently wronged husband, according to the ancient Moslem rule of "forty, save one."

Kunta's own thoughts about getting married cooled somewhat as he watched and listened to the angry testimony of injured wives and husbands before the Council. Men charged that their wives failed to respect them, were unduly lazy, were unwilling to make love when their turn came, or were just generally impossible to live with. Unless an accused wife presented a strong counterargument, with some witnesses to bear her out, the senior elders usually told the husband to go that day and set any three possessions of his wife's outside her hut and then utter toward those possessions, three times, with witnesses present, the words, "I divorce you!"

A wife's most serious charge — certain to bring out every woman in the village if it was suspected in advance — was to claim that her husband was not a man, meaning that he was inadequate with her in bed. The elders would appoint three old persons, one from the family of the defiant wife, another from the family of the husband, and the third from among the elders themselves. A date and time would be set for them to observe the wife and husband together in his bed. If two of the three voted that the wife was right, she won her divorce, and her family kept the dowry goats; but if two observers voted that the husband performed well, he not only got the goats back but also could beat the wife and divorce her if he wished to.

In the rains since Kunta had returned from manhood training, no case that had been considered by the Council filled him and his mates with as much anticipation as the one that began with gossip and whispering about two older members of their own kafo and a pair of Juffure's most eligible widows. On the day the matter finally came before the Council, nearly everyone in the village gathered early to assure themselves of the best possible seats. A number of routine old people's problems were settled first, and then came the case of Dembo Dabo and Kadi Tamba, who had been granted a divorce more than a rain before but now were back before the Council grinning widely and holding hands and asking permission to remarry. They stopped grinning when the senior elder told them sternly: "You insisted on divorce; therefore you may not remarry — until each of you has had another wife and husband in between."

The gasps from those in the rear were hushed by the drumtalk announcement of the next names to be called: "Tuda Tamba and Kalilu Conteh! Fanta Bedeng and Sefo Kela!" The two members of Kunta's kafo and the two widows stood up. The taller widow, Fanta Bedeng, spoke for all of them, sounding as if she had carefully practiced what to say; but nervousness still gripped her. "Tuda Tamba with her thirty-two rains and I with my thirty-three have small chance of catching more husbands,'' she said, and proceeded to ask the Council to approve of teriya friendships for her and Tuda Tamba to cook for the sleep with Sefo Kela and Kalilu Conteh, respectively.

Different elders asked a few questions of all four — the widows responding confidently, Kunta's friends uncertainly, in sharp contrast to their usual boldness of manner. And then the elders turned around, murmuring among themselves. The audience was so tense and quiet that a dropped groundnut could have been heard as the elders finally turned back around. The senior elder spoke: ''Allah would approve! You widows will have a man to use, and you new men will get valuable experience for when you marry later.''

The senior elder rapped his stick twice hard against the edge of the talking drum and glared at the buzzing women in the rear. Only when they fell silent was the next name called: ''Jankeh Jallon!'' Having but fifteen rains, she was thus the last to be heard. All of Juffure had danced and feasted when she found her way home after escaping from some toubob who had kidnaped her. Then, a few moons later, she became big with child, although unmarried, which caused much gossip. Young and strong, she might still have found some old man's acceptance as a third or fourth junior wife. But then the child was born: He was a strange pale tan color like a cured hide, and had very odd hair — and wherever Jankeh Jallon would appear thereafter, people would look at the ground and hurry elsewhere. Her eyes glistening with tears, she stood up now and asked the Council: What was she to do? The elders didn't turn around to confer; the senior elder said they would have to weigh the matter — which was a most serious and difficult one — until the next moon's Council meeting. And with that, he and the five other elders rose and left.

Troubled, and somehow unsatisfied, by the way the session had ended, Kunta remained seated for a few moments after most of his mates and the rest of the audience had gotten up — chattering among themselves — and headed back toward their huts. His head was still full of thoughts, when Binta brought in his evening meal, and he said not a word to her as he ate, nor she to him. Later, as he picked up his spear and his bow and arrow and ran with his wuolo dog to his sentry post — for this was his night to stand guard outside the village — Kunta was still thinking: about the tan baby with the strange hair, about his no doubt even stranger father, and about whether this toubob would have eaten Jankeh Jallon if she had not escaped from him.

CHAPTER 32

In the moonlit expanse of ripening fields of groundnuts, Kunta climbed the notched pole and sat down crosslegged on the lookout platform that was built into its sturdy fork, high above the ground. Placing his weapons beside him — along with the ax with which he planned the next morning, at last, to chop the wood for his drum frame — he watched as his wuolo dog went trotting and sniffing this way and that in the fields below. During Kunta's first moons on sentry duty, rains ago, he remembered snatching at his spear if so much as a rat went rustling through the grass. Every shadow seemed a monkey, every monkey a panther, and every panther a toubob, until his eyes and ears became seasoned to his task. In time, he found he could tell the difference between a snarl of a lion and that of a leopard. It took longer, however, for him to learn how to remain viligant through these long nights. When his thoughts began to turn inward, as they always did, he often forgot where he was and what he was supposed to be doing. But finally he learned to keep alert with half of his mind and yet still explore his private thoughts with the other.

Tonight, he was thinking about the teriya friendships that had been approved for his two friends by the Council of Elders. For several moons, they had been telling Kunta and his mates that they were going to take their case before the Council, but no one had really believed them. And now it was done. Perhaps at this very moment, he thought, they might be performing the teriya act in bed with their two widows. Kunta suddenly sat upright trying to picture what it must be like.

It was chiefly from his kafo's gossip that Kunta knew what little he did about under women's clothes. In marriage negotiations, he knew, girls' fathers had to guarantee them as virgins to get the best bride price. And a lot of bloodiness was connected with women, he knew that. Every moon they had blood; and whenever they had babies; and the night when they got married. Everyone knew how the next morning, the newlyweds' two mothers went to the hut to put into a woven basket the white pagne cloth the couple had slept on, taking its bloodiness as proof of the girl's virginity to the alimamo, who only then walked around the village drumtalking Allah's blessings on that marriage. If that white cloth wasn't bloodied, Kunta knew, the new husband would angrily leave the hut with the two mothers as his witnesses and shout loudly, "I divorce you!" three times for all to hear.

But teriya involved none of that — only new men sleeping with a willing widow and eating her cooking. Kunta thought for a little while about how Jinna M'Baki had looked at him, making no secret of her designs, amid the previous day's jostling crowd as the Council session ended.

Almost without realizing, he squeezed his hard foto, but he forced back the strong urge to stroke it because that would seem as if he was giving in to what that widow wanted, which was embarrassing even to think about. He didn't really want the stickiness with her, he told himself; but now that he was a man, he had every right, if he pleased, to *think* about teriya, which the senior elders themselves had shown was nothing for a man to be ashamed of.

Kunta's mind returned to the memory of some girls he and Lamin had passed in one village when returning from their gold-hunting trip. There had been about ten of them, he guessed, all beautifully black, in tight dresses, colorful beads, and bracelets, with high breasts and little hair plaits sticking up. They had acted so strangely as he went by that it had taken Kunta a moment to realize that the show they made of looking away whenever he looked at them meant not that they weren't interested in him but that they wanted him to be interested in *them*.

Females were so confusing, he thought.

333

Girls of their age in Juffure never paid enough attention to him even to look away. Was it because they knew what he was really like? Or was it because they knew he was far younger than he looked — too young to be worthy of their interest? Probably the girls in that village believed no traveling man leading a boy could have less than twenty or twenty-five rains, let alone his seventeen. They would have scoffed if they had known. Yet he was being sought after by a widow who knew very well how young he was. Perhaps he was lucky not to be older, Kunta thought. If he was, the girls of Juffure would be carrying on over him the way the girls of that village had, and he knew they all had just one thing on their minds: marriage. At least Jinna M'Baki was too old to be looking for anything more than a teriya friendship. Why would a man want to marry when he could get a woman to cook for him and sleep with him without getting married? There must be some reason. Perhaps it was because it was only through marrying that a man could have sons. That was a good thing.

But what would he have to teach those sons until he had lived long enough to learn something about the world — not just from his father, and from the arafang, and from the kintango, but also by exploring it for himself, as his uncles had done?

His uncles weren't married even yet, though they were older than his father, and most men of their rains had already taken second wives by now. Was Omoro considering taking a second wife? Kunta was so startled at the thought that he sat up straight. And how would his mother feel about it? Well, at least Binta, as the senior wife, would be able to tell the second wife her duties, and make certain she worked hard and set her sleeping turns with Omoro. Would there be trouble between the two women? No, he was sure Binta wouldn't be like the kintango's senior wife, whom it was commonly known shouted so much abuse at his junior wives, keeping them in such a turmoil, that he rarely got any peace.

Kunta shifted the position of his legs to let them hang for a while over the edge of his small perch, to keep the muscles from cramping. His wuolo dog was curled on the ground below him, its smooth brown fur shining in the moonlight, but he knew that the dog only seemed to be dozing, and that his nose and ears were alertly twitching for the night air's slightest smell or sound of warning to bound up racing and barking after the baboons that had lately been raiding the groundnut fields almost every night. During each long lookout duty, few things pleased Kunta more than when, maybe a dozen times in the course of a night, he would be jerked from his thoughts by sudden distant snarlings as a baboon was sprung upon in the brush by a big cat — especially if the baboon's growling turned into a scream quickly hushed, which meant that it had not escaped.

But it all was quiet now as Kunta sat on the edge of his platform and looked out across the fields. The only sign of life, in fact, beyond the tall grass, was the bobbing yellow light of a Fulani herdsman in the distance as he waved his grass torch to frighten away some animal, probably a hyena, that was roaming too close to his cows. So good were the Fulani at tending cattle that people claimed they could actually talk with their animals. And Omoro had told Kunta that each day, as part of their pay for herding, the Fulani would siphon a little blood from the cows' necks, which they mixed with milk and drank. What a strange people, thought Kunta. Yet though they were not Mandinka, they were from The Gambia, like him. How much stranger must be the people — and the customs — one would find beyond the borders of his land.

Within a moon after he returned from gold hunting with Lamin, Kunta had been restless to get on the road once again — this time for a *real* trip. Other young men of his kafo, he knew, were planning to travel somewhere as soon as the groundnuts and couscous got harvested, but none was going to venture far. Kunta, however, meant to put his eyes and feet upon that distant place called Mali, where, some three or four hundred rains before, according to Omoro and his uncles, the Kinte clan had begun. These forefather Kintes, he remembered, had won fame as blacksmiths, men who had conquered fire to make iron weapons that won wars and iron tools that made farming less hard. And from this original Kinte family, all of their descendants and all of the people who worked for them had taken the Kinte name. And some of that clan had moved to Mauretania, the birthplace of Kunta's holy-man grandfather.

So that no one else, even Omoro, would know about his plan until he wanted it known, Kunta had consulted in the strictest confidence with the arafang about the best route to Mali. Drawing a rough map in the dust, then tracing his finger along it, he had told Kunta that by following the banks of the Kamby Bolongo about six days in the direction of one's prayers to Allah, a traveler would reach Samo Island. Beyond there, the river narrowed and curved sharply to the left and began a serpent's twists and turns, with many confusing bolongs leading off as wide as the river, whose swampy banks couldn't be seen in some areas for the thickness of the mangroves growing sometimes as high as ten men. Where one could see the riverbanks, the schoolmaster told him, they abounded with monkeys, hippopotamus, giant crocodiles, and herds of as many as five hundred baboons.

But two to three days of that difficult traveling should bring Kunta to a second large island, where the low, muddy banks would rise into small cliffs matted with shrubs and small trees. The trail, which twisted alongside the river, would take him past villages of Bansang, Karantaba, and Diabugu. Soon afterward he would cross the eastern border of The Gambia and enter the Kingdom of Fulladu, and half day's walking from there, he would arrive at the village of Fatoto. Out of his bag, Kunta took the scrap of cured hide the arafang had given him. On it was the name of a colleague in Fatoto who he said would give Kunta directions for the next twelve to fourteen days, which would take him across a land called Senegal. Beyond that, said the arafang, lay Mali and Kunta's destination, Ka-ba, that land's main place. To go there and return, the arafang figured, would take about a moon — not counting whatever time Kunta chose to spend in Mali.

So many times had Kunta drawn and studied the route on his hut's dirt floor — erasing it before Binta brought his meals — that he could almost see it before him as he sat on his perch in the groundnut fields. Thinking about the adventures that awaited him along that trail — and in Mali — he could hardly contain his eagerness to be off. He was almost as eager to tell Lamin of his plans, not only because he wanted to share his secret, but also because he had decided to take his little brother along. He knew how much Lamin had boasted about that earlier trip with his brother. Since then, Lamin had also been through manhood training and would be a more experienced and trustworthy traveling companion. But Kunta's deepest reason for deciding to take him, he had to admit, was simply that he wanted company.

For a moment, Kunta sat in the dark smiling to himself, thinking of Lamin's face when the time would come for him to know. Kunta planned, of course, to drop the news in a very offhand way, as if he had just happened to think of it. But before then he must speak about it with Omoro, whom he knew now would feel no undue concern. In fact, he was sure that Omoro would be deeply pleased, and that even Binta, though she would worry, would be less upset than before. Kunta wondered what he might bring to Binta from Mali that she would treasure even more than her quills of gold. Perhaps some fine molded pots, or a bolt of beautiful cloth; Omoro and his uncles had said that the ancient Kinte women in Mali had been famed for the pots they made and for the brilliant patterns of cloth they wove, so maybe the Kinte women there still did those things.

When he returned from Mali, it occurred to Kunta, he might plan still another trip for a later rain. He might even journey to that distant place beyond endless sands where his uncles had told of the long caravans of strange animals with water stored in two humps on their backs.

Kalilu Conteh and Sefo Kela could have their old, ugly teriya widows; he, Kunta Kinte, would make a pilgrimage to Mecca itself. Happening at that moment to be staring in the direction of that holy city, Kunta became aware of a tiny, steady yellow light far across the fields. The Fulani herdsman over there, he realized, was cooking his breakfast. Kunta hadn't even noticed the first faint streaks of dawn in the east.

Reaching down to pick up his weapons and head home, he saw his ax and remembered the wood for his drum frame. But he was tired, he thought; maybe he'd chop the wood tomorrow. No, he was already halfway to the forest, and if he didn't do it now, he knew he would probably let it go until his next sentry duty, which was twelve days later. Besides, it wouldn't be manly to give in to his weariness. Moving his legs to test for any cramps and feeling none, he climbed down the notched pole to the ground, where his wuolo dog waited, making happy little barks and wagging his tail. After kneeling for his suba prayer, Kunta got up, stretched, took a deep breath of the cool morning air, and set off toward the bolong at a lope.

CHAPTER 33

The familiar perfumes of wild flowers
filled Kunta's nostrils as he ran, wetting
his legs, through grass glistening with
dew in the first rays of sunshine. Hawks
circled overhead looking for prey, and the
ditches beside the fields were alive with the
croaking of frogs. He veered away from
a tree to avoid disturbing a flock of
blackbirds that filled its branches like
shiny black leaves. But he might have
saved himself the trouble, for no sooner
had he passed by than an angry, raucous
cawing made him turn his head in time
to see hundreds of crows bullying the
blackbirds from their roost.

Breathing deeply as he ran, but still
not out of breath, he began to smell
the musky aroma of the mangroves as he

neared the low, thick underbrush that extended far back from the banks of the bolong. At the first sight of him, a sudden snorting spread among the wild pigs, which in turn set off a barking and snarling among the baboons, whose big males quickly pushed their females and babies behind them. When he was younger, he would have stopped to imitate them, grunting and jumping up and down, since this never failed to annoy the baboons, who would always shake their fists and sometimes throw rocks. But he was no longer a boy, and he had learned to treat all of Allah's creatures as he himself wished to be treated: with respect.

Fluttering white waves of egrets, cranes, storks, and pelicans rose from their sleeping places as he picked his way through the tangled mangrove down to the bolong. Kunta's wuolo dog raced ahead chasing watersnakes and big brown turtles down their mudslides into the water, where they left not even a ripple.

As he always did whenever he felt some need to come here after a night's lookout duty, Kunta stood awhile at the edge of the bolong, today watching a gray heron trailing its long, thin legs as it flew at about a spear's height above the pale green water, rippling the surface with each downbeat of its wings. Though the heron was looking for smaller game, he knew that this was the best spot along the bolong for kujalo, a big, powerful fish that Kunta loved to catch for Binta, who would stew it for him with onions, rice, and bitter tomatoes. With his stomach already rumbling for breakfast, it made him hungry just to think of it.

A little farther downstream, Kunta turned away from the water's edge along a path he himself had made to an ancient mangrove tree that he thought must know him, after countless visits, as well as he knew it. Pulling himself up into the lowest branch, he climbed all the way to his favorite perch near the top. From here, in the clear morning, with the sun warm on his back, he could see all the way to the next bend in the bolong, still carpeted with sleeping waterfowl, and beyond them to the women's rice plots, dotted with their bamboo shelters for nursing babies.

In which one of them, he wondered, had his mother put him when he was little? This place in the early morning would always fill Kunta with a greater sense of calm, and wonder, than anywhere else he knew of. Even more than in the village mosque, he felt here how totally were everyone and everything in the hands of Allah; and how everything he could see and hear and smell from the top of this tree had been here for longer than men's memories, and would be here long after he and his sons and his sons' sons had joined their ancestors.

Trotting away from the bolong toward the sun for a little while, Kunta finally reached the head-high grass surrounding the grove where he was going to pick out and chop a section of tree trunk just the right size for the body of his drum. If the green wood started drying and curing today, he figured it would be ready to hollow out and work on in a moon and a half, about the time he and Lamin would be returning from their trip to Mali. As he stepped into the grove, Kunta saw a sudden movement out of the corner of his eye. It was a hare, and the wuolo dog was after it in a flash as it raced for cover in the tall grass. He was obviously chasing it for sport rather than for food, since he was barking furiously; Kunta knew that a hunting wuolo never made noise if he was really hungry. The two of them were soon out of earshot, but Kunta knew that his dog would come back when he lost interest in the chase.

Kunta headed forward to the center of the grove, where he would find more trees from which to choose a trunk of the size, smoothness, and roundness that he wanted. The soft, mossy earth felt good under his feet as he walked deeper into the dark grove, but the air here was damp and cold, he noticed, the sun not being high enough or hot enough yet to penetrate the thick foliage overhead. Leaning his weapons and ax against a warped tree, he wandered here and there, occasionally stooping, his eyes and fingers examining for just the right trunk, one just a little bit larger — to allow for drying shrinkage — than he wanted his drum to be.

He was bending over a likely prospect

when he heard the sharp crack of a twig, followed by the squawk of a parrot overhead. It was probably the dog returning, he thought in the back of his mind. But no grown dog ever cracked a twig, he flashed, whirling in the same instant. In a blur, rushing at him, he saw a white face, a club upraised; heard heavy footfalls behind him. *Toubob!* His foot lashed up and caught the man in the belly — it was soft and he heard a grunt — just as something hard and heavy grazed the back of Kunta's head and landed like a treetrunk on his shoulder. Sagging under the pain, Kunta spun — turning his back on the man who lay doubled over on the ground at his feet — and pounded with his fists on the faces of two black men who were lunging at him with a big sack, and at another toubob swinging a short, thick club, which missed him this time as he sprang aside.

His brain screaming for any weapon, Kunta leaped into them — clawing, butting, kneeing, gouging — hardly feeling the club that was pounding against his back. As three of them went down with him, sinking to the ground under their combined weight, a knee smashed into Kunta's lower back, rocking him with such pain that he gasped. His open mouth meeting flesh, his teeth clamped, cut, tore. His numb fingers finding a face, he clawed deeply into an eye, hearing its owner howl as again the heavy club met Kunta's head.

Dazed, he heard a dog's snarling, a toubob screaming, then a sudden piteous yelp. Scrambling to his feet, wildly twisting, dodging, ducking to escape more clubbing, with blood streaming from his split head, he saw one black cupping his eye, one of the toubob holding a bloody arm, standing over the body of the dog, and the remaining pair circling him with raised clubs. Screaming his rage, Kunta went for the second toubob, his fists meeting and breaking the force of the descending club. Almost choking with the awful toubob stink, he tried desperately to wrench away the club. Why had he not *heard* them, *sensed* them, *smelled* them?

Just then the black's club smashed into Kunta once again, staggering him to his knees, and the toubob sprang loose. His head ready to explode, his body reeling, raging at his own weakness, Kunta reared up and roared, flailing blindly at the air, everything blurred with tears and blood and sweat. He was fighting for more than his life now. Omoro! Binta! Lamin! Suwadu! Madi! The toubob's heavy club crashed against his temple. And all went black.

CHAPTER 34

Kunta wondered if he had gone mad. Naked, chained, shackled, he awoke on his back between two other men in a pitch darkness full of steamy heat and sickening stink and a nightmarish bedlam of shrieking, weeping, praying, and vomiting. He could feel and smell his own vomit on his chest and belly. His whole body was one spasm of pain from the beatings he had received in the four days since his capture. But the place where the hot iron had been put between his shoulders hurt the worst.

A rat's thick, furry body brushed his cheek, its whiskered nose sniffing at his mouth. Quivering with revulsion, Kunta snapped his teeth together desperately and the rat ran away. In rage, Kunta snatched and kicked against the shackles that bound his wrists and ankles. Instantly, angry exclamations and jerking came back from whomever he was shackled to. The shock and pain adding to his fury, Kunta lunged upward, his head bumping hard against wood — right on the spot where he had been clubbed by the toubob back in the woods. Gasping and snarling, he and the unseen man next to him battered their iron cuffs at each other until both slumped back in exhaustion. Kunta felt himself starting to vomit again, and he tried to force it back, but couldn't. His already emptied belly squeezed up a thin, sour fluid that drained from the side of his mouth as he lay wishing that he might die.

He told himself that he mustn't lose control again if he wanted to save his strength and his sanity. After a while, when he felt he could move again, he very slowly and carefully explored his shackled right wrist and ankle with his left hand. They were bleeding. He pulled lightly on the chain; it seemed to be connected to the left ankle and wrist of the man he had fought with. On Kunta's left, chained to him by the ankles, lay some other man, someone who kept up a steady moaning, and they were all so close that their shoulders, arms, and legs touched if any of them moved even a little.

Remembering the wood he had bumped into with his head, Kunta drew himself upward again, just enough for it to bump gently; there wasn't enough space even to sit up. And behind his head was a wooden wall. I'm trapped like a leopard in a snare, he thought. Then he remembered sitting in the darkness of the manhood-training hut after being taken blindfolded to the jujuo so many rains before, and a sob welled up in his throat; but he fought it back. Kunta made himself think about the cries and groans he was hearing all around him. There must be many men here in the blackness, some close, some farther away, some beside him, others in front of him, but all in one room, if that's what this was. Straining his ears, he could hear still more cries, but they were muffled and came from below, beneath the splintery planking he lay on.

Listening more intently, he began to recognize the different tongues of those around him. Over and over, in Arabic, a Fulani was shouting, "Allah in heaven, help me!" And a man of the Serere tribe was hoarsely wailing what must have been the names of his family. But mostly Kunta heard Mandinkas, the loudest of them babbling wildly in the sira kango secret talk of men, vowing terrible deaths to all toubob. The cries of the others were so slurred with weeping that Kunta could identify neither their words nor their languages, although he knew that some of the strange talk he heard must come from beyond The Gambia.

As Kunta lay listening, he slowly began to realize that he was trying to push from his mind the impulse to relieve the demands of his bowels, which he had been forcing back for days. But he could hold it no longer, and finally the feces curled out between his buttocks. Revolted at himself, smelling his own addition to the stench, Kunta began sobbing, and again his belly spasmed, producing this time only a little spittle; but he kept gagging.

What sins was he being punished for in such a manner as this? He pleaded to Allah for an answer. It was sin enough that he hadn't prayed once since the morning he went for the wood to make his drum. Though he couldn't get onto his knees, and he knew not even which way was east, he closed his eyes where he lay and prayed, beseeching Allah's forgiveness.

Afterward, Kunta lay for a long time bathing dully in his pains, and slowly became aware that one of them, in his knotted stomach, was nothing more than hunger. It occurred to him that he hadn't eaten anything since the night before his capture. He was trying to remember if he had *slept* in all that time, when suddenly he saw himself walking along a trail in the forest; behind him walked two blacks, ahead of him a pair of toubob with their strange clothes and their long hair in strange colors. Kunta jerked his eyes open and shook his head; he was soaked in sweat and his heart was pounding. It had been a nightmare; or was the nightmare this stinking blackness? No, it was as real as the scene in the forest in his dream had been. Against his will, it all came back to him.

After fighting the black slatees and the toubob so desperately in the grove of trees, he remembered awakening — into a wave of blinding pain — and finding himself gagged, blindfolded, and bound with his wrists behind him and his ankles hobbled with knotted rope. Thrashing to break free, he was jabbed savagely with sharp sticks until blood ran down his legs. Yanked onto his feet and prodded with the sticks to begin moving, he stumbled ahead of them as fast as his hobbles would permit.

Somewhere along the banks of the bolong — Kunta could tell by the sounds, and the feel of the soft ground beneath his feet — he was shoved down into a canoe. Still blindfolded, he heard the slatees grunting, rowing swiftly, with the toubob hitting him whenever he struggled. Landing, again they walked, until finally that night they reached a place where they threw Kunta on the ground, tied him with his back to a bamboo fence and, without warning, pulled off his blindfold. It was dark, but he could see the pale face of the toubob standing over him, and the silhouettes of others like him on the ground nearby. The toubob held out some meat for him to bite off a piece. He turned his head aside and clamped his jaws. Hissing with rage, the toubob grabbed him by the throat and tried to force his mouth open. When Kunta kept it shut tight, the toubob drew back his fist and punched him hard in the face.

Kunta was let alone the rest of the night. At dawn, he began to make out — tied to other bamboo trunks — the figures of the other captured people, eleven of them — six men, three girls, and two children — all guarded closely by armed slatees and toubob. The girls were naked; Kunta could only avert his eyes; he never had seen a woman naked before. The men, also naked, sat with murderous hatred etched in their faces, grimly silent and crusted with blood from whip cuts. But the girls were crying out, one about dead loved ones in a burned village; another, bitterly weeping, rocked back and forth cooing endearments to an imaginary infant in her cradled arms; and the third shrieked at intervals that she was going to Allah.

In wild fury, Kunta lunged back and forth trying to break his bonds. A heavy blow with a club again knocked him senseless. When he came to, he found that he too was naked, that all of their heads had been shaved and their bodies smeared with red palm oil. At around noonday, two new toubob entered the grove. The slatees, now all grins, quickly untied the captives from the bamboo trunks, shouting to them to stand in a line. Kunta's muscles were knotted with rage and fear. One of the new toubob was short and stout and his hair was white. The other towered over him, tall and huge and scowling, with deep knife scars across his face, but it was the white-haired one before whom the slatees and the other toubob grinned and all but bowed.

Looking at them all, the white-haired one gestured for Kunta to step forward, and lurching backward in terror, Kunta screamed as a whip seared across his back.

A slatee from behind grappled him downward to his knees, jerking his head backward. The white-haired toubob calmly spread Kunta's trembling lips and studied his teeth. Kunta attempted to spring up, but after another blow of the whip, he stood as ordered, his body quivering as the toubob's fingers explored his eyes, his chest, his belly. When the fingers grasped his foto, he lunged aside with a choked cry. Two slatees and more lashings were needed to force Kunta to bend over almost double, and in horror he felt his buttocks being spread wide apart. Then the white-haired toubob roughly shoved Kunta aside and, one by one, he similarly inspected the others, even the private parts of the wailing girls. Then whips and shouted commands sent the captives all dashing around within the enclosure, and next springing up and down on their haunches.

After observing them, the white-haired toubob and the huge one with the knife-scarred face stepped a little distance away and spoke briefly in low tones. Stepping back, the white-haired one, beckoning another toubob, jabbed his finger at four men, one of them Kunta, and two of the girls. The toubob looked shocked, pointing at the others in a beseeching manner. But the white-haired one shook his head firmly. Kunta sat straining against his bonds, his head threatening to burst with rage, as the toubob argued heatedly. After a while, the white-haired one disgustedly wrote something on a piece of paper that the other toubob angrily accepted.

Kunta struggled and howled with fury as the slatees grabbed him again, wrestling him to a seated position with his back arched. Eyes wide with terror, he watched as the toubob withdrew from the fire a long, thin iron that the white-haired one had brought with him. Kunta was already thrashing and screaming as the iron exploded pain between his shoulders. The bamboo grove echoed with the screams of the others, one by one. Then red palm oil was rubbed over the peculiar LL shape Kunta saw on their backs.

Within the hour, they were hobbling in a line of clanking chains, with the slatees' ready whips flailing down on anyone who balked or stumbled. Kunta's back and shoulders were ribboned with bleeding cuts when late that night they reached two canoes hidden under thick, overhanging mangroves at the river's banks. Split into two groups, they were rowed through darkness by the slatees, with the toubob lashing out at any sign of struggle.

When Kunta saw a vast dark shape looming up ahead in the night, he sensed that this was his last chance. Springing and lunging amid shouts and screams around him, he almost upset the canoe in his struggle to leap overboard; but he was bound to the others and couldn't make it over the side. He almost didn't feel the blows of the whips and clubs against his ribs, his back, his face, his belly, his head — as the canoe bumped against the side of the great dark thing. Through the pain, he could feel the warm blood pouring down his face, and he heard above him the exclamations of many toubob. Then ropes were being looped around him, and he was helpless to resist. After being half pushed and half pulled up some strange rope ladder, he had enough strength left to twist his body wildly in another break for freedom; again he was lashed with whips, and hands were grabbing him amid an overwhelming toubob smell and the sound of women shrieking and loud toubob cursing.

Through swollen lids, Kunta saw a thicket of legs and feet all around him, and managing an upward glance while trying to shield his bleeding face with his forearm, he saw the short toubob with the white hair standing calmly making marks in a small book with a stubby pencil. Then he felt himself being snatched upright and shoved roughly across a flat space. He caught a glimpse of tall poles with thick wrappings of coarse white cloth. Then he was being guided, stumbling weakly down some kind of narrow steps, into a place of pitch blackness; at the same instant, his nose was assaulted by an unbelievable stink, and his ears by cries of anguish.

Kunta began vomiting as the toubob — holding dim yellowish flames that burned within metal frames carried by a ring — shackled his wrists and ankles, then shoved him backward, close between two other moaning men. Even in his terror, he sensed that lights bobbing in other directions meant that the toubob were taking those who had come with him to be shackled elsewhere. Then he felt his thoughts slipping; he thought he must be dreaming. And then, mercifully, he was.

CHAPTER 35

Only the rasping sound of the deck hatch being opened told Kunta if it was day or night. Hearing the latch click, he would jerk his head up — the only free movement that his chains and shackles would allow — and four shadowy toubob figures would descend, two of them with bobbing lights and whips guarding the other pair as they all moved along the narrow aisleways pushing a tub of food. They would thrust tin pans of the stuff up onto the filth between each two shacklemates. So far, each time the food had come, Kunta had clamped his jaws shut, preferring to starve to death until the aching of his empty stomach had begun to make his hunger almost as terrible as the pains from his beatings. When those on Kunta's level had been fed, the lights showed the toubob descending farther below with the rest of the food.

Less often than the feeding times, and usually when it was night outside, the toubob would bring down into the hold some new captives, screaming and whimpering in terror as they were shoved and lashed along to wherever they were to be chained into empty spaces along the rows of hard plank shelves.

One day, shortly after feeding time, Kunta's ears picked up a strange, muted sound that seemed to vibrate through the ceiling over his head. Some of the other men heard it too, and their moaning ended abruptly. Kunta lay listening intently; it sounded as if many feet were dashing about overhead. Then — much nearer to them in the darkness — came a new sound, as of some very heavy object being creaked very slowly upward.

Kunta's naked back felt an odd vibration from the hard, rough planking he lay on. He felt a tightening, a swelling within his chest, and he lay frozenly. About him he heard thudding sounds that he knew were

366

men lunging upward, straining against their chains. It felt as if all of his blood had rushed into his pounding head. And then terror went clawing into his vitals as he sensed in some way that this place was moving, taking them away. Men started shouting all around him, screaming to Allah and His spirits, banging their heads against the planking, thrashing wildly against their rattling shackles. "Allah, I will never pray to you less than five times daily!" Kunta shrieked into the bedlam, "Hear me! Help me!"

The anguished cries, weeping, and prayers continued, subsiding only as one after another exhausted man went limp and lay gasping for breath in the stinking blackness. Kunta *knew* that he would never see Africa again. He could feel clearly now, through his body against the planks, a slow, rocking motion, sometimes enough that his shoulders or arms or hips would press against the brief warmth of one of the men he was chained between. He had shouted so hard that he had no voice left, so his mind screamed it instead: "Kill toubob — and their traitor black helpers!"

He was sobbing quietly when the hatch opened and the four toubob came bumping down with their tub of food. Again he clamped his jaws against his spasms of hunger, but then he thought of something the kintango had once said — that warriors and hunters must eat well to have greater strength than other men. Starving himself meant that weakness would prevent him from killing toubob. So this time, when the pan was thrust onto the boards between him and the man next to him, Kunta's fingers also clawed into the thick mush. It tasted like ground maize boiled with palm oil. Each gulping swallow pained his throat in the spot where he had been choked for not eating before, but he swallowed until the pan was empty. He could feel the food like a lump in his belly, and soon it was rising up his throat. He couldn't stop it, and a moment later the gruel was back on the planking. He could hear, over the sound of his own retching, that of others doing the same thing.

As the lights approached the end of the long shelf of planks on which Kunta lay, suddenly he heard chains rattling, a head bumping, and then a man screaming hysterically in a curious mixture of Mandinka and what sounded like some toubob words. An uproarious burst of laughter came from the toubob with the feeding tub, then their whips lashing down, until the man's cries lapsed, into babbling and whimpering. Could it be? Had he heard an African speaking toubob? Was there slatee down there among them? Kunta had heard that toubob would often betray their black traitor helpers and throw them into chains.

After the toubob had gone on down to the level below, scarcely a sound was heard on Kunta's level until they reappeared with their emptied tub and climbed back up outside, closing the hatch behind them. At that instant, an angry buzzing began in different tongues, like bees swarming. Then, down the shelf from where Kunta lay, there was a heavy chain-rattling blow, a howl of pain and bitter cursing in the same hysterical Mandinka. Kunta heard the man shriek,

"You think I am toubob?" There were more violent, rapid blows and desperate screams. Then the blows stopped, and in the blackness of the hold came a high squealing — and then an awful gurgling sound, as of a man whose breath was being choked off. Another rattling of chains, a tattoo of bare heels kicking at the planks, then quiet.

Kunta's head was throbbing, and his heart was pounding, as voices around him began screaming, "Slatee! Slatees die!" Then Kunta was screaming along with them and joining in a wild rattling of chains — when suddenly with a rasping sound the hatch was opened, admitting its shaft of daylight and a group of toubob with lights and whips. They had obviously heard the commotion below them, and though now almost total silence had fallen in the hold, the toubob rushed among the aisles shouting and lashing left and right with their whips. When they left without finding the dead man, the hold remained silent for a long moment. Then, very quietly, Kunta heard a mirthless laugh from the end of the shelf next to where the traitor lay dead.

The next feeding was a tense one. As if the toubob sensed something amiss, their whips fell even more often than usual. Kunta jerked and cried out as a bolt of pain cut across his legs. He had learned that when anyone didn't cry from a blow, he would get a severe beating until he did. Then he clawed and gulped down the tasteless mush as his eyes followed the lights moving on down along the shelf.

Every man in the hold was listening when one of the toubob exclaimed something to the others. A jostling of lights could be seen, then more exclamations and cursings, and then one of the toubob rushed down the aisle and up through the hatch, and he soon returned with two more. Kunta could hear the iron cuffs and chains being unlocked. Two of the toubob then half carried, half dragged the body of the dead man along the aisle and up the hatch, while the others continued bumping their food tub along the aisles.

The food team was on the level below when four more toubob climbed down through the hatch and went directly to where the slatee had been chained. By twisting his head, Kunta could see the lights raised high. With violent cursing, two of the toubob sent their whips whistling down against flesh. Whoever was being beaten refused at first to scream; though just listening to the force of the blows was almost paralyzing to Kunta, he could hear the beaten man flailing against his chains in the agony of his torture — and of his grim determination not to cry out.

Then the toubob were almost shrieking their curses, and the lights could be seen changing hands as one man spelled the other with the lash. Finally the beaten man began screaming — first a Foulah curse, then things that could not be understood, though they too were in the Foulah tongue. Kunta's mind flashed a thought of a quiet, gentle Foulah tribe who tended Mandinka cattle — as the lashing sounds continued until the beaten man barely whimpered. Then the four toubob left, cursing, gasping, and gagging in the stink.

The moans of the Foulah shivered through the black hold. Then, after a while, a clear voice called out in Mandinka, "Share his pain! We must be in this place as one village!" The voice belonged to an elder. He was right. The Foulah's pains had been as Kunta's own. He felt himself about to burst with rage. He also felt, in some nameless way, a terror greater than he had ever known before, and it seemed to spread from the marrow of his bones. Part of him wanted to die, to escape all of this; but no, he must live to avenge it. He forced himself to lie absolutely still. It took a long while, but finally he felt his strain and confusion, even his body's pains, begin to ebb — except for the place between his shoulders where he had been burned with the hot iron. He found that his mind could focus better now on the only choice that seemed to lie before him and the others: Either they would all die in this nightmare place, or somehow the toubob would have to be overcome and killed.

CHAPTER 36

The stinging bites, then the itching of the body lice, steadily grew worse. In the filth, the lice as well as the fleas had multiplied by the thousands until they swarmed all over the hold. They were worst wherever the body crevices held any hair. Kunta's armpits, and around his foto, felt as if they were on fire, and his free hand scratched steadily wherever his shackled hand couldn't reach.

He kept having thoughts of springing up and running away; then, a moment later, his eyes would fill with tears of frustration, anger would rise in him, and he would fight it all back down until he felt again some kind of calm. The worst thing was that he couldn't *move* anywhere; he felt he wanted to *bite* through his chains. He decided that he must keep himself focused upon something, anything to occupy his mind or his hands, or else he would go mad — as some men in the hold seemed to have done already, judging from the things they cried out.

By lying very still and listening to the breathing sounds of the men on either side of him, Kunta had long since learned to tell when either of them was asleep or awake. He concentrated now upon hearing farther away from him. With more and more practice at listening intently to repeated sounds, he discovered that his ears after a while could discern their location almost exactly; it was a peculiar sensation, almost as if his ears were serving for eyes. Now and then, among the groans and curses that filled the darkness, he heard the thump of a man's head against the planks he lay on. And there was another odd and monotonous noise. It would stop at intervals, then resume after a while; it sounded as if two pieces of metal were being rubbed hard together, and after hearing more of it Kunta figured that someone was trying to wear the links of his chains apart. Kunta often heard, too, brief exclamations and janglings of chains as two men furiously fought, jerking their shackles against each other's ankles and wrists.

Kunta had lost track of time. The urine, vomit, and feces that reeked everywhere around him had spread into a slick paste covering the hard planking of the long shelves on which they lay. Just when he had begun to think he couldn't stand it any more, eight toubob came down the hatchway, cursing loudly. Instead of the routine food container, they carried what seemed to be some kind of long-handled hoes and four large tubs. And Kunta noticed with astonishment that they were not wearing any clothes at all.

The naked toubob almost immediately began vomiting worse than any of the others who had come before. In the glow of their lights, they all but sprang along the aisles in teams of two, swiftly thrusting their hoes up onto the shelves and scraping some of the mess into their tubs. As each tub was filled, the toubob would drag it back along the aisle and go bumping it up the steps through the open hatchway to empty it outside, and then they would return. The toubob were gagging horribly by now, their faces contorted grotesquely, and their hairy, colorless bodies covered with blobs of the mess they were scraping off the shelves. But when they finished their job and were gone, there was no difference in the hot, awful, choking stench of the hold.

The next time that more than the usual four toubob descended with their food tubs, Kunta guessed that there must be as many as twenty of them clumping down the hatch steps. He lay frozen. Turning his head this way and that, he could see small groups of toubob posting themselves around the hold, some carrying whips and guns, guarding others with lights upraised at the ends of each shelf of chained men. A knot of fear grew in Kunta's belly as he began hearing strange clicking sounds, then heavy rattlings. Then his shackled right ankle began jerking; with flashing terror he realized that the toubob were releasing him. Why? What terrible thing was going to happen now? He lay still, his right ankle no longer feeling the familiar weight of the chain, hearing all around the hold more clicking sounds and the rattling of chains being pulled. Then the toubob started shouting and lashing with their whips. Kunta knew that it meant for them to get down off their shelves. His cry of alarm joined a sudden bedlam of shrieks in different tongues as the men reared their bodies upward, heads thudding against the ceiling timbers.

The whips lashed down amid screams of pain as one after another pair of men went thumping down into the aisleways. Kunta and his Wolof shacklemate hugged each other on the shelf as the searing blows jerked them convulsively back and forth. Then hands clamped roughly around their ankles and hauled them across the shelf's mushy filth and into the tangle of other men in the aisleway, all of them howling under the toubob whips. Wrenching and twisting in vain to escape the pain, he glimpsed shapes moving against the light of the opened hatchway. The toubob were snatching men onto their feet — one pair after another — then beating and shoving them along, stumbling in the darkness, toward the hatchway's steps. Kunta's legs felt separated from the rest of his body as he went lurching alongside the Wolof, shackled by their wrists, naked, crusted with filth, begging not to be eaten.

The first open daylight in nearly fifteen days hit Kunta with the force of a hammer between his eyes. He reeled under the bursting pain, flinging his free hand up to cover his eyes. His bare feet told him that whatever they were walking on was moving slightly from side to side. Fumbling blindly ahead, with even his cupped hand and clamped eyelids admitting some tormenting light, trying futilely to breathe through his nostrils nearly plugged with snot, he gaped open his cracked lips and took a deep breath of sea air — the first of his life. His lungs convulsed from its rich cleanness, and he crumpled to the deck, vomiting alongside his shacklemate. All about him he heard more vomiting, chains clanking, lashes meeting flesh, and shrieks of pain amid toubob shouts and curses and

379

strange flapping sounds overhead.

When another whip ripped across his back, Kunta shrank to one side, hearing his Wolof partner gasp as the lash hit him. It kept tearing at them both until somehow they stumbled to their feet. He slit his eyes to see if he could escape some of the blows; but new pains stabbed into his head as their tormentor shoved them toward where Kunta could see the blurred forms of other toubob passing a length of chain through the shackles around each man's ankles. There had been more of them down there in the darkness than he had ever realized — and far more toubob than had ever gone below. In the bright sunlight, they looked even paler and more horrible, their faces pitted with the holes of disease, their peculiar long hair in colors of yellow or black or red, some of them even with hair around their mouths and under their chins. Some were bony, others fat, some had ugly scars from knives, or a hand, eye, or limb missing, and the backs of many were crisscrossed with deep scars. It flashed through Kunta's mind how his teeth had been counted and inspected, for several of these toubob he saw had but few teeth.

Many of them were spaced along the rail, holding whips, long knives, or some kind of heavy metal stick with a hole in the end, and Kunta could see beyond them an amazing sight — an unbelievable endlessness of rolling blue water. He jerked his head upward toward the slapping sounds above and saw that they came from giant white cloths billowing among huge poles and many ropes. The cloths seemed to be filled up with the wind. Turning about, Kunta saw that a high barricade of bamboo taller than any man extended completely across the width of the huge canoe. Showing through the barricade's center was the gaping black mouth of a huge, terrible-looking metal thing with a long, thick, hollow shaft, and the tips of more metal sticks like the ones the toubob had been holding at the rail. Both the huge thing and the sticks were pointed toward where he and the other naked men were grouped.

As their ankle shackles were being linked onto the new chain, Kunta got the chance to take a good look at his Wolof shacklemate for the first time. Like himself, the man was crusted from head to foot with filth. He seemed about the rains of Kunta's father Omoro, and the Wolof had that tribe's classic facial features, and he was very black of color. The Wolof's back was bleeding from where the whipping had cut into him, and pus was oozing from where an LL mark had been burned into his back. Kunta realised, as their eyes searched each other, that the Wolof was staring at him with the same astonishment. Amid the commotion, they had time to stare also at the other naked men, most of them gibbering in their terror. From the different facial features, tribal tattoos, and scarification marks, Kunta could tell that some were Foulah, Jola, Serere, and Wolof, like his partner, but most were Mandinkas — and there were some he could not be sure of. With excitement, Kunta saw the one he was sure must have killed the slatee. He was indeed a Foulah; blood from the beating he had received was crusted all over him.

They were all soon being shoved and whipped toward where another chain of ten men were being doused with buckets of seawater drawn up from over the side. Then other toubob with long-handled brushes were scrubbing the screaming men. Kunta screamed, too, as the drenching salt water hit him, stinging like fire in his own bleeding whip cuts and the burned place on his back. He cried even louder as the stiff brush bristles not only loosened and scraped off some of his body's crusted filth but also tore open his scabbed lash cuts. He saw the water frothing and pinkish at their feet. Then they were herded back toward the center of the deck, where they flopped down in a huddle. Kunta gawked upward to see toubob springing about on the poles like monkeys, pulling at the many ropes among the great white cloths. Even in Kunta's shock, the heat of the sun felt warm and good, and he felt an incredible sense of relief that his skin was freed of some of its filth.

A sudden chorus of cries brought the chained men jerking upright. About twenty women, most of them teen-aged, and four children, came running naked and without chains from behind the barricade, ahead of two grinning toubob with whips. Kunta instantly recognized the girls who had been brought on board with him — as with flooding rage he watched all of the toubob leering at their nakedness, some of them even rubbing their fotos. By sheer force of will, he fought the urge to go lunging after the nearest toubob despite their weapons. Hands clutched into fists, he sucked hard for air to keep breathing, wrenching his eyes away from the terrified women.

Then a toubob near the rail began pulling out and pushing in between his hands some peculiar folding thing that made a wheezing sound. Another joined in, beating on a drum from Africa, as other toubob now moved themselves into a ragged line with the naked men, women, and children staring at them. The toubob in the line had a length of rope, and each of them looped one ankle within it, as if that rope was a length of chain such as linked the naked men. Smiling now, they began jumping up and down together in short hops, keeping in time with the drumbeats and the wheezing thing. Then they and the other armed toubob gestured for the men in chains to jump in the same manner. But when the chained men continued to stand as if petrified, the toubobs' grins became scowls, and they began laying about with whips.

"Jump!" shouted the oldest woman suddenly, in Mandinka. She was of about the rains of Kunta's mother Binta. Bounding out, she began jumping herself. "Jump!" she cried shrilly again, glaring at the girls and children, and they jumped as she did. "Jump to kill toubob!" she shrieked, her quick eyes flashing at the naked men, her arms and hands darting in the movements of the warrior's dance. And then, as her meaning sank home one after another shackled pair of men began a weak, stumbling hopping up and down, their chains clanking against the deck. With his head down, Kunta saw the welter of hopping feet and legs, feeling his own legs rubbery under him as his breath came in gasps. Then the singing of the woman was joined by the girls. It was a happy sound, but the words they sang told how these terrible toubob had taken every woman into the dark corners of the canoe each night and used them like dogs. *"Toubob fa!"* (Kill toubob) they shrieked with smiles and laughter. The naked, jumping men joined in: *"Toubob fa!"* Even the toubob were grinning now, some of them clapping their hands with pleasure.

But Kunta's knees began to buckle beneath him and his throat went tight when he saw, approaching him, the short, stocky toubob with white hair, and with him the huge, scowling one with the knife-scarred face who also had been at that place where Kunta was examined and beaten and choked and burned before he was brought here. In an instant, as the other naked people saw these two, a sudden silence fell, and the only sound to be heard was that of great, slapping cloths overhead, for even the rest of the toubob had stiffened at their presence.

Barking out something hoarsely, the huge one cleared the other toubob away from the chained people. From his belt, there dangled a large ring of the slender, shiny things that Kunta had glimpsed others using as they had opened the chains. And then the white-haired one went among the naked people, peering closely at their bodies. Wherever he saw whip cuts badly festered, or pus draining from rat bites or burned places, he smeared on some grease from a can that the huge one handed to him. Or the huge one himself would sprinkle a yellowish powder from a container on wrists and ankles that became a sickly, moist, grayish color beneath the iron cuffs. As the two toubob moved nearer to him, Kunta shrank in fear and fury, but then the white-haired one was smearing grease on his festering places and the huge one was sprinkling his ankles and wrists with the yellowish powder, neither of them seeming even to recognize who Kunta was.

Then, suddenly, amid rising shouts among the toubob, one of the girls who had been brought with Kunta was springing wildly between frantic guards. As several of them went clutching and diving for her, she hurled herself screaming over the rail and went plunging downward. In the great shouting commotion, the white-haired toubob and the huge one snatched up whips and with bitter curses lashed the backs of those who had gone sprawling after, letting her slip from their grasp.

Then the toubob up among the cloths were yelling and pointing toward the water. Turning in that direction, the naked people saw the girl bobbing in the waves — and not far away, a pair of dark fins coursing swiftly toward her. Then came another scream — a blood-chilling one — then a frothing and thrashing, and she was dragged from sight, leaving behind only a redness in the water where she had been. For the first time, no whips fell as the chained people, sick with horror, were herded back into the dark hold and rechained into their places. Kunta's head was reeling. After the fresh air of the ocean, the stench smelled even worse than before, and after the daylight, the hold seemed even darker. When soon a new disturbance arose, seeming somewhat distant, his practiced ears told him that the toubob were driving up onto the deck the terrified men from the level below.

After a while, he heard near his right ear a low mutter. *"Jula?"* Kunta's heart leaped. He knew very little of the Wolof tongue, but he did know that Wolof and some others used the word *jula* to mean travelers and traders who were usually Mandinkas. And twisting his head a bit closer to the Wolof's ear, Kunta whispered, *"Jula.* Mandinka." For moments, as he lay tensely, the Wolof made no return sound. It went flashing through Kunta's head that if he could only speak many languages, as his father's brothers did — but he was ashamed to have brought them to this place, even in his thoughts.

"Wolof. Jebou Manga," the other man whispered finally, and Kunta knew that was his name.

"Kunta Kinte," he whispered back.

Exchanging a whisper now and then in their desperation to communicate, they picked at each other's minds to learn a new word here, another there, in their respective tongues. It was much as they had learned their early words as first-kafo children. During one of the intervals of silence between them, Kunta remembered how when he had been a lookout against the baboons in the groundnut fields at night, the distant fire of a Fulani herdsman had given him a sense of comfort and he had wished that there had been some way he could exchange words with this man he had never seen. It was as if that wish were being realized now, except that it was with a Wolof, unseen for the weeks they had been lying there shackled to each other.

Every Wolof expression Kunta had ever heard he now dragged from his memory. He knew that the Wolof was doing the same with Mandinka words, of which he knew more than Kunta knew of Wolof words. In another time of silence between them, Kunta sensed that the man who lay on his other side, who never had made any sound other than moaning in pain, was listening closely to them. Kunta realized from the low murmuring that spread gradually throughout the hold that once the men had actually been able to see each other up in the daylight, he and his own shacklemate weren't the only ones trying now to communicate with one another. The murmuring kept spreading. The hold would fall silent now only when the toubob came with the food tub, or with the brushes to clean the filth from the shelves. And there was a new quality to the quietness that would fall at these times; for the first time since they had been captured and thrown in chains, it was as if there was among the men a sense of being together.

CHAPTER 37

The next time the men were taken up onto the deck, Kunta made a point of looking at the man behind him in line, the one who lay beside him to the left when they were below. He was a Serere tribesman, much older than Kunta, and his body front and back was creased with whip cuts, some of them so deep and festering that Kunta felt badly for having wished sometimes that he might strike the man in the darkness for moaning so steadily in his pain. Staring back at Kunta, the Serere's dark eyes were full of fury and defiance. A whip lashed out even as they stood looking at each other — this time at Kunta, spurring him to move ahead. The force of the blow drove him nearly to his knees and triggered an explosion of rage.

With his throat ripping out almost an animal's cry, Kunta lunged off balance toward the toubob, only to fall, sprawling, dragging his shacklemate down with him, as the toubob nimbly sprang clear of them both. Men milled around them as the toubob, his eyes narrowing with hatred, brought the whip down over and over on both Kunta and the Wolof, like a slashing knife. Trying to roll away, Kunta was kicked heavily in his ribs. But somehow he and the gasping Wolof managed to stagger back up among the other men from their shelf who were shambling toward their dousing with buckets of seawater.

A moment later, the stinging saltiness of it was burning in Kunta's wounds, and his screams joined those of others over the sound of the drum and the wheezing thing that had again begun marking time for the chained men to jump and dance for the toubob. Kunta and the Wolof were so weak from their new beating that twice they stumbled, but whip blows and kicks sent them hopping clumsily up and down in their chains. So great was his fury that Kunta was barely aware of the women singing *"Toubob fa!"* And when he had finally been chained back down in his place in the dark hold, his heart throbbed with a lust to murder toubob.

Every few days the eight naked toubob would again come into the stinking darkness and scrape their tubs full of the excrement that had accumulated on the shelves where the chained men lay. Kunta would lie still with his eyes staring balefully in hatred, following the bobbing orange lights, listening to the toubob cursing and sometimes slipping and falling into the slickness underfoot — so plentiful now, because of the increasing looseness of the men's bowels, that the filth had begun to drop off the edges of the shelves down into the aisleway.

The last time they were on deck, Kunta had noticed a man limping on a badly infected leg. The chief toubob had applied grease to it, but it hadn't helped, and the man had begun to scream horribly in the darkness of the hold. When they next went on deck, he had to be helped up, and Kunta saw that the leg, which had been grayish before, had begun to rot and stink even in the fresh air. This time the man was kept up on deck when the rest were taken back below. A few days later, the women told the other prisoners in their singing that the man's leg had been cut off and that one of the women had been brought to tend him, but that the man had died that night and been thrown over the side. Starting then, when the toubob came to clean the shelves, they also dropped red-hot pieces of metal into pails of strong vinegar. The clouds of acrid steam left the hold smelling better, but soon it would again be overwhelmed by the choking stink. It was a smell that Kunta felt would never leave his lungs and skin.

The steady murmuring that went on in the hold whenever the toubob were gone kept growing in volume and intensity as the men began to communicate better and better with one another. Words not understood were whispered from mouth to ear along the shelves until someone who knew more than one tongue would send back their meanings. In the process, all of the men along each shelf learned new words in tongues they had not spoken before. Sometimes men jerked upward, bumping their heads, in the double excitement of communicating with each other and the fact that it was being done without the toubob's knowledge. Muttering among themselves for hours, the men developed a deepening sense of intrigue and of brotherhood. Though they were of different villages and tribes, the feeling grew that they were not from different peoples or places.

When the toubob next came to drive them up onto the deck, the chained men marched as if they were on parade. And when they descended again, several of those men who spoke several tongues managed to change their position in line in order to get chained at the ends of shelves, thus permitting more rapid relaying of translations. The toubob never seemed to notice, for they were either unable or unconcerned to distinguish one chained man from another.

Questions, and responses to them, had begun spreading in the hold. "Where are we being taken?" That brought a babble of bitterness. "Who ever returned to tell us?'' ''Because they were eaten!'' The question, ''How long have we been here?'' brought a rash of guesses of up to a moon, until the question was translated to a man who had been able to keep a count of daylights through a small air vent near where he was chained; he said that he counted eighteen days since the great canoe had sailed.

Because of intrusions by toubob with their food tub or their scrapers, an entire day might be used up in relaying of responses to a single statement or question. Anxious inquiries were passed along for men who might know each other. ''Is anyone here from Barrakunda village?'' someone asked one day, and after a time there came winging back from mouth to ear the joyous response, ''I, Jabon Sallah, am here!'' One day, Kunta nearly burst with excitement when the Wolof hastily whispered, ''Is anyone here from Juffure village?'' ''Yes, Kunta Kinte!'' he sent back breathlessly. He lay almost afraid to breathe for the hour that it took an answer to return: ''Yes, that was the name. I heard the drums of his grieving village." Kunta dissolved into sobs, his mind streaming with pictures of his family around a flapping white cockerel that died on its back as the village wadanela went to spread that sad news among all of the people who would then come to Omoro, Binta, Lamin, Suwadu, and the baby Madi, all of them squatting about and weeping as the village drums beat out the words to inform whoever might hear them far away that a son of the village named Kunta Kinte now was considered gone forever.

Days of talking sought answers to the question: "How could the toubob of this canoe be attacked and killed?" Did anyone have or know of anything that might be used as weapons? None did. Up on the deck, had anyone noticed any carelessness or weaknesses on the part of the toubob that could be useful to a surprise attack? Again, none had. The most useful information of any sort had come from the women's singing as the men danced in their chains: that about thirty toubob were riding with them on this big canoe. There had seemed to be many more, but the women were in a better position to count them. The women said also that there had been more toubob at the beginning of the voyage, but five had died. They had been sewn inside white cloths and thrown overboard while the white-haired chief toubob read from some kind of book. The women also sang that the toubob often fought and beat each other viciously, usually as a result of arguments over which ones would next use the women.

Thanks to their singing, not much happened up on the deck that wasn't quickly told to the men dancing in their chains, who then lay discussing it down in the hold. Then came the exciting new development that contact had been established with the men chained on the level yet below. Silence would fall in the hold where Kunta lay, and a question would be called out from near the hatchway: "How many are down there?" And after a time the answer would circulate on Kunta's level: "We believe about sixty of us."

The relaying of any information from

whatever source seemed about the only function that would justify their staying alive. When there was no news, the men would talk of their families, their villages, their professions, their farms, their hunts. And more and more frequently there arose disagreements about how to kill the toubob, and when it should be tried. Some of the men felt that, whatever the consequences, the toubob should be attacked the next time they were taken up on deck. Others felt that it would be wiser to watch and wait for the best moment. Bitter disagreements began to flare up. One debate was suddenly interrupted when the voice of an elder rang out, "Hear me! Though we are of different tribes and tongues, remember that we are the same people! We must be as one village, together in this place!"

Murmurings of approval spread swiftly within the hold. That voice had been heard before, giving counsel in times of special stress. It was a voice with experience and authority as well as wisdom. Soon the information passed from mouth to ear that the speaker had been the alcala of his village. After some time, he spoke again, saying now that some leader must be found and agreed upon, and some attack plan must be proposed and agreed upon before there could be any hope of overcoming the toubob, who were obviously both well organized and heavily armed. Again, the hold soon filled with mutterings of approval.

The new and comforting sense of closeness with the other men made Kunta feel almost less aware of the stink and filth, and even the lice and rats. Then he heard the new fear that was circulating — that yet another slatee was believed to be somewhere on the level of men below. One of the women had sung of having been among the group of chained people whom this slatee had helped to bring, blindfolded, onto this canoe. She had sung that it was night when her blindfold was removed, but she had seen the toubob give that slatee liquor, which he drank until he stumbled about drunkenly, and then the toubob, all howling with laughter, had knocked him unconscious and dragged him into the hold. The woman sang that though she was not able to tell in any definite way the face of that slatee, he was almost surely somewhere below in chains like the rest, in terror that he would be discovered and killed, as he now knew that one slatee had already. In the hold, the men discussed how probably this slatee, too, was able to speak some toubob words, and in hopes of saving his miserable life, he might try to warn the toubob of any attack plans he learned of.

It occurred to Kunta, as he shook his shackles at a fat rat, why he had known little of slatees until now. It was because none of them would dare to live among people in villages, where even a strong suspicion of who they were would bring about their instant death. He remembered that back in Juffure he often had felt that his own father Omoro and yet older men, when they sat around the night fires, would seem to be needlessly occupied with dark worries and gloomy speculations about dangers to which he and the other younger men privately thought they themselves would never succumb. But now he understood why the older men had worried about the safety of the village; they had known better than he how many slatee slithered about many of them in The Gambia. The despised tan-colored sasso borro children of toubob fathers were easy to identify; but not all. Kunta thought now about the girl of his village who had been kidnapped by toubob and then escaped, who had gone to the Council of Elders just before he had been taken away, wanting to know what to do about her sasso borro infant, and he wondered what the Council of Elders had decided for her to do.

Some few slatees, he learned now, from the talk in the hold, only supplied toubob canoes with such goods as indigo, gold, and elephants' teeth. But there were hundreds of others who helped toubob to burn villages and capture people. Some of the men told how children were enticed with slices of sugar cane; then bags were thrown over their heads. Others said the slatees had beaten them mercilessly during the marches after their capture. One man's wife, big with child, had died on the road.

The wounded son of another was left bleeding to die from whip cuts. The more Kunta heard, the more his rage became as great for others as for himself.

He lay there in the darkness hearing the voice of his father sternly warning him and Lamin never to wander off anywhere alone; Kunta desperately wished that he had heeded his father's warnings. His heart sank with the thought that he would never again be able to listen to his father, that for the rest of whatever was going to be his life, he was going to have to think for himself.

"All things are the will of Allah!" That statement — which had begun with the alcala — went from mouth to ear, and when it came to Kunta from the man lying on his left side, he turned his head to whisper the words to his Wolof shacklemate. After a moment, Kunta realized that the Wolof hadn't whispered the words on to the next man, and after wondering for a while why not, he thought that perhaps he hadn't said them clearly, so he started to whisper the message once again. But abruptly the

Wolof spat out loudly enough to be heard across the entire hold, "If your Allah wills this, give me the devil!" From elsewhere in the darkness came several loud exclamations of agreement with the Wolof, and arguments broke out here and there.

Kunta was deeply shaken. The shocked realization that he lay with a pagan burned into his brain, faith in Allah being as precious to him as life itself. Until now he had respected the friendship and the wise opinions of his older shacklemate. But now Kunta knew that there could never be any more companionship between them.

CHAPTER 38

Up on the deck now, the women sang of having to steal and hide a few knives, and some other things that could be used as weapons. Down in the hold, even more strongly than before, the men separated into two camps of opinion. The leader of the group that felt the toubob should be attacked without delay was a fierce-looking, tattooed Wolof. On the deck, every man had seen him dancing wildly in his chains while baring his sharply filed teeth at the toubob, who clapped for him because they thought he was grinning. Those who believed in the wisdom of further watchful preparation were led by the tawny Foulah who had been beaten for choking the slatee to death.

There were a few followers of the

Wolof who exclaimed that the toubob should be attacked when many of them were in the hold, where the chained men could see better than they and the element of surprise would be greatest — but those who urged this plan were dismissed as foolish by the others, who pointed out that the bulk of the toubob would still be up on the deck, and thus able to kill the chained men below like so many rats. Sometimes when the arguments between the Wolof and the Foulah would reach the point of shouting, the alcala would intervene, commanding them to be quieter lest their discussion be overheard by the toubob.

Whichever leader's thinking finally prevailed, Kunta was ready to fight to the death. Dying held no fear for him any more. Once he had decided that he would never see his family and home again, he felt the same as dead already. His only fear now was that he might die without at least one of the toubob also dead by his hand. But the leader toward whom Kunta was most inclined — along with most of the men, he felt — was the cautious, whip-scarred Foulah. Kunta had found out by now that most of the men in the hold were Mandinkas, and every Mandinka knew well that the Foulah people were known for spending years, even their entire lives if need be, to avenge with death any serious wrong ever done to them. If someone killed a Foulah and escaped, the Foulah's sons would never rest until one day they found and killed the murderer.

"We must be as one behind the leader we agree upon," the alcala counseled. There was angry muttering from those who followed the Wolof, but when it had become clear that most of the men sided with the Foulah, he promptly issued his first order. "We must examine toubob's every action with the eyes of hawks. And when the time comes, we must be warriors." He advised them to follow the counsel of the woman who had told them to look happy when they jumped on deck in their chains. That would relax the toubob's guard, which would make them easier to take by surprise. And the Foulah also said that every man should locate with his eyes any weaponlike object that he could swiftly grab and use. Kunta was very pleased with himself, for during his times up on deck, he had already spotted a spike, tied loosely beneath a space of railing, which he intended to snatch and use as a spear to plunge into the nearest toubob belly. His fingers would clutch around the handle he imagined in his hands every time he thought of it.

Whenever the toubob would jerk the hatch cover open and climb down among them, shouting and wielding their whips, Kunta lay as still as a forest animal. He thought of what the kintango had said during manhood training, that the hunter should learn from what Allah himself had taught the animals — how to hide and watch the hunters who sought to kill them. Kunta had lain for hours thinking how the toubob seemed to *enjoy* causing pain. He remembered with loathing the times when toubob would laugh as they lashed the men — particularly those whose bodies were covered with bad sores — and then disgustedly wipe off the ooze that splattered onto them. Kunta lay also bitterly picturing the toubob in his mind as they forced the women into the canoe's dark corners in the nights; he imagined that he could hear the women screaming. Did the toubob have no women of their own? Was that why they went like dogs after others' women? The toubob seemed to respect nothing at all; they seemed to have no gods, not even any spirits to worship.

The only thing that could take Kunta's mind off the toubob — and how to kill them — was the rats, which had become bolder and bolder with each passing day. Their nose whiskers would tickle between Kunta's legs as they went to bite a sore that was bleeding or running with pus. But the lice preferred to bite him on the face, and they would suck at the liquids in the corners of Kunta's eyes, or the snot draining from his nostrils. He would squirm his body, with his fingers darting and pinching to crush any lice that he might trap between his nails. But worse even than the lice and rats was the pain in Kunta's shoulders, elbows, and hips, stinging now like fire from the weeks of steady rubbing against the hard, rough boards beneath him. He had seen the raw patches on other men when they were on deck, and his own cries joined theirs whenever the big canoe pitched or rolled somewhat more than usual.

And Kunta had seen that when they were up on the deck, some of the men had begun to act as if they were zombies — their faces wore a look that said that they were no longer afraid, because they no longer cared whether they lived or died. Even when the whips of the toubob lashed them, they would react only slowly. When they had been scrubbed of their filth, some were simply unable to try jumping in their chains, and the white-haired chief toubob, with a look of worry, would order the others to permit those men to sit, which they did with their foreheads between their knees and the thin, pinkish fluid draining down their raw backs. Then the chief toubob would force their heads backward and into their upturned mouths pour some stuff that they would usually choke up. And some of them fell limply

411

on their sides, unable to move, and toubob would carry them back into the hold. Even before these men died, which most of them did, Kunta knew that in some way they had willed themselves to die.

But in obedience to the Foulah, Kunta and most of the men tried to keep acting happy as they danced in their chains, although the effort was like a canker in their souls. It was possible to see, though, that when the toubob were thus made more relaxed, fewer whips fell on backs, and the men were allowed to remain on the sunlit deck for longer periods than before. After enduring the buckets of seawater and the torture of the scrubbing brushes, Kunta and the rest of the men sat resting on their haunches and watched the toubobs' every move — how they generally spaced themselves along the rails; how they usually kept their weapons too close to be grabbed away. No chained man's eye missed it whenever any toubob leaned his gun briefly against the rails. While they sat on the deck, anticipating the day when they would kill the toubob,

Kunta worried about the big metal thing that showed through the barricade. He knew that at whatever cost in lives, that weapon would have to be overwhelmed and taken, for even though he didn't know exactly what it was, he knew that it was capable of some terrible act of destruction, which was of course why the toubob had placed it there.

He worried also about those few toubob who were always turning the wheel of the big canoe, a little this way, a little that way, while staring at a round brownish metal thing before them. Once, when they were down in the hold, the alcala spoke his own thought: "If those toubob are killed, who will run this canoe?" And the Foulah leader responded that those toubob needed to be taken alive. "With spears at their throats," he said, "they will return us to our land, or they will die." The very thought that he might actually see his land, his home, his family once again sent a shiver down Kunta's spine. But even if that should happen, he thought he would have to live to be very old if he was ever to forget, even a little bit, what the toubob had done to him.

There was yet another fear within Kunta — that the toubob might have the eyes to notice how differently he and the other men danced in their chains on the deck, for now they were really dancing; they couldn't help their movements from showing what was deep in their minds: swift gestures of hurling off shackles and chains, then clubbing, strangling, spearing, killing. While they were dancing, Kunta and the other men would even whoop out hoarsely their anticipation of slaughter. But to his great relief, when the dancing ended, and he could again contain himself, he saw that the unsuspecting toubob only grinned with happiness. Then one day up on the deck, the chained people suddenly stood rooted in astonishment and stared — along with the toubob — at a flight of hundreds of flying fish that filled the air above the water like silvery birds. Kunta was watching, dumfounded, when suddenly he heard a scream. Whirling, he saw the fierce tattooed Wolof in the act of snatching a metal stick from a toubob.

Swinging it like a club, he sent the toubob's brains spraying onto the deck; as other toubob snapped from their frozen positions of shock, he battered another to the deck. It was done so swiftly that the Wolof, bellowing with rage, was clubbing his fifth toubob when the flash of a long knife lopped off his head cleanly at the shoulders. His head hit the deck before his body had crumpled down, and both spurted blood from their stumps. The eyes in the face were still open, and they looked very surprised.

Amid shoutings of panic, more and more toubob scrambled to the scene, rushing out of doors and sliding like monkeys down from among the billowing white cloths. As the women shrieked, the shackled men huddled together in a circle. The metal sticks barked flame and smoke; then the big black barrel exploded with a thunderous roar and a gushing cloud of heat and smoke just over their heads, and they screamed and sprawled over each other in horror.

From behind the barricade bolted the chief toubob and his scar-faced mate, both of them screaming in rage. The huge one struck the nearest toubob a blow that sent blood spurting from his mouth, then all of the other toubob were a mass of screaming and shouting as with their lashes and knives and firesticks they rushed to herd the shackled men back toward the opened hatch. Kunta moved, not feeling the lashes that struck him, still awaiting the Foulah's signal to attack. But almost before he realized it, they were below and chained back in their dark places and the hatch cover had been slammed down.

But they were not alone. In the commotion, a toubob had been trapped down there with them. He dashed this way and that in the darkness, stumbling and bumping into the shelves, screaming in terror, scrambling up when he fell and dashing off again. His howlings sounded like some primeval beast's. *"Toubob fa!"* somebody shouted, and the other voices joined him: *"Toubob fa!" Toubob fa!"* They shouted, louder and louder, as more and more men joined the chorus. It was as if the toubob knew they meant it for him, and pleading sounds came from him as Kunta lay silent as if frozen, none of his muscles able to move. His head was pounding, his body poured out sweat, he was gasping to breathe. Suddenly the hatch cover was snatched open and a dozen toubob came pounding down the stairs into the dark hold. Some of their whips had slashed down onto the trapped toubob before he could make them realize he was one of them.

Then, under viciously lashing whips, the men were again unchained and beaten, kicked back up onto the deck, where they were made to watch as four toubob with heavy whips beat and cut into a pulpy mess the headless body of the Wolof. The chained men's naked bodies shone with sweat and blood from their cuts and sores, but scarcely a sound came from among them. Every one of the toubob was heavily armed now, and murderous rage was upon their faces as they stood in a surrounding ring, glaring and breathing heavily. Then the whips lashed down again as the naked men were beaten back down into the hold and rechained in their places.

For a long while, no one dared even to whisper. Among the torrent of thoughts and emotions that assailed Kunta when his terror had subsided enough for him to think at all was the feeling that he wasn't alone in admiring the courage of the Wolof, who had died as a warrior was supposed to. He remembered his own tingling anticipation that the Foulah leader would at any instant signal an attack — but that signal hadn't come. Kunta was bitter, for whatever might have happened would have been all over now; and why not die now? What better time was going to come? Was there any reason to keep hanging onto life here in this stinking darkness? He wished desperately that he could communicate as he once did with his shacklemate, but the Wolof was a pagan.

Mutterings of anger at the Foulah's failure to act were cut short by his dramatic message: The attack, he announced would come the next time the men on their level of the hold were on deck being washed and jumping in their chains, when the toubob seemed most relaxed. "Many among us will die," the

Foulah said, "as our brother has died for us — but our brothers below will avenge us."

There was grunting approval in the murmurings that circulated now. And Kunta lay in the darkness listening to the raspings of a stolen file rubbing against chains. He knew for weeks that the file marks had been carefully covered with filth so that the toubob wouldn't see. He lay fixing in his mind the faces of those who turned the great wheel of the canoe, since their lives were the only ones to be spared.

But during that long night in the hold, Kunta and the other men began to hear an odd new sound they had never heard before. It seemed to be coming through the deck from over their heads. Silence fell rapidly in the hold and, listening intently, Kunta guessed that stronger winds must be making the great white cloths flap much harder than usual. Soon there was another sound, as if rice was falling onto the deck; he guessed after a while that it must be rain pelting down. Then he was sure that he heard, unmistakably, the muffled crack and rumble of heavy thunder.

Feet could be heard pounding on the deck overhead, and the big canoe began to pitch and shudder. Kunta's screams were joined by others' as each movement up and down, or from side to side, sent the chained men's naked shoulders, elbows, and buttocks — already festered and bleeding — grinding down even harder against the rough boards beneath them, grating away still more of the soft, infected skin until the muscles underneath began rubbing against the boards. The hot, lancing pains that shot from head to foot almost blacked him out, and it was as if from afar that he became dimly aware of the sound of water pouring down into the hold — and of shrieks amid a bedlam of terror.

The water poured more and more rapidly into the hold until Kunta heard the sound of something heavy, like some great coarse cloth, being dragged over the deck above. Moments later, the flood subsided to a trickle — but then Kunta began to sweat and gag. The toubob had covered the holes above them to shut out the water, but in so doing they had cut off all air from the outside, trapping the heat and stench entirely within the hold. It was beyond tolerance, and the men began to choke and vomit, rattling their shackles frantically and screaming in panic. Kunta's nose, throat, and then his lungs felt as if they were being stuffed with blazing cotton. He was gasping for more breath to scream with. Surrounded by the wild frenzy of jerking chains and suffocating cries, he didn't even know it when both his bladder and his bowels released themselves.

Sledgehammer waves crashed on the hull, and the timbers behind their heads strained against the pegs that held them together. The choked screams of the men down in the hold grew louder when the great canoe plunged sickeningly downward, shuddering as tons of ocean poured across her. Then, miraculously, she rose again under the torrential rains that beat down on her like hailstones. As the next mountainous broadside drove her back down again, and up again — heeling, rolling, trembling — the noise in the hold began to abate as more and more of the chained men fainted and went limp.

When Kunta came to, he was up on deck, amazed to find himself still alive. The orange lights, moving about, made him think at first they were still below. Then he took a deep breath and realized it was fresh air. He lay sprawled on his back, which was exploding with pains so terrible that he couldn't stop crying, even in front of the toubob. He saw them far overhead, ghostly in the moonlight, crawling along the crossarms of the tall, thick poles; they seemed to be trying to unroll the great white cloths. Then, turning his pounding head toward a loud noise, Kunta saw still more toubob stumbling up through the open hatchway, staggering as they dragged the limp, shackled forms of naked men up onto the deck of the canoe, dumping them down near Kunta and others already piled up like so many logs.

Kunta's shacklemate was trembling violently and gagging between moans. And Kunta's own gagging wouldn't stop as he watched the white-haired chief toubob and the huge scarred one shouting and cursing at the others, who were slipping and falling in the vomit underfoot, some of it their own as they continued to drag up bodies from below.

The great canoe was still pitching heavily, and drenching spray now and then splashed over the quarterdeck. The chief toubob had difficulty keeping his balance, now moving hurriedly, as another toubob followed him with a light. One or the other of them would turn upward the face of each limp, naked man, and the light would be held close; the chief toubob would peer closely and sometimes he would put his fingers on one wrist of that shackled man. Sometimes, then, cursing bitterly, he would bark an order and the other toubob would lift and drop the man into the ocean.

Kunta knew these men had died below. He asked himself how Allah, of whom it was said that He was in all places at all times, could possibly be here. Then he thought that even to question such a thing would make him no better than the pagan shuddering and moaning alongside him.

And he turned his thoughts to prayer for the souls of the men who had been thrown over the side, joined already with their ancestors. He envied them.

CHAPTER 39

By the time the dawn came, the weather had calmed and cleared, but the ship still rolled in heavy swells. Some of the men who still lay on their backs, or on their sides, showed almost no signs of life; others were having dreadful convulsions. But along with most of the other men, Kunta had managed to get himself into a sitting position that relieved somewhat the horrible pains in his back and buttocks. He looked dully at the backs of those nearby; all were bleeding afresh through blood already dried and clotted, and he saw what seemed to be bones showing at the shoulders and elbows. With a vacant look in another direction, he could see a woman lying with her legs wide apart; her private parts, turned in his direction, were

425

smudged with some strange grayish-yellowish paste, and his nose picked up some indescribable smell that he knew must come from her.

Now and then one of the men who were still lying down would try to raise himself up. Some would only fall back, but among those who succeeded in sitting up, Kunta noticed, was the Foulah leader. He was bleeding heavily, and his expression was of one who wasn't part of what was going on around him. Kunta didn't recognize many of the other men he saw. He guessed that they must be from the level below his. These were the men whom the Foulah had said would avenge the dead from the first level after the toubob were attacked. The attack. Kunta didn't have the strength even to think about it any more.

In some of the faces around him, including that of the man he was shackled to, Kunta saw that death was etched. Without knowing why, he was sure they were going to die. The face of the Wolof was grayish in color, and each time he gasped to breathe there was a bubbling sound in his nose. Even the Wolof's shoulder and elbow bones, which showed through the raw flesh, had a grayish look. Almost as if he knew that Kunta was looking at him, the Wolof's eyes fluttered open and looked back at Kunta — but without a sign of recognition. He was a pagan, but . . . Kunta extended a finger weakly to touch the Wolof on the arm. But there was no sign of any awareness of Kunta's gesture, or of how much it had meant.

Although his pains didn't subside, the warm sun began to make Kunta feel a little better. He glanced down and saw, in a pool around where he sat, the blood that had drained from his back — and a shuddering whine forced itself up his throat. Toubob who were also sick and weak were moving about with brushes and buckets, scrubbing up vomit and feces, and others were bringing tubs of filth up from below and dumping it over the side. In the daylight, Kunta vacantly noted their pale, hairy skins, and the smallness of their fotos.

After a while he smelled the steam of

boiling vinegar and tar through the gratings as the chief toubob began to move among the shackled people applying his salve. He would put a plaster of cloth smeared with powder wherever the bones showed through, but seeping blood soon made the plasters slip and fall off. He also opened some of the men's mouths — including Kunta's — and forced down their throats something from a black bottle.

At sunset, those who were well enough were fed — maize boiled with red palm oil and served in a small tub they dipped into with their hands. Then each of them had a scoopful of water brought by a toubob from a barrel that was kept at the foot of the biggest of the poles on deck. By the time the stars came out, they were back below in chains. The emptied spaces on Kunta's level, where men had died, were filled with the sickest of the men from the level below, and their moans of suffering were even louder than before.

For three days Kunta lay among them in a twilight of pain, vomiting, and fever, his cries mingled with theirs. He was also among those racked with fits of deep, hoarse coughing. His neck was hot and swollen, and his entire body poured with sweat. He came out of his stupor only once, when he felt the whiskers of a rat brush along his hip; almost by reflex his free hand darted out and trapped the rat's head and foreparts in its grasp. He couldn't believe it. All the rage that had been bottled up in him for so long flooded down his arm and into his hand. Tighter and tighter he squeezed — the rat wriggling and squaling frantically — until he could feel the eyes popping out, the skull crunching under his thumb. Only then did the strength ebb from his fingers and the hand open to release the crushed remains.

A day or two later, the chief toubob began to enter the hold himself, discovering each time — and unchaining — at least one more lifeless body. Gagging in the stench, the others holding up lights for him to see by, he applied his salve and powder and forced the neck of his black bottle into the mouths of those still living. Kunta fought not to scream with pain whenever the fingers touched the grease to his back or the bottle to his lips. He also shrank from the touch of those pale hands against his skin; he would rather have felt the lash. And in the light's orange glow, the faces of the toubob had a kind of paleness without features that he knew would never leave his mind any more than the stink in which he lay.

Lying there in filth and fever, Kunta didn't know if they had been down in the belly of this canoe for two moons or six, or even as long as a rain. The man who had been lying near the vent through which they had counted the days was dead now. And there was no longer any communication among those who had survived.

Once when Kunta came jerking awake from a half sleep, he felt a nameless terror and sensed that death was near him. Then after a while, he realized that he could no longer hear the familiar wheezing of his shacklemate beside him. It was a long time before Kunta could bring himself to reach out a hand and touch the man's arm. He recoiled in horror, for it was cold and rigid. Kunta lay shuddering. Pagan or not, he and the Wolof had talked together, they had lain together. And now he was alone.

When the toubob came down again, bringing the boiled corn, Kunta cringed as their gagging and muttering came closer. Then he felt one of them shaking the body of the Wolof and cursing. Then Kunta heard food being scraped as usual into his own pan, which was thrust up between him and the still Wolof, and the toubob moved on down the shelf. However starved his belly was, Kunta couldn't think of eating.

After a while two toubob came and unshackled the Wolof's ankle and wrist from Kunta's. Numb with shock, he listened as the body was dragged and bumped down the aisle and up the stairs. He wanted to shove himself away from that vacant space, but the instant he moved, the raking of his exposed muscles against the boards made him scream in agony. As he lay still, letting the pain subside, he could hear in his mind the death wailings of the women of the Wolof's village, mourning his death.

"Toubob fa!" he screamed into the stinking darkness, his cuffed hand jangling the chain of the Wolof's empty cuff.

The next time he was up on deck, Kunta's glance met the gaze of one of the toubob who had beaten him and the Wolof. For an instant they looked deeply into each other's eyes, and though the toubob's face and eyes tightened with hatred, this time no whip fell upon Kunta's back. As Kunta was recovering from his surprise, he looked across the deck and for the first time since the storm, saw the women. His heart sank. Of the original twenty, only twelve remained. But he felt a pang of relief that all four of the children had survived.

There was no scrubbing this time — the wounds of the men's backs were too bad — and they jumped in their chains only weakly, this time to the beat of the drum alone; the toubob who had squeezed the wheezing thing was gone. As well as they could, in their pain, the women who were left sang that quite a few more toubob had been sewn into white cloths and dropped overboard.

With a great weariness in his face, the white-haired toubob was moving among the naked people with his salve and bottle when a man with the empty shackles of a dead partner dangling from his wrist and ankle bolted from where he stood and raced to the rail. He had scrambled halfway over it when one of the nearby toubob managed to catch up with him and grab the trailing chain just as he leaped. An instant later his body was banging against the side of the great canoe and the deck was ringing with his strangled howls. Suddenly, unmistakably, amid the cries, Kunta heard some toubob words. A hissing rose from the chained men; it was the other slatee, without question. As the man flailed against the hull — screaming *"Toubob fa!"* and then begging for mercy — the chief toubob went over to the tail and looked down. After listening for a moment, he abruptly jerked the chain from the other toubob and let the slatee drop screaming into the sea. Then, without a word, he went back to greasing and powdering wounds as if nothing had happened.

Though their whips fell less often, the guards seemed to act terrified of their prisoners now. Each time the prisoners were brought up on deck, the toubob ringed them closely, with firesticks and knives drawn, as if at any moment the shackled people might attack. But as far as Kunta was concerned, though he despised the toubob with all his being, he didn't care about killing them any more. He was so sick and weak that he didn't even care if he lived or died himself. Up on the deck he would simply lie down on his side and close his eyes. Soon he would feel the chief toubob's hands smearing salve on his back again. And then, for a while, he would feel nothing but the warmth of the sun and smell only the fresh ocean breeze, and the pain would dissolve into a quiet haze of waiting — almost blissfully — to die and join his ancestors.

Occasionally, down in the hold, Kunta would hear a little murmuring here and there, and he wondered what they could find to talk about. And what was the point? His Wolof shacklemate was gone, and death had taken some of those who had translated for the others. Besides, it took too much strength to talk any more. Each day Kunta felt a little worse, and it didn't help to see what was happening to some of the other men. Their bowels had begun to drain out a mixture of clotted blood and thick, grayish-yellow, horribly foul-smelling mucus.

When they first smelled and saw the putrid discharge, the toubob became agitated. One of them went rushing back up through the hatch, and minutes later the chief toubob descended. Gagging, he gestured sharply for the other toubob to unshackle the screaming men and remove them from the hold. More toubob soon returned with lights, hoes, brushes, and buckets. Vomiting and gasping curses, they scraped, scrubbed, and scrubbed again the shelves from which sick men had been taken away. Then they poured boiling vinegar on those places and moved the men lying next to those places to other empty spaces farther away.

But nothing helped, for the bloody contagion — which Kunta heard the toubob call "the flux" — spread and spread. Soon he too began to writhe with pains in his head and back, then to roast and shiver with fever and chills, and finally to feel his insides clenching and squeezing out the stinking blood and ooze. Feeling as if his entrails were coming out along with the discharge, Kunta nearly fainted from the pain. Between screams, he cried out things he could hardly believe he was uttering: "Omoro — Omar the Second Caliph, third after Muhammad the Prophet! Kairaba — Kairaba means peace!" Finally his voice was all but gone from shrieking and could hardly be heard amid the sobbing of the others. Within two days, the flux had afflicted nearly every man in the hold.

By now the bloody globs were dripping down off the shelves into the aisleways, and there was no way for the toubob to avoid brushing against it or stepping on it — cursing and vomiting — whenever they went into the hold. Each day now the men would be taken up on deck while the toubob took down buckets of vinegar and tar to boil into steam to clean the hold.

Kunta and his mates stumbled up through the hatch and across to where they would flop down on the deck, which would soon be fouled with the blood from their backs and the discharge from their bowels. The smell of the fresh air would seem to go all through Kunta's body, from his feet to his head and then, when they were returned to the hold, the vinegar and tar smell would do the same, although the smell of it never killed the stench of the flux.

In his delirium, Kunta saw flashing glimpses of his Grandma Yaisa lying propped up on one arm on her bed talking to him for the last time, when he was but a small boy; and he thought of old Grandmother Nyo Boto, and the stories she would tell when he was back in the first kafo, about the crocodile who was caught in a trap by the river when the boy came along to set it free. Moaning and babbling, he would claw and kick when the toubob came anywhere near him.

Soon most of the men could no longer walk at all, and toubob had to help them up onto the deck so that the white-haired one could apply his useless salve in the light of day. Every day someone died and was thrown overboard, including a few more of the women and two of the four children — as well as several of the toubob themselves. Many of the surviving toubob were hardly able to drag themselves around any more, and one manned the big canoe's wheel while standing in a tub that would catch his flux mess.

The nights and the days tumbled into one another until one day Kunta and the few others from below who yet could manage to drag themselves up the hatch steps stared over the rail with dull astonishment at a rolling carpet of gold-colored seaweed floating on the surface of the water as far as they could see. Kunta knew that the water couldn't continue forever, and now it seemed that the big canoe was about to go over the edge of the world — but he didn't really care. Deep within himself, he sensed that he was nearing the end; he was unsure only of by what means he was going to die.

Dimly he noted that the great white

sheets were dropping, no longer full of wind as they had been. Up among the poles, the toubob were pulling their maze of ropes to move the sheets this way and that, trying to pick up any little breeze. From the toubob down on the deck, they drew up buckets of water and sloshed them against the great cloths. But still the great canoe remained becalmed, and gently it began to roll back and forth upon the swells.

All the toubob were on the edges of their tempers now, the white-haired one even shouting at his knife-scarred mate, who cursed and beat the lesser toubob more than before, and they in turn fought with each other even more than they had before. But there were no further beatings of the shackled people, except on rare occasions, and they began to spend almost all the daylight hours up on the deck, and — to Kunta's amazement — they were given a full pint of water every day.

When they were taken up from the hold one morning, the men saw hundreds of flying fish piled up on the deck. The women sang that the toubob had set lights out on deck the night before to lure them, and they had flown aboard and floundered about in vain trying to escape. That night they were boiled with the maize, and the taste of fresh fish startled Kunta with pleasure. He wolfed the food down, bones and all.

When the stinging yellow powder was sprinkled next against Kunta's back, the chief toubob applied a thick cloth bandage against his right shoulder. Kunta knew that meant his bone had begun showing through, as was the case with so many other men already, especially the thinner ones, who had the least muscle over their bones. The bandaging made Kunta's shoulder hurt even more than before. But he hadn't been back down in the hold for long before the seeping blood made the soaked bandage slip loose. It didn't matter. Sometimes his mind would dwell on the horrors he had been through, or on his deep loathing of all toubob; but mostly he just lay in the stinking darkness, eyes gummy with some yellowish matter, hardly aware that he was still alive.

He heard other men crying out, or beseeching Allah to save them, but he neither knew nor cared who they were. He would drift off into fitful, moaning sleep, with jumbled dreams of working in the fields back in Juffure, of leafy green farms, of fish leaping from the glassy surface of the bolong, of fat antelope haunches roasting over glowing coals, of gourds of steaming tea sweetened with honey. Then, drifting again into wakefulness, he sometimes heard himself mouthing bitter, incoherent threats and begging aloud, against his will, for a last look at his family. Each of them — Omoro, Binta, Lamin, Suwadu, Madi — was a stone in his heart. It tortured him to think that he had caused them grief. Finally he would wrench his mind away to something else, but it wouldn't help. His thoughts would always drift to something like the drum he had been going to make for himself. He'd think about how he would have practiced on it at night while guarding the groundnut fields, where no one could hear his mistakes. But then he would remember the day he had gone to chop down the tree trunk for the drum, and it would all come flooding back.

Among the men who were still alive, Kunta was one of the last who were able to climb down unassisted from their shelf and up the steps to the deck. But then his wasting legs began trembling and buckling under him and finally he, too, had to be half carried and half dragged to the deck. Moaning quietly, with his head between his knees, rheumy eyes clamped tight, he sat limply until his turn came to be cleaned. The toubob now used a large soapy sponge lest a hard-bristled brush do further damage to the men's gouged and bleeding backs. But Kunta was still better off than most, who were able only to lie on their sides, seeming almost as if they had stopped breathing.

Among them all, only the remaining women and children were reasonably healthy; they hadn't been shackled and chained down within the darkness, filth, stench, lice, fleas, rats, and contagion. The oldest of the surviving women, one of about Binta's rains — Mbuto was her name, a Mandinka of the village of

Kerewan — had such stateliness and dignity that even in her nakedness it was as if she wore a robe. The toubob didn't even stop her from moving with comforting words among the shackled men lying sick on the deck, rubbing fevered chests and foreheads. "Mother! Mother!" Kunta whispered when he felt her soothing hands, and another man, too weak to speak, just gaped his jaw in an attempt to smile.

Finally, Kunta could no longer even eat without help. The draining shreds of muscle in his shoulders and elbows refused to lift his hands enough for him to claw into the food pan. Often now the feeding was done with the men up on deck, and one day Kunta's fingernails were scrabbling to get over the edges of the pan when the scar-faced toubob noticed it. He barked an order at one of the lesser toubob, who proceeded to force into Kunta's mouth a hollow tube and pour the gruel through it. Gagging on the tube, Kunta gulped and slobbered the food down, then sprawled out on his belly.

The days were growing hotter, and even

up on the deck everyone was sweltering in the still air. But after a few more days, Kunta began to feel a breath of cooling breeze. The big cloths up on the tall poles started to snap again and soon were billowing in the wind. The toubob up above were springing about like monkeys again, and soon the big canoe was cutting through the water with froth curling at her bow.

The next morning, more toubob than usual came thudding down through the hatch, and much earlier than ever before. With great excitement in their words and movements, they rushed along the aisles, unchaining the men and hurriedly helping them upward. Stumbling up through the hatch behind a number who were ahead of him, Kunta blinked in the early-morning light and then saw the other toubob and the women and children standing at the rails. The toubob were all laughing, cheering, and gesturing wildly. Between the scabbed backs of the other men, Kunta squinted and then saw . . .

Though still blurred in the distance, it was unmistakably some piece of Allah's earth. These toubob really did have some place to put their feet upon — the land of toubabo doo — which the ancient forefathers said stretched from the sunrise to the sunset. Kunta's whole body shook. The sweat came popping out and glistened on his forehead. The voyage was over. He had lived through it all. But his tears soon flooded the shoreline into a gray, swimming mist, for Kunta knew that whatever came next was going to be yet worse.

CHAPTER 40

Back down in the darkness of the hold, the chained men were too afraid to open their mouths. In the silence, Kunta could hear the ship's timbers creaking, the muted *ssss* of the sea against the hull, and the dull clumpings of toubob feet rushing about on the deck overhead.

Suddenly some Mandinka began shrieking the praises of Allah, and soon all the others had joined him — until there was a bedlam of praise and praying and of chains being rattled with all the strength the men could muster. Amid the noise, Kunta didn't hear the hatch when it scraped open, but the jarring shaft of daylight stilled his tongue and jerked his head in that direction. Blinking his eyes to compress the mucus in them, he watched dimly as the toubob entered with their lanterns and began to herd them — with unusual haste — back onto the deck. Wielding their long-handled brushes once again, the toubob ignored the men's screams as they scrubbed the encrusted filth from their festering bodies, and the chief toubob moved down the line sprinkling his yellow powder. But this time, where the muscles were rubbed through deeply, he signaled for his big assistant to apply a black substance with a wide, flat brush. When it touched Kunta's raw buttocks, the rocketing pain smashed him dizzily to the deck.

As he lay with his whole body feeling as if it were on fire, he heard men howling anew in terror, and snapping his head up, he saw several of the toubob engaged in what could only be preparing the men to be eaten. Several of them, in pairs, were pushing first one chained man and then the next into a kneeling position where he was held while a third toubob brushed onto his head a white frothing stuff and then, with a narrow, gleaming thing, raked the hair off his scalp, leaving blood trickling down across his face.

When they reached Kunta and seized him, he screamed and struggled with all his might until a heavy kick in the ribs left him gasping for breath while the skin of his head numbly felt the frothing and the scraping. Next the chained men's bodies were oiled until they shone, and then they were made to step into some odd loincloth that had two holes the legs went through and that also covered their private parts. Finally, under the close scrutiny of the chief toubob, they were chained prostrate along the rails as the sun reached the center of the sky.

Kunta lay numbly, in a kind of stupor. It came into his mind that when they finally ate his flesh and sucked the bones, his spirit would already have escaped to Allah. He was praying silently when barking shouts from the chief toubob and his big helper made him open his eyes in time to watch the lesser toubob dashing up the tall poles. Only this time their grunts, as they strained at the ropes, were mixed with excited shouts and laughter. A moment later most of the great white sheets slackened and crumpled downward.

Kunta's nostrils detected a new smell in the air; actually, it was a mingling of many smells, most of them strange and unknown to him. Then he thought he heard new sounds in the distance, from across the water. Lying on the deck, with his crusty eyes half shut, he couldn't tell from where. But soon the sounds grew closer, and as they did, his fearful whimperings joined those of his mates. As the sounds got louder, so did their praying and gibbering — until finally, in the light wind, Kunta could smell the bodies of many unfamiliar toubob. Just then the big canoe bumped hard against something solid and unyielding, and it lurched heavily, rocking back and forth until, for the first time since they left Africa four and a half moons before, it was secured by ropes and fell still.

The chained men sat frozen with terror. Kunta's arms were locked around his knees, and his eyes were clamped shut as if he were paralyzed. For as long as he could, he held his breath against the sickening wave of smells, but when something clumped heavily onto the deck, he slit his eyes open and saw two new toubob stepping down from a wide plank holding a white cloth over their noses. Moving briskly, they shook hands with the chief toubob, who was now all grins, clearly anxious to please them. Kunta silently begged Allah's forgiveness and mercy as the toubob began rushing along the rails unchaining the black men and gesturing with shouts for them to stand up. When Kunta and his mates clutched at their chains — not wanting to let go of what had become almost a part of their bodies — the whips began to crack, first over their heads, then against their backs. Instantly, amid screams, they let go of the chains and stumbled to their feet.

Over the side of the big canoe, down on the dock, Kunta could see dozens of toubob stamping, laughing, pointing in their excitement, with dozens more running from all directions to join them. Under the whips, they were driven in a stumbling single file up over the side and down the sloping plank toward the waiting mob. Kunta's knees almost buckled under him as his feet touched the toubob earth, but other toubob with cocked whips kept them moving closely alongside the jeering crowd, their massed smell like the blow of a giant fist in Kunta's face. When one black man fell, crying out to Allah, his chains pulled down the men ahead of and behind him. Whips lashed them all back up again as the toubob crowd screamed in excitement.

The impulse to dash and escape surged wildly in Kunta, but the whips kept his chained line moving. They trudged past toubob riding in extraordinary two-wheeled and four-wheeled vehicles drawn by huge animals that looked a little like donkeys; then past a toubob throng milling around in some kind of marketplace stacked with colorful piles of what seemed to be fruits and vegetables. Finely clothed toubob regarded them with expressions of loathing, while more roughly clad toubob pointed and hooted with enjoyment. One of the latter, he noticed, was a she toubob, her stringy hair the color of straw. After seeing the hungry way the toubob on the great canoe had lusted after the black women, he was amazed to see that the toubob had women of their own; but looking at this specimen, he could understand why they preferred Africans.

Kunta darted a glance sideways as they passed a group of toubob screaming crazily around a flurry of two cocks fighting with each other. And hardly had that din faded behind them when they came upon a shouting crowd leaping this way and that to avoid being bowled over by three toubob boys as they raced and dove after a squealing, filthy swine that looked shiny with grease. Kunta couldn't believe his eyes.

As if lightning had struck him, Kunta then glimpsed two black men who were not from the big canoe — a Mandinka and a Serere, there was no doubt. He jerked his head around to stare as they walked quietly behind a toubob. He and his mates weren't alone after all in this terrible land! And if these men had been allowed to live, perhaps they too would be spared from the cooking cauldron. Kunta wanted to rush over and embrace them;

but he saw their expressionless faces and the fear in their downcast eyes. And then his nose picked their smell; there was something wrong with it. His mind reeled; he couldn't comprehend how black men would docilely follow behind a toubob who wasn't watching them or even carrying a weapon, rather than try to run away — or kill him.

He didn't have time to think about it further, for suddenly they found themselves at the open door of a large, square house of baked mud bricks in oblong shapes with iron bars set into a few open spaces along the sides. The chained men were whipped inside the wide door by the toubob guarding it, then into a large room. Kunta's feet felt cool on the floor of hard-packed earth. In the dim light that came through the two iron-barred openings, his blinking eyes picked out the forms of five black men huddled along one wall. They didn't so much as lift their heads as the toubob locked the wrists and ankles of Kunta and his mates in thick iron cuffs attached to short chains that were bolted to the walls.

Along with the others, Kunta then huddled down himself, with his chin against his clasped knees, his mind dazed and reeling with all that he had seen and heard and smelled since they had gotten off the great canoe. After a little while, another black man entered. Without looking at anyone, he put down some tins of water and food before each man and quickly left. Kunta wasn't hungry, but his throat was so dry that finally he couldn't stop himself from sipping a small amount of the water; it tasted strange. Numbly, he watched through one of the iron-barred spaces as the daylight faded into darkness.

The longer they sat there, the deeper Kunta sank into a kind of nameless terror. He felt that he would almost have preferred the dark hold of the big canoe, for at least he had come to know what to expect next there. He shrank away whenever a toubob came into the room during the night; their smell was strange and overpowering. But he was used to the other smells — sweat, urine, dirty bodies, the stink as some chained man went through the agony of relieving his bowels amid the others' mingled praying and cursing and moaning and rattling of their chains.

Suddenly all the noises ceased when a toubob came in carrying a light such as those that had been used on the big canoe, and behind him, in the soft yellowish glow, another toubob who was striking with his whip some new black one who was crying out in what sounded like the toubob tongue. That one was soon chained, and the two toubob left. Kunta and his mates remained still, hearing the newcomer's piteous sounds of suffering and pain.

The dawn was near, Kunta sensed, when from somewhere there came into his head as clearly as when he had been in manhood training the high, sharp voice of the kintango: "A man is wise to study and learn from the animals." It was so shocking that Kunta sat bolt upright. Was it finally some message from Allah? What could be the meaning of learning from the animals — here, now? He was himself, if anything, like an animal in a trap. His mind pictured animals he had seen in traps. But sometimes the animals escaped before they were killed. Which ones were they?

Finally, the answer came to him. The animals he had known to escape from their traps were those that had not gone raging around within the trap until they were weakened to exhaustion; those that escaped had made themselves wait quietly, conserving their strength until their captors came, and the animal seized upon their carelessness to explode its energies in a desperate attack — or more wisely — a flight toward freedom.

Kunta felt intensely more alert. It was his first positive hope since he had plotted with the others to kill the toubob on the big canoe. His mind fastened upon it now: escape. He must appear to the toubob to be defeated. He must not rage or fight yet; he must seem to have given up any hope.

But even if he managed to escape, where would he run? Where could he hide in this strange land? He knew the country around Juffure as he knew his own hut, but here he knew nothing whatever. He didn't even know if toubob had forests, or if they did, whether he would find in them the signs that a hunter would use. Kunta told himself that these problems would simply have to be met as they came.

As the first streaks of dawn filtered through the barred windows, Kunta dropped fitfully off to sleep. But no sooner had he closed his eyes, it seemed, than he was awakened by the strange black one bringing containers of water and food. Kunta's stomach was clenched with hunger, but the food smelled sickening, and he turned away. His tongue felt foul and swollen. He tried to swallow the slime that was in his mouth, and his throat hurt with the effort.

He looked dully about him at his mates from the big canoe; they all seemed unseeing, unhearing — drawn within themselves. Kunta turned his head to study the five who were in the room when they arrived. They wore ragged toubob clothing. Two of them were of the light brown sasso borro skin color that the elders had said resulted from some toubob taking a black woman. Then Kunta looked at the newcomer who had been brought in during the night; he sat slumped forward, the dried blood caked in his hair and staining the toubob garment he wore, and one of his arms hung in an awkward way that told Kunta it had been broken.

More time passed, and finally Kunta fell asleep again — only to be awakened once more, this time much later, by the arrival of another meal. It was some kind of steaming gruel, and it smelled even worse than the last thing they'd set in front of him. He shut his eyes not to see it, but when nearly all of his mates snatched up the containers and began wolfing the stuff down, he figured it might not be so bad after all. If he was ever going to escape from this place, thought Kunta, he would need strength. He would force himself to eat a little bit — but just a little. Seizing the bowl, he brought it to his open mouth and gulped and swallowed until the gruel was gone. Disgusted with himself, he banged the bowl back down and began to gag, but he forced it down again. He had to keep the food inside him if he was going to live.

From that day on, three times a day, Kunta forced himself to eat the hated food. The black one who brought it came once each day with a bucket, hoe, and a shovel to clean up after them. And once each afternoon, two toubob came to paint more of the stinging black liquid over the men's worst open sores, and sprinkle the yellow powder over the smaller sores. Kunta despised himself for the weakness that made him jerk and moan from the pain along with the others.

Through the barred window, Kunta counted finally six daylights and five nights. The first four nights, he had heard faintly from somewhere, not far away, the screams of women whom he recognized from the big canoe. He and his mates had had to sit there, burning with humiliation at being helpless to defend their women, let alone themselves. But it was even worse tonight, for there were no cries from the women. What new horror had been visited upon them?

Nearly every day, one or more of the strange black men in toubob clothes would be shoved stumbling into the room and chained. Slumped against the wall behind them, or curled down on the floor, they always showed signs of recent beatings, seeming not to know where they were or to care what might happen to them next. Then, usually before another day had passed, some important-acting toubob would enter the room holding a rag over his nose, and always one of those recent prisoners would start shrieking with terror — as that toubob kicked and shouted at him; then that black one would be taken away.

Whenever he felt that each bellyful of food had settled, Kunta would try to make his mind stop thinking in an effort to sleep. Even a few minutes of rest would blot out for that long a time this seemingly unending horror, which for whatever reason was the divine will of Allah. When Kunta couldn't sleep, which was most of the time, he would try to force his mind onto things other than his family or his village, for when he thought of them he would soon be sobbing.

CHAPTER 41

Just after the seventh morning gruel, two toubob entered the barred room with an armload of clothes. One frightened man after another was unchained and shown how to put them on. One garment covered the waist and legs, a second the upper body. When Kunta put them on, his sores — which had begun to show signs of healing — immediately started itching.

In a little while, he began to hear the sound of voices outside; quickly it grew louder and louder. Many toubob were gathering — talking, laughing — not far beyond the barred window. Kunta and his mates sat in their toubob clothes gripped with terror at what was about to happen — whatever it might be.

When the two toubob returned, they

461

quickly unchained and marched from the room three of the five black ones who had originally been there. All of them acted somehow as if this had happened to them enough times before that it no longer mattered. Then, within moments, there was a change in the toubob sounds from outside; it grew much quieter, and then one toubob began to shout. Struggling vainly to understand what was being said, Kunta listened uncomprehendingly to the strange cries: "Fit as a fiddle! Plenty of spirit in this buck!" And at brief intervals other toubob would interrupt with loud exclamations: "Three hundred and fifty!" "Four hundred!" "Five!" And the first toubob would shout: "Let's hear six! Look at him! Works like a mule!"

Kunta shuddered with fear, his face running with sweat, breath tight in his throat. When four toubob came into the room — the first two plus two others — Kunta felt paralyzed. The new pair of toubob stood just within the doorway holding short clubs in one hand and small metal objects in the other. The other two moved along Kunta's side of the wall unlocking the iron cuffs. When anyone cried out or scuffled, he was struck with a short, thick, leather strap. Even so, when Kunta felt himself touched, he came up snarling with rage and terror. A blow against his head made it seem to explode; he felt only dimly a jerking at the chain on his cuffs. When his head began to clear, he was the first of the chained line of six men stumbling through a wide doorway out into the daylight.

"Just picked out of the trees!" The shouting one was standing on a low wooden platform with hundreds of other toubobs massed before him. As they gaped and gestured, Kunta's nose recoiled from the thickness of their stink. He glimpsed a few black ones among the toubob, but their faces seemed to be seeing nothing. Two of them were holding in chains two of the black ones who had just been brought from the barred room. Now the shouting one began striding rapidly down the line of Kunta and his companions, his eyes appraising them from head to foot. Then he walked back up the line thrusting the butt of his whip against their chests and bellies, all the while making his strange cries: "Bright as monkeys! Can be trained for anything!" Then back at the end of the line, he prodded Kunta roughly toward the raised platform. But Kunta couldn't move, except to tremble; it was as if his senses had deserted him. The whip's butt seared across the scabbing crust of his ulcerated buttocks; nearly collapsing under the pain, Kunta stumbled forward, and the toubob clicked the free end of his chain into an iron thing.

"Top prime — young and supple!" the toubob shouted. Kunta was already so numb with terror that he hardly noticed as the toubob crowd moved in more closely around him. Then, with short sticks and whip butts, they were pushing apart his compressed lips to expose his clenched teeth, and with their bare hands prodding him all over — under his armpits, on his back, his chest, his genitals. Then some of those who had been inspecting Kunta began to step back and make strange cries.

"Three hundred dollars! . . . three fifty!" The shouting toubob laughed scornfully. "Five hundred! . . . six!" He sounded angry. "This is a choice young nigger! Do I hear seven fifty?"

"Seven fifty!" came a shout.

He repeated the cry several times, then shouted "Eight!" until someone in the crowd shouted it back. And then, before he had a chance to speak again, someone else shouted, "Eight fifty!"

No other calls came. The shouting toubob unlocked Kunta's chain and jerked him toward the toubob who came stepping forward. Kunta felt an impulse to make his move right then, but he knew he would never make it — and anyway, he couldn't seem to move his legs.

He saw a black one moving forward behind the toubob to whom the shouter had handed his chain. Kunta's eyes entreated this black one, who had distinctly Wolof features, *My Brother, you come from my country.* . . . But the black one seemed not even to see Kunta as, jerking hard on the chain so that Kunta came stumbling after him, they began moving through the crowd. Some of the younger toubob laughed, jeered, and poked at Kunta with sticks as they passed, but finally they left them behind and the black one stopped at a large box sitting up off the ground on four wheels behind one of those enormous donkeylike animals he had seen on his way here from the big canoe.

With an angry sound, the black one grasped Kunta around the hips and boosted him up over the side and onto the floor of the box, where he crumpled into a heap, hearing the free end of his chain click again into something beneath a raised seat at the front end of the box behind the animal.

Two large sacks of what smelled like some kind of grain were piled near where Kunta lay. His eyes were shut tight; he felt as if he never wanted to see anything again — especially this hated black slatee.

After what seemed a very long time, Kunta's nose told him that the toubob had returned. The toubob said something, and then he and the black one climbed onto the front seat, which squeaked under their weight. The black one made a quick sound and flicked a leather thong across the animal's back; instantly it began pulling the rolling box ahead.

Kunta was so dazed that for a while he didn't even hear the chain locked to his ankle cuff rattling against the floor of the box. He had no idea how far they had traveled when his next clear thought came, and he slit his eyes open far enough to study the chain at close range. Yes, it was smaller than the one that had bound him on the big canoe; if he collected his strength and sprang, would this one tear loose from the box?

Kunta raised his eyes carefully to see the backs of the pair who sat ahead, the toubob sitting stiffly at one end of the plank seat, the black one slouched at the other end. They both sat staring ahead as if they were unaware that they were sharing the same seat. Beneath it — somewhere in the shadow — the chain seemed to be securely fastened; he decided that it was not yet time to jump.

The odor of the grain sacks along side him was overpowering, but he could also smell the toubob and his black driver — and soon he smelled some other black

467

people, quite nearby. Without making a sound, Kunta inched his aching body upward against the rough side of the box, but he was afraid to lift his head over the side, and didn't see them.

As he lay back down, the toubob turned his head around, and their eyes met. Kunta felt frozen and weak with fear, but the toubob showed no expression and turned his back again a moment later. Emboldened by the toubob's indifference, he sat up again — this time a little farther — when he heard a singing sound in the distance gradually growing louder. Not far ahead of them he saw a toubob seated on the back of another animal like the one pulling the rolling box. The toubob held a coiled whip, and a chain from the animal was linked to the wrist cuffs of about twenty blacks — or most of them were black, some brown — walking in a line ahead of him.

Kunta blinked and squinted to see better. Except for two fully clothed women, they were all men and all bare from their waist up, and they were singing with deep mournfulness. He listened very carefully to the words, but they made no sense whatever to him. As the rolling box slowly passed them, neither the blacks nor the toubob so much as glanced in their direction, though they were close enough to touch. Most of their backs, Kunta saw, were crisscrossed with whip scars, some of them fresh, and he guessed at some of their tribes: Foulah, Yoruba, Mauretanian, Wolof, Mandinka. Of those he was more certain than of the others, most of whom had had the misfortune to have toubob for fathers.

Beyond the blacks, as far as Kunta's runny eyes would let him see, there stretched vast fields of crops growing in different colors. Alongside the road was a field painted with what he recognized as maize. Just as it was back in Juffure after the harvest, the stalks were brown and stripped of ears.

Soon afterward, the toubob leaned over, took some bread and some kind of meat out of the sack beneath the seat, broke off a piece of each, and set them on the seat between him and the black one, who picked it up with a tip of his hat and began to eat. After a few moments the black one turned in his seat, took a long look at Kunta, who was watching intently, and offered him a chunk of bread. He could smell it from where he lay, and the fragrance made his mouth water, but he turned his head away. The black one shrugged and popped it into his own mouth.

Trying not to think about his hunger, Kunta looked out over the side of the box and saw, at the far end of a field, what appeared to be a small cluster of people bent over, seemingly at work. He thought they must be black, but they were too far away to be sure. He sniffed the air, trying to pick up their scent, but couldn't.

As the sun was setting, the box passed another like it, going in the opposite direction, with a toubob at the reins and three first-kafo black children riding behind him. Trudging in chains behind the box were seven adult blacks, four men wearing ragged clothes and three women in coarse gowns. Kunta wondered why these were not also singing; then he saw the deep despair on their faces as they flashed past. He wondered where toubob was taking them.

As the dusk deepened, small black bats began squeaking and darting jerkily here and there, just as they did in Africa. Kunta heard the toubob say something to the black one, and before much longer the box turned off onto a small road. Kunta sat up and soon, in the distance, saw a large white house through the trees. His stomach clutched up: What in the name of Allah was to happen now? Was it here that he was going to be eaten? He slumped back down in the box and lay as if he were lifeless.

CHAPTER 42

As the box rolled closer and closer to the house, Kunta began to smell — and then hear — more black people. Raising himself up on his elbows, he could just make out three figures in the early dusk as they approached the wagon. The largest among them was swinging one of those small flames Kunta had become familiar with when the toubob had come down into the dark hold of the big canoe; only this one was enclosed in something clear and shiny rather than in metal. He had never seen anything like it before; it looked hard, but you could see through it as if it weren't there. He didn't have the chance to study it more closely, though, for the three blacks quickly stepped to one side as a new toubob strode past them and up to the box, which promptly stopped beside him. The two toubob greeted one another, and then one of the blacks held up the flame so that the toubob in the box could see better as he climbed down to join the other one. They clasped hands warmly and then walked off together toward the house.

Hope surged in Kunta. Would the black ones free him now? But he no sooner thought of it than the flame lit their faces as they stood looking at him over the sides of the wagon; they were laughing at him. What kind of blacks were these who looked down upon their own kind and worked as goats for the toubob? Where had they come from? They looked as Africans looked, but clearly they were not of Africa.

Then the one who had driven the rolling box clucked at the animal and snapped the thongs and the box moved ahead. The other blacks walked alongside, still laughing, until it stopped again. Climbing down, the driver walked back and in the light of the flame jerked roughly at Kunta's chain, making threatening sounds as he unlocked it under the seat, and then gestured for Kunta to get out.

Kunta fought down the impulse to leap for the throats of the four blacks. The odds were too high; his chance would come later. Every muscle in his body seemed to be screaming as he forced himself onto his knees and began to crab backward in the box. When he took too long to suit them, two of the blacks grabbed Kunta, hoisted him roughly over the side, and half dropped him onto the ground. A moment later the driver had clicked the free end of Kunta's chain around a thick pole.

As he lay there, flooded with pain, fear, and hatred, one of the blacks set before him two tin containers. In the light of the flame, Kunta could see that one was nearly filled with water, and the other held some strange-looking, strange-smelling food. Even so, the saliva ran in Kunta's mouth and down in his throat; but he didn't permit even his eyes to move. The black ones watching him laughed.

Holding up the flame, the driver went over to the thick pole and lunged heavily against the locked chain, clearly for Kunta to see that it could not be broken. Then he pointed with his foot at the water and the food, making threatening sounds, and the others laughed again as the four of them walked away.

Kunta lay there on the ground in the darkness, waiting for sleep to claim them, wherever they had gone. In his mind, he saw himself rearing up and surging desperately again and again against the chain, with all of the strength that he could muster, until it broke and he could escape to . . . Just then he smelled a dog approaching him, and heard it curiously sniffing. Somehow he sensed that it was not his enemy. But then, as the dog came closer, he heard the sound of chewing and the click of teeth on the tin pan. Though he wouldn't have eaten it himself, Kunta leaped up in rage, snarling like a leopard. The dog raced away, and from a short distance started barking. Within a moment, a door had squeaked open nearby and someone was running toward him with a flame. It was the driver, and Kunta sat staring with cold fury as the driver anxiously examined the chain around the base of the post, and next where the chain was attached to the iron cuff around Kunta's ankle. In the dim yellow light, Kunta saw the driver's expression of satisfaction at the empty food plate. With a hoarse grunt, he walked back to his hut, leaving Kunta in the darkness wishing that he could fasten his hands around the throat of the dog.

After a while, Kunta groped around for the container of water and drank some of the contents, but it didn't make him feel any better; in fact, the strength felt drained from his body; it seemed as if he were only a shell. Abandoning the idea of breaking the chain — for now, anyway — he felt as if Allah had turned His back — but why? What thing so terrible had he ever done? He tried to review everything of any significance that he had ever done — right or wrong — up to the morning when he was cutting a piece of wood to make himself a drum and then, too late, heard a twig snap. It seemed to him that every time in his life when he had been punished, it had been because of carelessness and inattention.

Kunta lay listening to the crickets, the whir of night birds, and the barking of distant dogs — and once to the sudden squeak of a mouse, then the crunch of its bones breaking in the mouth of an animal that had killed it. Every now and then he would tense up with the urge to run, but he knew that even if he were able to rip loose his chain, its rattling would swiftly awaken someone in the huts nearby.

He lay this way — with no thought of sleeping — until the first streaks of dawn. Struggling as well as his aching limbs would let him into a kneeling position, he began his suba prayer. As he was pressing his forehead against the earth, however, he lost his balance and almost fell over on his side; it made him furious to realize how weak he had become.

As the eastern sky slowly brightened, Kunta reached again for the water container and drank what was left. Hardly had he finished it when approaching footsteps alerted him to the return of the four black men. Hurriedly they hoisted Kunta back into the rolling box, which was driven to the large white house, where the toubob was waiting to get onto the seat again. And before he knew it they were back on the main road, headed in the same direction as before.

For a time in the clearing day, Kunta lay staring vacantly at the chain rattling across the floor of the box to where it was locked under the seat. Then, for a while, he let his eyes bore with hatred at the backs of the toubob and the black ahead. He wished he could kill them. He made himself remember that if he was to survive, having survived so much until now, that he must keep his senses collected, he must keep control of himself, he must not expend his energy until he knew that it was the right time.

It was around midmorning when Kunta heard what he knew instantly was a blacksmith pounding on metal; lifting his head, Kunta strained his eyes to see and finally located the sound somewhere beyond a thick growth of trees they were passing. He saw that much forest had been freshly cut, and stumps grubbed up, and in some places, as the rolling box lurched along, Kunta saw and smelled grayish smoke rising from where dry brush was being burned. He wondered if the toubob were thus fertilizing the earth for the next season's crops, as it was done in Juffure.

Next, in the distance ahead, he saw a small square hut beside the road. It seemed to be made of logs, and in a cleared plot of earth before it, a toubob man was plodding behind a brown bullock. The toubob's hands were pressing down hard against the curving handles of some large thing pulled by the bullock that was tearing through the earth. As they came nearer, Kunta saw two more toubob — pale and thin — squatting on their haunches under a tree, three equally skinny swine were rooting around them, and some chickens were pecking for food. In the hut's doorway stood a she toubob with red hair. Then, dashing past her, came three small toubob shouting and waving toward the rolling box. Catching sight of Kunta, they shrieked with laughter and pointed; he stared at them as if they were hyena cubs. They ran alongside the wagon for a good way before turning back, and Kunta lay realizing that he had seen with his own eyes an actual family of toubob.

Twice more, far from the road, Kunta saw large white toubob houses similar to the ones where the wagon had stopped the night before. Each was the height of two houses, as if one were on top of another; each had in front of it a row of three or four huge white poles as big around — and almost as tall — as trees; nearby each was a group of small dark huts where Kunta guessed the blacks lived; and surrounding each was a vastness of cotton fields, all of them recently harvested, flecked here and there with a tuft of white.

Somewhere between these two great houses, the rolling box overtook a strange pair of people walking along the side of the road. At first Kunta thought they were black, but as the wagon came closer he saw that their skin was reddish-brown, and they had long black hair tied to hang down their backs like a rope, and they walked quickly, lightly in shoes and loincloths that seemed to be made of hide, and they carried bows and arrows. They weren't toubob, yet they weren't of Africa either; they even smelled different. What sort of people were they? Neither one seemed to notice the rolling box as it went by, enveloping them in dust.

As the sun began to set, Kunta turned his face toward the east, and by the time he had finished his silent evening prayer to Allah, dusk was gathering. He was getting so weak, after two days without accepting any of the food he had been offered, that he had to lie down limply in the bottom of the rolling box, hardly caring any more about what was happening around him.

But Kunta managed to raise himself up again and look over the side when the box stopped a little later. Climbing down, the driver hung one of those lights against the side of the box, got back in his seat, and resumed the trip. After a long while the toubob spoke briefly, and the black one replied; it was the first time since they had started out that day that the two of them had exchanged a sound. Again the box stopped, and the driver got out and tossed some kind of coverlet to Kunta, who ignored it. Climbing back up onto the seat, the driver and the toubob pulled coverlets over themselves and set out once again.

Though he was soon shivering, Kunta refused to reach for the coverlet and draw it over him, not wishing to give them that satisfaction. They offer me cover, he thought, yet they keep me in chains; and my own people not only stand by and let it happen but actually do the toubob's dirty business for him. Kunta knew only that he must escape from this dreadful place — or die in the attempt. He dared not dream that he would ever see Juffure again, but if he did, he vowed that all of The Gambia would learn what the land of toubob was really like.

Kunta was nearly numb with cold when the rolling box turned suddenly off the main road and onto a bumpier and smaller one. Again he forced his aching body upward far enough to squint into the darkness — and there in the distance he saw the ghostly whiteness of another of the big houses. As on the previous night, the fear of what would befall him now coursed through Kunta as they pulled up in front of the house — but he couldn't even smell any signs of the toubob or black ones he expected to greet them.

When the box finally stopped, the toubob on the seat ahead of him dropped to the ground with a grunt, bent and squatted down several times to uncramp his muscles, then spoke briefly to the driver with a gesture back at Kunta, and then walked away toward the big house.

Still no other blacks had appeared, and as the rolling box creaked on ahead toward the nearby huts, Kunta lay in the back feigning indifference. But he was tense in every fiber, his pains forgotten. His nostrils detected the smell of other blacks nearby; yet no one came outside. His hopes rose further. Stopping the box near the huts, the black one climbed heavily and clumsily to the ground and trudged over to the nearest hut, the flame bobbing in his hand. As he pushed the door open, Kunta watched and waited, ready to spring, for him to go inside; but instead he turned and came back to the box. Putting his hands under the seat, he unclicked Kunta's chain and held the loose end in one hand as he walked around to the back of the box. Yet something made Kunta still hold back. The black one jerked the chain sharply and barked something roughly to Kunta. As the black one stood watching carefully, Kunta struggled onto all fours — trying to look even weaker than he felt — and began crawling backward as slowly and clumsily as possible. As he had hoped, the black one lost patience, leaned close, and with one powerful arm, levered Kunta up and over the end of the wagon, and his upraised knee helped to break Kunta's fall to the ground.

At that instant, Kunta exploded upward — his hands clamping around the driver's big throat like the bone-cracking jaws of a hyena. The flame dropped to the ground as the black one lurched backward with a hoarse cry; then he came storming back upright with his big hands pounding, tearing, and clawing at Kunta's face and forearms. But somehow Kunta found the strength to grip the throat even tighter as he twisted his body desperately to avoid the driver's clublike blows with thrashing fists, feet, and knees. Kunta's grip would not be broken until the black one finally stumbled backward and then down, with a deep gurgling sound, and then went limp.

Springing up, fearing above all another barking dog, Kunta slipped away like a shadow from the fallen driver and the overturned flame. He ran bent low, legs crashing through frosted stalks of cotton. His muscles, so long unused, screamed with pain, but the cold, rushing air felt good upon his skin, and he had to stop himself from whooping out loud with the pleasure of feeling so wildly free.

CHAPTER 43

The thorny brambles and vines of the
brush at the edge of the forest seemed to
reach out and tear at Kunta's legs.
Ripping them aside with his hands, he
plunged on — stumbling and falling,
picking himself up again — deeper and
deeper into the forest. Or so he thought,
until the trees began to thin and he burst
suddenly into more low brush. Ahead of
him was another wide cottonfield, and
beyond it yet another big white house with
small dark huts beside it. With shock and
panic, Kunta sprang back into the woods,
realizing that all he had done was cross a
narrow stretch of forest that separated two
great toubob farms. Crouching behind a
tree, he listened to the pounding of his
heart and head, and began to feel a

486

stinging in his hands, arms, and feet. Glancing down in the bright moonlight, he saw that they were cut and bleeding from the thorns. But what alarmed him more was that the moon was already down in the sky; it would soon be dawn. He knew that whatever he was going to do, he had little time to decide.

Stumbling back into motion, Kunta knew after only a little while that his muscles would not carry him much farther. He must retreat into the thickest part of the forest he could find and hide there. So he went clawing his way back, sometimes on all fours, his feet and arms and legs tangling in the vines, until at last he found himself in a dense grove of trees. Though his lungs were threatening to burst, Kunta considered climbing one of them, but the softness of the thick carpeting of leaves under his feet told him that many of the trees' leaves had fallen off, which could make him easily seen, so that his best concealment would be on the ground.

Crawling again, he settled finally — just as the sky began to lighten — in a place of deep undergrowth. Except for the wheeze of his own breath, everything was very still, and it reminded him of his long, lonely vigils guarding the groundnut fields with his faithful wuolo dog. It was just then that he heard in the distance the deep baying of a dog. Perhaps he had heard it only in his mind, he thought, snapping to alertness and straining his ears. But it came again — only now there were two of them. He didn't have much time.

Kneeling toward the east, he prayed to Allah for deliverance, and just as he finished, the deep-throated baying came again, closer this time. Kunta decided it was best to stay hidden where he was, but when he heard the howling once again — closer still — just a few minutes later, it seemed that they knew exactly where he was and his limbs wouldn't let him remain there a moment longer. Into the underbrush he crawled again, hunting for a deeper, even more secreted place. Every inch among the brambles raking at his hands and knees was torture, but with every cry from the dogs he scrambled faster and faster. Yet the barking grew ever louder and closer, and Kunta was sure that he could hear now the shouting of men behind the dogs.

He wasn't moving fast enough; springing up he began to run — stumbling through the brambles — as quickly and quietly as his exhaustion would permit. Almost immediately he heard an explosion; the shock buckled his knees and sent him sprawling into a tangle of briars.

The dogs were snarling at the very edge of the thicket now. Quivering in terror, Kunta could even smell them. A moment later they were thrashing through the underbrush straight for him. Kunta made it up onto his knees just as the two dogs came crashing through the brush and leaped on him, yowling and slavering and snapping as they knocked him over, then sprang backward to lunge at him again. Snarling himself, Kunta fought wildly to fend them off, using his hands like claws while he tried to crab backward away from them. Then he heard the men shouting from the edge of the brush, and again there was an explosion, this time much louder. As the dogs relented somewhat in their attack, Kunta heard the men cursing and slashing through the brush with knives.

Behind the growling dogs, he saw first the black one he had choked. He held a huge knife in one hand, a short club and a rope in the other, and he looked murderous. Kunta lay bleeding on his back, jaws clenched to keep from screaming, expecting to be chopped into bits. Then Kunta saw the toubob who had brought him here appear behind the black one, his face reddish and sweating. Kunta waited for the flash and the explosion that he had learned on the big canoe could come from the firestick that a second toubob — one he hadn't seen before — pointed at him now. But it was the black one who now rushed forward furiously, raising his club, when the chief toubob shouted.

The black one halted, and the toubob shouted at the dogs, who drew farther back. Then the toubob said something to the black one, who now moved forward uncoiling his rope. A heavy blow to Kunta's head sent him into a merciful

490

numbing shock. He was dimly aware of being trussed up so tightly that the rope bit into his already bleeding skin; then of being half lifted from among the brambles and made to walk. Whenever he lost his balance and fell down a whip seared across his back. When they finally reached the forest's edge, Kunta saw three of the donkeylike animals tied near several trees.

As they approached the animals, he tried to bolt away again, but a vicious yank on the free end of the rope sent him tumbling down — and earned him a kick in the ribs. Now the second toubob, holding the rope, moved ahead of Kunta, jerking him stumbling toward a tree where the animals were tied. The rope's free end was thrown over a lower limb, and the black one hauled on it until Kunta's feet barely touched the ground.

The chief toubob's whistling whip began to lash against Kunta's back. He writhed under the pain, refusing to make any sound, but each blow felt as if it had torn him in half. Finally he began screaming, but the lashing went on.

Kunta was hardly conscious when at last

the whip stopped falling. He sensed vaguely that he was being lowered and crumpling onto the ground; then that he was being lifted and draped across the back of one of the animals; then he was aware of movement.

The next thing Kunta knew — he had no idea how much time had passed — he was lying spread-eagled on his back in some kind of hut. A chain, he noticed, was attached to an iron cuff on each wrist and ankle, and the four chains were fixed to the base of four poles at the corners of the hut. Even the slightest movement brought such excruciating pain that for a long while he lay completely still, his face wet with sweat and his breath coming in quick, shallow gasps.

Without moving, he could see that a small, square, open space above him was admitting daylight. Out of the corner of his eye, he could see a recessed place in the wall, and within it a mostly burned log and some ashes. On the other side of the hut, he saw a wide, flat, lumpy thing of cloth on the floor, with corn shucks showing through its holes; he guessed it might be used as a bed.

As dusk showed through the open space above him, Kunta heard — from very nearby — the blowing of a strange-sounding horn. And before much more time had passed, he heard the voices of what he smelled were many black people passing near where he was. Then he smelled food cooking. As his spasms of hunger mingled with the pounding of his head and the stabbing pains in his back and his thorn-cut arms and legs, he berated himself for not having waited for a better time to escape, as a trapped animal would have done. He should have first observed and learned more of this strange place and its pagan people.

Kunta's eyes were closed when the hut's door squeaked open; he could smell the black one he had choked, who had helped to catch him. He lay still and pretended to be asleep — until a vicious kick in the ribs shot his eyes wide open. With a curse, the black one set something down just in front of Kunta's face, dropped a covering over his body, and went back out, slamming the door behind him.

The smell of the food before him hurt Kunta's stomach almost as much as the pain in his back. Finally, he opened his eyes. There was some kind of mush and some kind of meat piled upon a flat, round tin, and a squat, round gourd of water beside it. His spread-eagled wrists made it impossible to pick them up, but both were close enough for him to reach with his mouth. Just as he was about to take a bite, Kunta smelled that the meat was the filthy swine, and the bile from his stomach came spewing up and onto the tin plate.

Through the night, he lay drifting into and out of sleep and wondering about these black ones who looked like Africans but ate pig. It meant that they were all strangers — or traitors — to Allah. Silently he begged Allah's forgiveness in advance if his lips would ever touch any swine without his realizing it, or even if he ever ate from any plate that any swine meat had ever been on.

Soon after the dawn showed again through the square opening, Kunta heard the strange horn blow once more; then came the smell of food cooking, and the voices of the black ones hurrying back and forth. Then the man he despised returned, bringing new food and water. But when he saw that Kunta had vomited over the untouched plate that was already there, he bent down with a string of angry curses and rubbed the contents into Kunta's face. Then he set the new food and water before him, and left.

Kunta told himself that he would choke the food down later; he was too sick even to think about it now. After a little while, he heard the door open again; this time he smelled the stench of toubob. Kunta kept his eyes clamped shut, but when the toubob muttered angrily, he feared another kick and opened them. He found himself staring up at the hated face of the toubob who had brought him here; it was flushed with rage. The toubob made cursing sounds and told him with threatening gestures that if he didn't eat the food, he would get more beating. Then the toubob left.

Kunta managed to move his left hand far enough for the fingers to scratch up a small mound of the hard dirt where the toubob's foot had been. Pulling the dirt closer, Kunta pressed his eyes shut and appealed to the spirits of evil to curse forever the womb of the toubob and his family.

CHAPTER 44

Kunta had counted four days and three nights in the hut. And each night he had lain listening to the singing from the huts nearby — and feeling more African than he ever felt in his own village. What kind of black people they must be, he thought, to spend their time *singing* here in the land of the toubob. He wondered how many of these strange black ones there were in all of toubob land, those who didn't seem to know or care who or what they were.

Kunta felt a special closeness to the sun each time it rose. He recalled what an old man who had been an alcala had said down in the darkness of the big canoe: "Each day's new sun will remind us that it rose in our Africa, which is the navel of the earth."

Although he was spread-eagled by four chains, he had practiced until he had learned a way to inch forward or backward on his back and buttocks to study more closely the small but thick iron rings, like bracelets, that fastened the chains to the four poles at the hut's corners. The poles were about the size of his lower leg, and he knew there was no hope of his ever breaking one, or of pulling one from the hard-packed earth floor, for the upper ends went up through the hut's roof. With his eyes and then his fingers, Kunta carefully examined the small holes in the thick metal rings; he had seen his captors insert a narrow metal thing into these holes and turn them, making a *click* sound. When he shook one of the rings, it made the chain rattle — loud enough for someone to hear — so he gave that up. He tried putting one of the rings in his mouth and biting it as hard as he could, finally one of his teeth cracked, lancing pains through his head.

Seeking some dirt preferable to that of the floor in order to make a fetish to the spirits, Kunta scraped out with his fingers a piece of the reddish, hardened mud chinking between the logs. Seeing short, black bristles within the mud, he inspected one curiously, when he realized that it was a hair from the filthy swine, he flung it away — along with the dirt — and wiped off the hand that had held it.

On the fifth morning, the black one entered shortly after the wake-up horn had blown, and Kunta tautened when he saw that along with his usual short, flat club, the man carried two thick iron cuffs. Bending down, he locked each of Kunta's ankles within the cuffs, which were connected by a heavy chain. Only then did he unlock the four chains, one by one, that had kept Kunta spread-eagled. Free to move at last, Kunta couldn't help himself from springing upward — only to be struck down by the black one's waiting fist. As Kunta began pushing himself back upward, a booted foot dug viciously into his ribs. Stumbling upward once again in agony and rage, he was knocked down even harder. He hadn't realized how much the days of lying on his back had sapped his strength, and he lay now fighting for breath as the black one stood over him with an expression that told Kunta he would keep knocking him down until he learned who was the master.

Now the black one gestured roughly for Kunta to get up. When he couldn't raise his body even onto his hands and knees, the black one jerked him to his feet with a curse and shoved him forward, the ankle cuffs forcing Kunta to hobble awkwardly.

The full force of daylight in the doorway blinded him at first, but after a moment he began to make out a line of black people walking hastily nearby in single file, followed closely by a toubob riding a "hoss," as he had heard that strange animal called. Kunta knew from his smell that he was the one who had held the rope after Kunta had been trapped by the dogs. There were about ten or twelve blacks — the women with red or white rags tied on their heads, most of the men and children wearing ragged straw hats; but a few were bareheaded, and as far as he could see, none of them wore a single saphie charm around their necks or arms. But some of the men carried what seemed to be long, stout knives, and the line seemed to be heading in the direction of the great fields. He thought that it must have been they whom he had heard at night doing all that singing. He felt nothing but contempt for them. Turning his blinking gaze, Kunta counted the huts they had come from: There were ten, including his own — all very small, like his, and they didn't have the stout look of the mud huts of his village, with their roofs or sweet-smelling thatch. They were arranged in rows of five each — positioned, Kunta noticed, so that whatever went on among the blacks living there could be seen from the big white house.

Abruptly the black one began jabbing at Kunta's chest with his finger, then exclaiming, "You — you Toby!" Kunta didn't understand, and his face showed it, so the black one kept jabbing him and saying the same thing over and over. Slowly it dawned on Kunta that the black one was attempting to make him understand something he was saying in the strange toubob tongue.

When Kunta continued to stare at him

dumbly, the black one began jabbing at his own chest. "Me Samson!" he exclaimed. "Samson!" He moved his jabbing finger again to Kunta. "You To-by! Toby. Massa say you name Toby!"

When what he meant began to sink in, it took all of Kunta's self-control to grip his flooding rage without any facial sign of the slightest understanding. He wanted to shout "I am Kunta Kinte, first son of Omoro, who is the son of the holy man Kairaba Kunta Kinte!"

Losing patience with Kunta's apparent stupidity, the black one cursed, shrugged his shoulders, and led him hobbling into another hut, where he gestured for Kunta to wash himself in a large, wide tin tub that held some water. The black one threw into the water a rag and a brown chunk of what Kunta's nose told him was something like the soap that Juffure women made of hot melted fat mixed with the lye of water dripped through wood ashes. The black one watched, scowling, as Kunta took advantage of the opportunity to wash himself. When he was through, the black one tossed to him some different toubob garments to cover his chest and legs, then a frayed hat of yellowish straw such as the others wore. How would these pagans fare under the heat of Africa's sun, Kunta wondered.

The black one led him next to still another hut. Inside, an old woman irritably banged down before Kunta a flat tin of food. He gulped down the thick gruel, and a bread resembling munko cake, and washed it down with some hot brown beefy-tasting broth from a gourd cup. Next they went to a narrow, cramped hut whose smell told of its use in advance. Pretending to pull down his lower garment, the black one haunched over a large hole cut into a plank seat and grunted heavily as if he were relieving himself. A small pile of corncobs lay in one corner, and Kunta didn't know what to make of them. But he guessed that the black one's purpose was to demonstrate the toubob's ways — of which he wished to learn all that he could, the better to escape.

As the black one led him past the next few huts, they went by an old man seated in some strange chair; it was rocking slowly back and forth as he wove dried cornshucks into what Kunta guessed was a broom. Without looking up, the old man cast toward him a not unkindly glance, but Kunta ignored it coldly.

Picking up one of the long, stout knives that Kunta had seen the others carrying, the black one motioned with his head toward the distant field, grunting and gesturing for Kunta to follow him. Hobbling along in the iron cuffs — which were chafing his ankles — Kunta could see in the field ahead that the females and the younger blacks were bending up and down, gathering and piling dried cornstalks behind the older men in front of them, who slashed down the stalks with swishing blows of their long knives.

Most of the men's backs were bared and glistening with sweat. His eyes searched for any of the branding-iron marks such as his back bore — but he saw only the scars that had been left by whips. The toubob rode up on his "hoss," exchanged words briefly with the black one, then fixed a threatening stare on Kunta as the black one gestured for his attention.

Slashing down about a dozen cornstalks,

the black one turned, bent, and made motions for Kunta to pick them up and pile them as the others were doing. The toubob jerked his horse closer alongside Kunta, his whip cocked and the scowl on his face making his intent clear if Kunta should refuse to obey. Enraged at his helplessness, Kunta bent down and picked up two of the cornstalks. Hesitating, he heard the black one's knife swishing ahead. Bending over again, he picked up two more cornstalks, and two more. He could feel the stares of other black ones upon him from adjacent rows, and could see the feet of the toubob's horse. He could feel the relief of the other blacks, and at last the horse's feet moved away.

Without raising his head, Kunta saw that the toubob rode this way or that to wherever he saw someone who wasn't working swiftly enough to please him, and then with an angry shout, his lash would go cracking down across a back.

Off in the distance, Kunta saw that there was a road. On it, a few times during the hot afternoon, through the sweat pouring down his forehead and stinging in his eyes, he caught glances of a lone rider on a horse, and twice he saw a wagon being drawn. Turning his head the other way, he could see the edge of the forest into which he had tried to escape. And from where he was piling the cornstalks now, he could see the forest's narrowness which had helped him to get caught, because he had not noticed that narrowness before. After a while, Kunta had to stop glancing in that direction, for the urge to spring up and bound toward those trees was almost irresistible. Each step he took, in any case, reminded him that he would never get five steps across the field wearing those iron hobbles. As he worked through the afternoon, Kunta decided that before he tried his next escape, he must find some kind of weapon to fight dogs and men with. No servant of Allah should ever fail to fight if he is attacked, he reminded himself. If it was dogs or men, wounded buffalo or hungry lions, no son of Omoro Kinte would ever entertain the thought of giving up.

It was after sundown when the horn

sounded once again — this time in the distance. As Kunta watched the other blacks hurrying into a line, he wished he could stop thinking of them as belonging to the tribes they resembled, for they were but unworthy pagans not fit to mingle with those who had come with him on the big canoe.

But how stupid the toubob must be to have those of Fulani blood — even such poor specimens as these — picking up cornstalks instead of tending cattle; anyone knew that the Fulani were born to tend cattle, that indeed Fulani and cattle *talked* together. This thought was interrupted as the toubob on his "hoss" cracked the whip to direct Kunta to the end of the line. As he obeyed, the squat, heavy woman at the end of the line took several quick forward steps, trying to get as far as possible from Kunta. He felt like spitting on her.

As they began to march — each step chafing at his ankles, which had been rubbed raw and were beginning to seep blood — Kunta heard some hounds barking far away. He shivered, remembering those that had tracked him and attacked him. Then his mind flashed a memory of how his own wuolo had died fighting the men who had captured him in Africa.

Back in his hut, Kunta kneeled and touched his forehead to the hard dirt floor in the direction in which he knew the next sun would rise. He prayed for a long time to make up for the two prayers he had been unable to perform out in the field, which would certainly have been interrupted by a lash across his back from the toubob who rode the "hoss."

After finishing his prayer, Kunta sat bolt upright and spoke softly for a while in the secret sira kango tongue, asking his ancestors to help him endure. Then — pressing between his fingers a pair of cock's feathers he had managed to pick up without being noticed while "Samson" had led him around that morning — he wondered when he would get the chance to steal a fresh egg. With the feathers of the cock and some finely crushed fresh eggshell, he would be able to prepare a powerful fetish to the spirits, whom he would ask to bless the dust where his last footsteps had touched in his village. If that dust was blessed, his footprints would one day reappear in Juffure, where every man's footprints were recognizable to his neighbors, and they would rejoice at this sign that Kunta Kinte was still alive and that he would return safely to his village. Someday.

For the thousandth time, he relived the nightmare of his capture. If only the cracking twig that alerted him had snapped a single footstep earlier, he could have leaped and snatched up his spear. Tears of rage came welling up into Kunta's eyes. It seemed to him that for moons without end, all that he had known was being tracked and attacked and captured and chained.

No! He would not allow himself to act this way. After all, he was a man now, seventeen rains of age, too old to weep and wallow in self-pity. Wiping away the tears, he crawled onto his thin, lumpy mattress of dried cornshucks and tried to go to sleep — but all he could think of was the name "To-by" he had been given, and rage rose in him once more. Furiously, he kicked his legs in frustration — but the movement only gouged the iron cuffs deeper into his ankles, which made him cry again.

Would he ever grow up to be a man like Omoro? He wondered if his father still thought of him; and if his mother had given to Lamin, Suwadu, and Madi the love that had been taken away from her when he was stolen. He thought of all of Juffure, and of how he had never realized more than now how very deeply he loved his village. As it had often been on the big canoe, Kunta lay for half the night with scenes of Juffure flashing through his mind, until he made himself shut his eyes and finally sleep came.

CHAPTER 45

With each passing day, the hobbles on his ankles made it more and more difficult and painful for Kunta to get around. But he kept on telling himself that the chances of gaining freedom depended upon continuing to force himself to do whatever was wanted of him, all behind a mask of complete blankness and stupidity. As he did so, his eyes, ears, and nose would miss nothing — no weapon he might use, no toubob weakness he might exploit — until finally his captors were lulled into removing the cuffs. Then he would run away again.

Soon after the conch horn blew each morning, Kunta would limp outside to watch as the strange black ones emerged from their huts, the sleepiness still in their faces, and splashed themselves with water from buckets drawn up in the well nearby. Missing the sound of the village women's pestles thumping the couscous for their families' morning meals, he would enter the hut of the old cooking woman and bolt down whatever she gave him — except for any filthy pork.

As he ate each morning, his eyes would search the hut for a possible weapon he might take without being detected. But apart from the black utensils that hung on hooks above her fireplace, there were only the round, flat tin things upon which she gave him what he ate with his fingers. He had seen her eating with a slender metal object that had three or four closely spaced points to stab the food with. He wondered what it was, and thought that although it was small it might be useful — if he could ever catch her eyes averted for a moment when the shiny object was within reach.

One morning, as he was eating his gruel, watching as the cooking woman cut a piece of meat with a knife he hadn't seen before and plotting what he would do with it if it were in his hands instead of hers, he heard a piercing squeal of agony from outside the hut. It was so close to his thoughts that he nearly jumped from his seat. Hobbling outside, he found the others already lined up for work — many of them still chewing the last bites of "breakfast," lest they get a lashing for being late — while there on the ground beside them lay a swine thrashing about with blood pulsing from its cut throat as two black men lifted it into a steaming pot of water, then withdrew it and scraped off the hair. The swine's skin was the color of a toubob, he noticed, as they suspended it by the heels, slit open its belly, and pulled out its insides. Kunta's nose stifled at the spreading smell of guts, and as he marched off with the others toward the fields, he had to suppress a shudder of revulsion at the thought of having to live among these pagan eaters of such a filthy animal.

There was frost on the cornstalks every morning now, and a haziness hung low over the fields until the heat of the climbing sun would burn it away. Allah's powers never ceased to amaze Kunta — that even in a place as distant as this toubob land was across the big water, Allah's sun and moon still rose and crossed the sky; though the sun was not so hot nor the moon so beautiful as in Juffure. It was only the people in this accursed place who seemed not of Allah's doing. The toubob were inhuman, and as for the blacks, it was simply senseless to try to understand them.

When the sun reached the middle of the sky, again the conch horn blew, signaling another lineup for the arrival of a wooden sled pulled by an animal similar to a horse, but more resembling a huge donkey, which Kunta had overheard being spoken of as a "mule." Walking beside the sled was the old cooking woman, who proceeded to pass out flat cakes of bread and a gourdful of some kind of stew to each person in the line, who either stood or sat and gulped it down, then drank some water dipped from a barrel that was also on the sled. Every day, Kunta warily smelled the stew before tasting it, to make sure he didn't put any swine meat into his mouth, but it usually contained only vegetables and no meat that he could see or smell at all. He felt better about eating the bread, for he had seen some of the black women making corn into meal by beating it in a mortar with a pestle of stone, about as it was done in Africa, although Binta's pestle was made of wood.

Some days they served foods Kunta knew of from his home, such as groundnuts, and kanjo — which was called "okra" — and so-so, which was called "black-eyed peas." And he saw how much these black ones loved the large fruit that he heard here being called "watermelon." But he saw that Allah appeared to have denied these people the mangoes, the hearts of palm, the breadfruits, and so many of the other delicacies that grew almost anywhere one cared to look on the vines and trees and bushes in Africa.

Every now and then the toubob who had brought Kunta to this place — the one they called "massa" — rode out into the fields when they were working. In his whitish straw hat, as he spoke to the toubob field boss, he gestured with a long, slender, plaited leather switch, and Kunta noticed that the toubob "oberseer" grinned and shuffled almost as much as the blacks whenever he was around.

Many such strange things happened each day, and Kunta would sit thinking about them back in his hut while he waited to find sleep. These black ones seemed to have no concern in their lives beyond pleasing the toubob with his lashing whip. It sickened him to think how these black ones jumped about their work whenever they saw a toubob, and how, if that toubob spoke a word to them, they rushed to do whatever he told them to. Kunta couldn't fathom what had happened to so destroy their minds that they acted like goats and monkeys. Perhaps it was because they had been born in this place rather than in Africa, because the only homes they had ever known were the toubob's huts of logs glued together with mud and swine bristles. These black ones had never known what it meant to sweat under the sun not for toubob masters but for themselves and their own people.

But no matter how long he stayed among them, Kunta vowed never to become *like* them, and each night his mind would go exploring again into ways to escape from this despised land. He couldn't keep from reviling himself almost nightly for his previous failure to get away. Playing back in his mind what it had been like among the thorn bushes and the slavering dogs, he knew that he must have a better plan for the next time. First he had to make himself a saphie charm to insure safety and success. Then he must either find or make some kind of weapon. Even a sharpened stick could have speared through those dogs' bellies, he thought, and he could have been away again before the black one and the toubob had been able to cut their way through the underbrush to where they had found him fighting off the dogs. Finally, he must acquaint himself with the surrounding countryside so that when he escaped again, he would know where to look for better hiding places.

Though he often lay awake half the night, restless with such thoughts, Kunta always awoke before the first crowing of the cocks, which always aroused the other fowl. The birds in this place, he noticed, merely twittered and sang — nothing like the deafening squawks of great flocks of green parrots that had opened the morning in Juffure. There didn't seem to be any parrots here, or monkeys either, which always began the day at home by chattering angrily in the trees overhead, breaking off sticks and hurling them to the ground at the people underneath. Nor had Kunta seen any goats here — a fact he found no less incredible than that these people kept swine in pens — "pigs" or "hogs," they called them — and even *fed* the filthy things.

But the squealing of the swine, it seemed to Kunta, was no uglier than the language of the toubob who so closely resembled them. He would have given anything to hear even a sentence of Mandinka, or any other African tongue. He missed his chain mates from the big canoe — even those who weren't Moslem

— and he wondered what had happened to them. Where had they been taken? To other toubob farms such as this one? Wherever they were, were they longing as he was to hear once again the sweetness of their own tongues — and yet feeling shut out and alone, as he did, because they knew nothing of the toubob language?

Kunta realized that he would have to learn something of this strange speech if he was ever to understand enough about the toubob or his ways to escape from him. Without letting anyone know, he already recognized some words: "pig," "hog," "watermelon," "black-eyed peas," "oberseer," "massa," and especially "yessuh, massa," which was about the only thing he ever heard the black ones say to them. He had also heard the black ones describe the she toubob who lived with "massa" in the big white house as "the missus." Once, from a distance, Kunta had glimpsed her, a bony creature the color of a toad's underbelly, as she walked around cutting off some flowers among the vines and bushes that grew alongside the big house.

Most of the other toubob words that Kunta heard still confused him. But behind his expressionless mask, he tried hard to make sense of them, and slowly he began to associate various sounds with certain objects and actions. But one sound in particular was extremely puzzling to him, though he heard it exclaimed over and over nearly every day by toubob and blacks alike. What, he wondered, was a "nigger"?

CHAPTER 46

With the cutting and piling of the
cornstalks at last completed, the
"oberseer" began assigning different
blacks to a variety of tasks after the conch
horn blew each dawn. One morning Kunta
was given the job of snapping loose from
their thick vines and piling onto a
"wagon," as he'd learned they called the
rolling boxes, a load of large, heavy
vegetables the color of overripe mangoes
and somewhat resembling the big gourds
that women in Juffure dried out and cut
in half to make household bowls. The
blacks here called them "punkins."

Riding with the "punkins" on the
wagon to unload them at a large building
called the "barn," Kunta was able to see
that some of the black men were sawing a

big tree into thick sections and splitting them with axes and wedges into firewood that children were stacking into long rows as high as their heads. In another place, two men were hanging over thin poles the large leaves of what his nose told him was the filthy pagan tobacco; he had smelled it once before on one of the trips he had taken with his father.

As he rode back and forth to the "barn," he saw that just as it was done in his own village, many things were being dried for later use. Some women were collecting a thick brown "sagegrass," he heard them call it, and tying it into bundles. And some of the garden's vegetables were being spread out on cloths to dry. Even moss — which had been gathered by groups of children and plunged into boiling water — was being dried as well; he had no idea why.

It turned his stomach to watch — and listen — as he passed a pen where still more swine were being butchered. Their hair, too, he noticed, was being dried and saved — probably for mortar — but the thing that really sickened him was to see the swines' bladders being removed, blown up, tied at the ends, and hung up to dry along a fence; Allah only knew for what unholy purpose.

When he had finished harvesting and storing the "punkins," Kunta was sent with several others to a grove of trees, the limbs of which they were told to shake vigorously so that the nuts growing in them would fall to the ground, where they were picked up by first-kafo children carrying baskets. Kunta picked up one of the nuts and hid it in his clothes to try later when he was alone; it wasn't bad.

When the last of these tasks was done, the men were put to work repairing things that needed it. Kunta helped another man fix a fence. And the women seemed to be busy in a general cleaning of the big white house and their own huts. He saw some of them washing things, first boiling them in a large black tub, then rubbing them up and down against a wrinkled piece of tin in soapy water; he wondered why none of them knew how to wash clothing properly by beating it against rocks.

Kunta noticed that the whip of the

"oberseer" seemed to strike down upon someone's back much less often than before. He felt in the atmosphere something similar to the time in Juffure when the harvest had all been put safely into the storehouses. Even before the evening's conch horn would blow to announce the end of the day's work, some of the black men would begin cavorting and prancing and singing among themselves. The "oberseer" would wheel his horse around and brandish his whip, but Kunta could tell he didn't really mean it. And soon the other men would join in, and then the women — singing words that made no sense at all to Kunta. He was so filled with disgust for all of them that he was glad when the conch horn finally signaled for them to return to their huts.

In the evenings, Kunta would sit down sideways just inside the doorway of his hut, heels flat against the packed dirt floor to minimize the iron cuffs' contact with his festering ankles. If there was any light breeze, he enjoyed feeling it blowing against him, and thinking about the fresh carpet of gold and crimson leaves he would find under the trees the next morning. At such times, his mind would wander back to harvest-season evenings in Juffure, with the mosquitoes and other insects tormenting the people as they sat around the smoky night fires and settled into long conversations that would be punctuated now and then by the distant snarling of leopards and the screaming of hyenas.

One thing he didn't hear, it occurred to him, and hadn't heard since he left Africa, was the sound of drums. The toubob probably didn't allow these black people to have any drums; that had to be the reason. But why? Was it because the toubob knew and feared how the sound of the drums could quicken the blood of everyone in a village, until even the little children and the toothless old ones would dance wildly? Or how the rhythm of the drums would drive wrestlers to their greatest feats of strength? Or how the hypnotic beat could send warriors into a frenzy against their enemies? Or perhaps the toubob were simply afraid to allow a form of communication they couldn't understand that could travel the distance between one farm and another.

But these heathen blacks wouldn't understand drumtalk any better than the toubob. Kunta was forced to concede, though — if only with great reluctance — that these pagan blacks might not be totally irredeemable. Ignorant as they were, some of the things they did were purely African, and he could tell that they were totally unaware of it themselves. For one thing, he had heard all his life the very same sounds of exclamation, accompanied by the very same hand gestures and facial expressions. And the way these blacks moved their bodies was also identical. No less so was the way these blacks laughed when they were among themselves — with their whole bodies, just like the people of Juffure.

And Kunta had been reminded of Africa in the way that black women here wore their hair tied up with strings into very tight plaits — although African women often decorated their plaits with colorful beads. And the women of this place knotted cloth pieces over their heads, although they didn't tie them correctly. Kunta saw that even some of these black men wore their hair in short plaits too, as some men did in Africa.

Kunta also saw Africa in the way that black children here were trained to treat their elders with politeness and respect. He saw it in the way that mothers carried their babies with their plump little legs straddling the mothers' bodies. He noticed even such small customs as how the older ones among these blacks would sit in the evenings rubbing their gums and teeth with a finely crushed end of a twig, which would have been lemongrass root in Juffure. And though he found it difficult to understand how they could do it here in toubob land, Kunta had to admit that these blacks' great love of singing and dancing was unmistakably African.

But what really began to soften his heart somewhat toward these strange people was the fact that over the past moon, their great showing of distaste for him had continued only when the "oberseer" or the "massa" was around.

When Kunta came by anywhere the blacks were among themselves, most of them by now would quickly nod, and he would notice their expressions of concern for the worsening condition of his left ankle. Though he always coldly ignored them and hobbled on, he would sometimes find himself later almost wishing that he had returned their nods.

One night, when Kunta had fallen asleep but drifted again into wakefulness, as he often did, he lay staring up into the darkness and feeling that Allah had somehow, for some reason, *willed* him to be here in this place amid the lost tribe of a great black family that reached its roots back among the ancient forefathers; but unlike himself, these black ones in this place had no knowledge whatsoever of who they were and where they'd come from.

Feeling around him, in some strange way, the presence of his holy-man grandfather, Kunta reached out into the darkness. There was nothing to be felt, but he began speaking aloud to the Alquaran Kairaba Kunta Kinte, imploring him to make known the purpose of his mission here, if there be any. He was startled to hear the sound of his own voice. Up to this moment in the toubob's land, he had never uttered a sound addressed to anyone but Allah, except for those cries that had been torn from him by a lash.

The next morning, as he joined the others in line for the march to work, Kunta almost caught himself saying, "Mornin," as he had heard them greet each other every day. But though he knew enough toubob words by now not only to understand a good deal of what was said to him but also to make himself somewhat understood as well, something made him decide to continue keeping that knowledge to himself.

It occurred to Kunta that these blacks masked their true feelings for the toubob as carefully as he did his changing attitude toward *them*. He had by now many times witnessed the blacks' grinning faces turn to bitterness the instant a toubob turned his head away. He had seen them break their working tools on purpose, and then act totally unaware of how it happened as the "oberseer" bitterly cursed them for their clumsiness. And he had seen how blacks in the field, for all their show of rushing about whenever the toubob was nearby, were really taking twice as much time as they needed to do whatever they were doing.

He was beginning to realize, too, that like the Mandinkas' own secret sira kango language, these blacks shared some kind of communication known only among themselves. Sometimes when they were working out in the field, Kunta's glance would catch a small, quick gesture or movement of the head. Or one of them would utter some strange, brief exclamation; at unpredictable intervals another, and then another, would repeat it, always just beyond the hearing of the "oberseer" as he rode about on his horse. And sometimes with him right there among them, they would begin singing something that told Kunta — even though he couldn't understand it — that some message was being passed, just as the women had done for the men on the big canoe.

When darkness had fallen among the huts and the lamp lights no longer glowed from the windows in the big house, Kunta's sharp ears would detect the swift rustlings of one or two blacks slipping away from "slave row" — and a few hours later, slipping back again. He wondered where they were going and for what — and why they were crazy enough to come back. And the next morning in the fields, he would try to guess which of them had done it. Whoever it was, he thought he just might possibly learn to trust them.

Two huts away from Kunta, the blacks would seat themselves around the small fire of the old cooking woman every evening after "supper," and the sight would fill Kunta with a melancholy memory of Juffure, except that the women here sat with the men, and some of both sexes were puffing away on pagan tobacco pipes that now and then glowed dully in the gathering darkness. Listening intently from where he sat just inside his doorway, Kunta could hear them talking over the rasping of the crickets and the distant hooting of owls in the forest. Though he couldn't understand the words, he felt the bitterness in their tone.

Even in the dark, Kunta by now could picture in his mind the face of whichever black was talking. His mind had filed away the voices of each of the dozen adults, along with the name of the tribe he felt that particular one most resembled. He knew which ones among them generally acted more carefree, and which seldom even smiled, a few of them not even around the toubob.

These evening meetings had a general pattern that Kunta had learned. The usual first talker was usually the woman who cooked in the big house. She mimicked things said by both the "massa" and the "missus." Then he heard the big black one who had captured him imitating the "oberseer," and he listened with astonishment as the others all but choked trying to stifle their laughter, lest they be heard in the big white house.

But then the laughter would subside and they would sit around talking among themselves. Kunta heard the helpless, haunted tone of some, and the anger of others, even though he grasped only a little of what they discussed. He had the feeling that they were recalling things that had happened to them earlier in their lives. Some of the women in particular would be talking and then suddenly break into tears. Finally the talking would grow quiet as one of the women began to sing, and the others joined in. Kunta couldn't understand the words — "No-body knows de troubles I'se seed" — but he felt the sadness in the singing.

At last there came a voice that Kunta knew was the oldest man among them, the one who sat in the rocking chair and wove things of cornshucks, and who blew the conch horn. The others would bow their heads, and he would begin speaking slowly what Kunta guessed was some kind of prayer, though it was certainly not to Allah. But Kunta remembered what was said by the old alcala down in the big canoe: "Allah knows every language." While the prayer continued, Kunta kept hearing the same odd sound exclaimed sharply by both the old man and others who kept interrupting him with it: "Oh Lawd!" He wondered if this "Oh Lawd" was their Allah.

A few days later, the night winds began to blow with a coldness beyond any that Kunta had ever felt, and he woke up to find the last leaves stripped from the trees. As he stood shivering in line to go out to the fields, he was bewildered when the "oberseer" directed everyone into the barn instead. Even the massa and the missus were there, and with them four other finely dressed toubob who watched and cheered as the blacks were separated into two groups and made to race each other at ripping off and flinging aside the whitened, dried outside shucks from the piled harvest of corn.

Then the toubob and the blacks — in two groups — ate and drank their fill. The old black man who prayed at night then took up some kind of musical instrument with strings running down its length — it reminded Kunta of the ancient kora from his own homeland — and began to make some very odd music on it by jerking some kind of wand back and forth across the strings. The other blacks got up and began to dance — wildly — as the watching toubob, even the "oberseer," gleefully clapped and shouted from the sidelines. Their faces reddened with excitement, all the toubob suddenly stood up, and as the blacks shrank to the side, they clapped their way out into the middle of the floor and began to dance in an awkward way while the old man played as if he had gone mad and the other blacks jumped up and down and clapped and screamed as if they were seeing the greatest performance of their lives.

It made Kunta think of a story he had been told by his beloved old Grandmother Nyo Boto when he was in the first kafo. She had told how the king of a village had called together all of the musicians and commanded them to play their very best for him to dance for the people, including even the slaves. And the people were all delighted and they left all singing loudly to the skies and there had never been another king like him.

Back in his hut later that night reflecting upon what he had seen, it occurred to Kunta that in some strong, strange, and very deep way, the blacks and the toubob had some *need* for each other. Not only during the dancing in the barn, but also on many other occasions, it had seemed to him that the toubob were at their happiest when they were close around the black ones — even when they were beating them.

CHAPTER 47

Kunta's left ankle had become so infected that pus draining from the wound all but covered the iron cuff with a sickly yellow slickness, and his crippled limping finally caused the "oberseer" to take a close look. Turning his head away, he told Samson to remove the cuffs.

It was still painful to raise his foot, but Kunta was so thrilled to be unfettered that he hardly felt it. And that night, after the others had gone to bed and all had become still, Kunta limped outside and stole away once again. Crossing a field in the opposite direction from the one he had fled across the last time, he headed toward what he knew was a wider, deeper forest on the other side. He had reached a ravine and was clambering up the far side on his belly when he heard the first sound of a movement in the distance. He lay still with his heart pounding as he heard heavy footfalls approaching and finally the hoarse voice of Samson cursing and shouting, "Toby! Toby!" Gripping a stout stick he had sharpened into a crude spear, Kunta felt strangely calm, almost numb, as his eyes coldly watched the bulky silhouette moving quickly this way and that in the brush at the top of the ravine. Something made him sense that Samson feared for himself if Kunta succeeded in getting away. Closer and closer he stalked — Kunta coiled tight but motionless as a stone — and then the moment came. Hurling the spear with all his might, he grunted slightly with the pain it caused and Samson, hearing him, sprang instantly to one side; it missed him by a hair.

Kunta tried to run, but the weakness of his ankles made him hardly able to keep upright, and when he whirled to fight, Samson was upon him, slamming with his greater weight behind each blow, until Kunta was driven to the earth. Hauling him back upward, Samson kept pounding, aiming only at his chest and belly, as Kunta tried to keep his body twisting as he gouged and bit and clawed. Then one massive blow sent him crashing down again, this time to stay. He couldn't even move to defend himself any further.

Gasping for breath, Samson tied Kunta's wrists tightly together with a rope, and then began jerking Kunta along by its free end, back toward the farm, kicking him savagely whenever he stumbled or faltered, and cursing him every step of the way.

It was all Kunta could do to keep staggering and lurching behind Samson. Dizzy from pain and exhaustion — and disgust with himself — he grimly anticipated the beatings he would receive when they reached his hut. But when they finally arrived — shortly before dawn — Samson only gave him another kick or two and then left him alone lying in a heap.

Kunta was so used up that he trembled. But with his teeth he began to gnash and tear at the fibers of the rope binding his wrists together, until his teeth hurt like flashes of fire. But the rope finally came apart just as the conch horn blew. Kunta lay weeping. He had failed again, and he prayed to Allah.

Through the days that followed, it was as if he and Samson shared some secret pact of hatred. Kunta knew how closely he was being watched; he knew that Samson was waiting for any excuse to hurt him in a manner the toubob would approve. Kunta responded by going through the motions of doing whatever work he was given to do as if nothing had happened — but even faster and more efficiently than before. He had noticed how the "oberseer" paid less attention to those who worked the hardest or did the most grinning. Kunta couldn't bring himself to grin, but with grim satisfaction he noted that the more he sweated, the less often the lash fell across his back.

One evening after work, Kunta was passing near the barn when he spotted a thick iron wedge lying half concealed among some of the sawed sections of trees where the "oberseer" had two men splitting firewood. Glancing around quickly in all directions, and seeing no one watching, Kunta snatched up the wedge and, concealing it in his shirt, hurried to his hut. Using it to dig a hole in the hard dirt floor, he placed the wedge in the hole, packed the loose dirt back over it, then beat it down carefully with a rock until the floor looked completely undisturbed.

He spent a sleepless night worrying that a wedge discovered missing might cause all of the cabins to be searched. He felt better when there was no outcry the following day, but he still wasn't sure just how he might employ the wedge to help himself escape, when that time came again.

What he really wanted to get his hands on was one of those long knives that the "oberseer" would issue to a few of the men each morning. But each evening he would see the "oberseer" demanding the knives back and counting them carefully. With one of those knives, he could cut brush to move more quickly within a forest, and if he had to, he could kill a dog — or a man.

One cold afternoon almost a moon later — the sky bleak and slaty — Kunta was on his way across one of the fields to help another man repair a fence when, to his astonishment, what looked like salt began to fall from the sky, at first lightly, then more rapidly and thickly. As the salt became a flaky whiteness, he heard the blacks nearby exclaiming, "Snow!" and guessed that was what they called it. When he bent down to pick some of it up, it was cold to his touch — and even colder when he licked it off a finger with his tongue. It stung, and it had no taste whatever. He tried to smell it, but not only did there seem to be no odor either, it also disappeared into watery nothingness. And wherever he looked on the ground was a whitish film.

But by the time he reached the other side of the field, the "snow" had stopped and even begun to melt away. Hiding his amazement, Kunta composed himself and nodded silently to his black partner, who was waiting by the broken fence. They set to work — Kunta helping the other man to string a kind of metal twine that he called "wire." After a while they reached a place almost hidden by tall grass, and as the other man hacked some of it down with the long knife he carried, Kunta's eyes were gauging the distance between where he stood and the nearest woods. He knew that Samson was nowhere near and the "oberseer" was keeping watch in another field that day. Kunta worked busily, to give the other man no suspicion of what was in his mind. But his breath came tensely as he stood holding the wire tight and looking down on the head of the man bent over his work. The knife had been left a few steps behind them, where the choppng of the brush had stopped.

With a silent prayer to Allah, Kunta clasped his hands together, lifted them high, and brought them down across the back of the man's neck with all the violence of which his slight body was capable. The man crumpled without a sound, as if he had been poleaxed. Within a moment, Kunta had bound the man's ankles and wrists with the wire. Snatching up the long knife, Kunta suppressed the impulse to stab him — this was not the hated Samson — and went running toward the woods, bent over almost double. He felt a lightness, as if he were running in a dream, as if this weren't really happening at all.

He came out of it a few moments later — when he heard the man he had left live yelling at the top of his lungs. He should have killed him, Kunta thought furious with himself, as he tried to run yet faster. Instead of fighting his way deeply into the underbrush when he reached the woods, he skirted it this time. He knew that he had to achieve distance first, then concealment. If he got far enough fast enough, he would have time to find a good place to hide and rest before moving on under cover of the night.

Kunta was prepared to live in the woods as the animals did. He had learned many things about this toubob land by now, together with what he already knew from Africa. He would capture rabbits and other rodents with snare traps and cook them over a fire that wouldn't smoke. As he ran, he stayed in the area where the brush would conceal him but wasn't thick enough to slow him down.

By nightfall, Kunta knew that he had run a good distance. Yet he kept going, crossing gullies and ravines, and for quite a way down the bed of a shallow stream. Only when it was completely dark did he allow himself to stop, hiding himself in a spot where the brush was dense but from which he could easily run if he had to. As he lay there in the darkness, he listened carefully for the sound of dogs. But there was nothing but stillness all around him. Was it possible? Was he really going to make it this time?

Just then he felt a cold fluttering on his face, and reached up with his hand. "Snow" was falling again! Soon he was covered — and surrounded — by whiteness as far as he could see. Silently it fell, deeper and deeper, until Kunta began to fear he was going to be buried in it; he was already freezing. Finally he couldn't stop himself from leaping up and running to look for better cover.

He had run a good way when he stumbled and fell; he wasn't hurt, but when he looked back, he saw with horror that his feet had left a trail in the snow so deep that a blind man could follow him. He knew that there was no way he could erase the tracks, and he knew that the morning was now not far away. The only possible answer was more distance. He tried to increase his speed, but he had been running most of the night, and his breath was coming in labored gasps. The long knife had begun to feel heavy; it would cut brush, but it wouldn't melt "snow." The sky was beginning to lighten in the east when he heard, far ahead of him, the faint sound of conch horns. He changed course in the next stride. But he had the sinking feeling that there was nowhere he could find to rest safely amid this blanketing whiteness.

When he heard the distant baying of the dogs, a rage flooded up in him such as he had never felt before. He ran like a hunted leopard, but the barking grew louder and louder, and finally, when he glanced back over his shoulder for the tenth time, he saw them gaining on him. The men couldn't be far behind. Then he heard a gun fire, and somehow it propelled him forward even faster than before. But the dogs caught up with him anyway. When they were but strides away, Kunta whirled and crouched down, snarling back at them. As they came lunging forward with their fangs bared, he too lunged at them, slashing open the first dog's belly with a single sideways swipe of the knife; with another blur of his arm, he hacked the blade between the eyes of the next one.

Springing away, Kunta began running again. But soon he heard the men on horses crashing through the brush behind him, and he all but dove for the deeper brush where the horses couldn't go. Then there was another shot, and another — and he felt a flashing pain in his leg. Knocked down in a heap, he had staggered upright again when the toubob shouted and fired again, and he heard the bullets thud into trees by his head. Let them kill me, thought Kunta; I will die as a man should. Then another shot hit the same leg, and it smashed him down like a giant fist. He was snarling on the ground when he saw the "oberseer" and another toubob coming toward him with their guns leveled and he was about to leap up and force them to shoot him again and be done with it, but the wounds in his leg wouldn't let him rise.

The other toubob held his gun at Kunta's head as the "oberseer" jerked off Kunta's clothing until he stood naked in the snow, the blood trickling down his leg and staining the whiteness at his feet. Cursing with each breath, the "oberseer" knocked Kunta all but senseless with his fist; then both of them tied him facing a large tree, with his wrists bound on the other side.

The lash began cutting into the flesh across Kunta's shoulders and back, with the "oberseer" grunting and Kunta shuddering under the force of each blow. After a while Kunta couldn't stop himself from screaming with the pain, but the beating went on until his sagging body pressed against the tree. His shoulders and back were covered with long, half-opened bleeding welts that in some places exposed the muscles beneath. He couldn't be sure, but the next thing Kunta knew he had the feeling he was falling. Then he felt the coldness of the snow against him and everything went black.

He came to in his hut, and along with his senses, pain returned — excruciating and enveloping. The slightest movement made him cry out in agony; and he was back in chains. But even worse, his nose informed him that his body was wrapped from feet to chin in a large cloth soaked with grease of the swine. When the old cooking woman came in with food, he tried to spit at her, but succeeded only in throwing up. He thought he saw compassion in her eyes.

Two days later, he was awakened early in the morning by the sounds of festivities. He heard black people outside the big house shouting "Christmas gif', Massa!," and he wondered what they could possibly have to celebrate. He wanted to die, so that his soul could join the ancestors; he wanted to be done forever with misery unending in this toubob land, so stifling and stinking that he couldn't draw a clean breath in it. He boiled with fury that instead of beating him like a man, the toubob had stripped him naked. When he became well, he would take revenge — and he would escape again. Or he would die.

CHAPTER 48

When Kunta finally emerged from his hut, again with both of his ankles shackled, most of the other blacks avoided him, rolling their eyes in fear of being near him, and moving quickly elsewhere, as if he were a wild animal of some kind. Only the old cooking woman and the old man who blew the conch horn would look at him directly.

Samson was nowhere to be seen. Kunta had no idea where he had gone, but Kunta was glad. Then, a few days later, he saw the hated black one bearing the unhealed marks of a lash; he was gladder still. But at the slightest excuse, the lash of the toubob "oberseer" fell once again on Kunta's back as well.

He knew every day that he was being

watched as he went through the motions of his work, like the others moving more quickly when the toubob came anywhere near, then slowing down as they left. Unspeaking, Kunta did whatever he was ordered to do. And when the day was over, he carried his melancholy — deep within himself — from the fields back to the dingy little hut where he slept.

In his loneliness, Kunta began talking to himself, most often in imaginary conversations with his family. He would talk to them mostly in his mind, but sometimes aloud. "Fa," he would say, "these black ones are not like us. Their bones, their blood, their sinews, their hands, their feet are not their own. They live and breathe not for themselves but for the toubob. Nor do they own anything at all, not even their own children. They are fed and nursed and bred for others."

"Mother," he would say, "these women wear cloths upon their heads, but they do not know how to tie them; there is little that they cook that does not contain the meat or the greases of the filthy swine; and many of them have lain down with the toubob, for I see their children who are cursed with the sasso-borro half color."

And he would talk with his brothers Lamin, Suwadu, and Madi, telling them that even the wisest of the elders could never really adequately impress upon them the importance of realizing that the most vicious of the forest animals was not half as dangerous as the toubob.

And so the moons passed in this way, and soon the spikes of "ice" had fallen and melted into water. And before long after that, green grass came peeping through the dark-reddish earth, the trees began to show their buds, and the birds were singing once again. And then came the plowing of the fields and the planting of the endless rows. Finally the sun's rays upon the soil made it so hot that Kunta was obliged to step quickly, and if he had to stop, to keep his feet moving to prevent them from blistering.

Kunta had bided his time and minded his own business, waiting for his keepers to grow careless and take their eyes off him once again. But he had the feeling that even the other blacks were still keeping an eye on him, even when the "oberseer" and the other toubob weren't around. He had to find some way not to be so closely watched. Perhaps he could take advantage of the fact that the toubob didn't look at blacks as people but as things. Since the toubob's reactions to these black things seemed to depend on how those things acted, he decided to act as inconspicuous as possible.

Though it made him despise himself, Kunta forced himself to start behaving the way the other blacks did whenever the toubob came anywhere near. Hard as he tried, he couldn't bring himself to grin and shuffle, but he made an effort to appear co-operative, if not friendly; and he made a great show of looking busy. He had also learned a good many more toubob words by now, always keenly listening to everything that was said around him, either out in the fields or around the huts at night, and though he still chose not to speak himself, he began to make it clear that he could understand.

Cotton — one of the main crops on the farm — grew quickly here in the toubob's land. Soon its flowers had turned into hard green bolls and split open, each filled with fluffy balls, until the fields as far as Kunta could see were vast seas of whiteness, dwarfing the fields he had seen around Juffure. It was time to harvest, and the wake-up horn began blowing earlier in the morning, it seemed to Kunta, and the whip of the "oberseer" was cracking in warning even before the "slaves," as they were called, could tumble from their beds.

By watching others out in the field, Kunta soon learned that a hunched position made his long canvas sack seem to drag less heavily behind him as the endlessly repeated handfuls of cotton from the bolls slowly filled his sack. Then he would drag it to be emptied in the wagon that waited at the end of the rows. Kunta filled his sack twice a day, which was about average, although there were some — hated and envied by the others for bending their backs so hard to please the toubob, and succeeding at it — who could pick cotton so fast that their hands seemed a blur; by the time the horn blew at dusk, their sacks would have been filled and emptied into the wagon at least three times.

When each cotton wagon was filled, it was taken to a storehouse on the farm, but Kunta noticed that the overflowing wagons of tobacco harvested in the larger fields adjoining his were driven away somewhere down the road. Four days passed before it returned empty — just in time to pass another loaded wagon on its way out. Kunta also began seeing other loaded tobacco wagons, doubtlessly from other farms, rolling along the main road in the distance, drawn sometimes by as many as four mules. Kunta didn't know where the wagons were going, but he knew they went a long way, for he had seen the utter exhaustion of Samson and other drivers when they had returned from one of their trips.

Perhaps they would go far enough to take him to freedom. Kunta found it hard to get through the next several days in his excitement with this tremendous idea. He ruled out quickly any effort to hide on one of this farm's wagons; there would be no time without someone's eyes too near for him to slip unnoticed into a load of tobacco. It must be a wagon moving along the big road from some other farm. Using the pretext of going to the outhouse late that night, Kunta made sure that no one was about, then went to a place where he could see the road in the moonlight. Sure enough — the tobacco wagons were traveling at night. He could see the flickering lights each wagon carried, until finally those small specks of brightness would disappear in the distance.

He planned and schemed every minute, no details of the local tobacco wagons escaping his notice. Picking in the fields, his hands fairly flew; he even made himself grin if the "oberseer" rode anywhere near. And all the time he was thinking how he would be able to leap onto the rear end of a loaded, rolling wagon at night and burrow under the tobacco without being heard by the drivers up front because of the bumping wagon's noise, and unseen not only because of the darkness but also because of the tall mound of leaves between the drivers and the rear of the wagon. It filled him with revulsion even to think of having to touch and smell the pagan plant he had managed to stay away from all his life, but if that was the only way to get away, he felt sure that Allah would forgive him.

CHAPTER 49

Waiting one evening soon afterward behind the "outhouse," as the slaves called the hut where they went to relieve themselves, Kunta killed with a rock one of the rabbits that abounded in the woods nearby. Carefully he sliced it thinly and dried it as he had learned in manhood training, for he would need to take some nourishment along with him. Then, with a smooth rock, he honed the rusted and bent knife blade he had found and straightened, and wired it into a wooden handle that he had carved. But even more important than the food and the knife was the saphie he had made — a cock's feather to attract the spirits, a horse's hair for strength, a bird's wishbone for success — all tightly wrapped and sewn within a small square of gunnysacking with a needle he had made from a thorn. He realized the foolishness of wishing that his saphie might be blessed by a holy man, but any saphie was better than no saphie at all.

He hadn't slept all night, but far from being tired, it was all Kunta could do not to burst with excitement — to keep from slowing any emotion at all — throughout the next day's working in the fields. For tonight would be the night. Back in his hut after the evening meal, his hands trembled as he pushed into his pocket the knife and the dried slices of rabbit, then tied his saphie tightly around his upper right arm. He could hardly stand hearing the familiar early-night routine of the other blacks; for each moment, which seemed to be taking forever to pass, might bring some unexpected occurrence that could ruin his plan. But the bone-weary field hands' mournful singing and praying soon ended. To let them get safely asleep, Kunta waited as much longer as he dared.

Then, grasping his homemade knife, he eased out into the dark night. Sensing no one about, he bent low and ran as fast as he could go, plunging after a while into a small, thick growth of brush just below where the big road curved. He huddled down, breathing hard. Suppose no more wagons were coming tonight? The thought lanced through him. And then a nearly paralyzing, worse fear: Suppose the driver's helper sits as a rear lookout? But he had to take the chance.

He heard a wagon coming minutes before he saw its flickering light. Teeth clenched, muscles quivering, Kunta felt ready to collapse. The wagon seemed barely crawling. But finally, it was directly across from him and slowly passing. Two dim figures sat on its front seat. Feeling like screaming, he lunged from the growth of brush. Trotting low behind the squeaking, lurching wagon, Kunta awaited the road's next rough spot; then his outstretched hand clawed over the tailboard, and he was vaulting upward, over the top, and into the mountain of tobacco. He was on board!

Frantically he went burrowing in. The leaves were packed together far more tightly than he had expected, but at last his body was concealed. Even after pawing open an air space to breathe more freely — the stench of the filthy weed almost made him sick — he had to keep moving his back and shoulders a bit this way or that, trying to get comfortable under the pressing weight. But finally he found the right position, and the rocking motion of the wagon, cushioned by the leaves, which were very warm around him, soon made him drowsy.

A loud bump brought him awake with a sickening start, and he began to think about being discovered. Where was the wagon going, and how long would it take to get there? And when it arrived, would he be able to slip away unseen? Or would he find himself trailed and trapped again? Why had he not thought of this before? A picture flashed into his mind of the dogs, and Samson, and the toubob with their guns, and Kunta shuddered. Considering what they did to him last time, he knew that this time his *life* would depend upon not getting caught.

But the more he thought of it, the stronger his urge grew to leave the wagon now. With his hands, he parted the leaves enough to poke his head out. Out in the moonlight were endless fields and countryside. He couldn't jump out now. The moon was bright enough to help his pursuers as much as it could help him. And the longer he rode, the less likely it was that the dogs could ever track him. He covered up the hole and tried to calm himself; but every time the wagon lurched, he feared that it was going to stop, and his heart would nearly leap from his chest.

Much later, when he opened the hole again and saw that it was nearing dawn, Kunta made up his mind. He had to leave the wagon right now, before he came any closer to the enemy of open daylight. Praying to Allah, he grasped the handle of his knife and began to wriggle out of his hole. When his entire body was free, he waited again for the wagon to lurch. It seemed to take an eternity, but when it finally did he made a light leap — and was on the road. A moment later he was out of sight in the bushes.

Kunta swung in a wide arc to avoid two toubob farms where he could see the familiar big house with the small, dark huts nearby. The sounds of their wake-up horns floated across the still air to his ears, and as the dawn brightened, he was slashing through underbrush deeper and deeper into what he knew was a wide expanse of forest. It was cool in the dense woods, and the dew that sprinkled onto him felt good, and he swung his knife as if it were weightless, grunting in his pleasure with each swing. During the early afternoon, he happened upon a small stream of clear water tippling over mossy rocks, and frogs jumped in alarm as he stopped to drink from it with his cupped hands. Looking around and feeling safe enough to rest for a while, he sat down on the bank and reached into his pocket. Taking out a piece of the dried rabbit and swashing it around in the stream, he put it in his mouth and chewed. The earth was springy and soft beneath him, and the only sounds he could hear were made by the toads and the insects and the birds. He listened to them as he ate, and watched sunlight stippling the leafy boughs above him with splashes of gold among the green; and he told himself that he was glad he didn't have to run as hard or as steadily as he had before, for exhaustion had made him an easy prey.

On and on he ran, for the rest of the afternoon, and after pausing for his sundown prayer, he went on still farther until darkness — and weariness — forced him to stop for the night. Lying on his bed of leaves and grass, he decided that later he would build himself a shelter of forked sticks with a roof of grass, as he had learned in manhood training. Sleep claimed him quickly, but several times during the night he was awakened by mosquitoes, and he heard the snarlings of wild animals in the distance as they made their kills.

Up with the first rays of the sun, Kunta quickly sharpened his knife and then was off again. Awhile later he came upon what was clearly a trail where a number of men had walked; although he could see that it had not been used in a long time, he ran back into the woods as fast as he could go.

Deeper and deeper into the forest, his knife kept slashing. Several times he saw snakes, but on the toubob farm he had learned that they would not attack unless they were frightened or cornered, so he let them slither away. Now and then he would imagine that he heard a dog barking somewhere, and he would shiver, for more than men, he feared dogs' noses.

Several times during the day, Kunta got into foliage so dense that in some places even his knife wasn't stout enough to clear a path, and he had to return and find another way. Twice he stopped to sharpen his knife, which seemed to be getting dull more and more often, but when it didn't work any better afterward, he suspected that the constant slashing at briars, bushes, and vines had begun to sap his strength. So he paused to rest again, ate some more rabbit — and some wild blackberries — and drank water that he found in cupped leaves of plants at the bases of the trees. That night he rested by another stream, plunging into sleep the moment he lay down, deaf to the cries of animals and night birds, insensible even to the buzzing and biting of the insects that were drawn to his sweaty body.

It wasn't until the next morning that Kunta began to think about where he was going. He hadn't let himself think of it before. Since he couldn't know where he was going because he didn't have any idea where he was, he decided that his only course was to avoid nearness to any other human beings, black or toubob, and to keep running toward the sunrise. The maps of Africa he'd seen as a boy showed the big water to the west, so he knew that eventually he'd reach it if he kept moving east. But when he thought about what might happen then, even if he wasn't caught; of how he would ever be able to cross the water, even if he had a boat; of how he would ever get safely to the other side, even if he knew the way — he began to get deeply frightened. Between prayers, he fingered the saphie charm on his arm even as he ran.

That night, as he lay hidden beneath a bush, he found himself thinking of the Mandinkas' greatest hero, the warrior Sundiata, who had been a crippled slave so meanly treated by his African master that he had escaped and gone hiding in the swamps, where he found and organized other escaped ones into a conquering army that carved out the vast Mandinka Empire. Maybe, Kunta thought as he set out again on this fourth day, he could find other escaped Africans somehow here in the land of toubob, and maybe they would be as desperate as he was to feel their toes once again in the dust of their native land. Maybe enough of them together could build or steal a big canoe. And then . . .

Kunta's reverie was interrupted by a terrible sound. He stopped in his tracks. No, it was impossible! But there was no mistake; it was the baying of hounds. Wildly he went hacking at the brush, stumbling and falling and scrambling up again. Soon he was so tired that when he fell again, he just sat there, very still, clutching the handle of his knife and listening. But he heard nothing now — nothing but the sounds of the birds and the insects.

Had he really heard the dogs? The thought tormented him. He didn't know which was his worst enemy: the toubob or his own imagination. He couldn't afford to assume that he hadn't really heard them, so he started running again; the only safety was to keep moving. But soon — exhausted not only by having to race so far and so fast, but also by fear itself — he had to rest again. He would close his eyes for just a moment, and then get going again.

He awoke in a sweat, sitting bolt upright. It was pitch dark! He had slept the day away! Shaking his head, he was trying to figure out what had wakened him when suddenly he heard it again: the baying of dogs, this time much closer than before. He sprang up and away so frantically that it was several moments before it flashed upon his mind that he had forgotten his long knife. He dashed back where he had lain, but the springy vines were a maze, and though he knew — maddeningly — that he had to be within arm's length of it, no amount of groping and scrabbling enabled him to lay his hand on it.

As the baying grew steadily louder, his stomach began to churn. If he didn't find it, he knew he would get captured again — or worse. With his hands jerking around everywhere underfoot, he finally grabbed hold of a rock about the size of his fist. With a desperate cry, he snatched it up and bolted into the deep brush.

All that night, like one possessed, he ran deeper and deeper into the forest — tripping, falling, tangling his feet in vines, stopping only for moments to catch his breath. But the hounds kept gaining on him, closer and closer, and finally, soon after dawn, he could see them over his shoulder. It was like a nightmare repeating itself. He couldn't run any farther. Turning and crouching in a little clearing with his back against a tree, he was ready for them — right hand clutching a stout limb he had snapped off another tree while he was running at top speed, left hand holding the rock in a grip of death.

The dogs began to lunge toward Kunta, but with a hideous cry he lashed the club at them so ferociously that they retreated and cowered just beyond its range, barking and slavering, until the two toubob appeared on their horses.

Kunta had never seen these men before. The younger one drew a gun, but the older one waved him back as he got down off his horse and walked toward Kunta. He was calmly uncoiling a long black whip.

Kunta stood there wild-eyed, his body shaking, his brain flashing a memory of toubob faces in the wood grove, on the big canoe, in the prison, in the place where he had been sold, on the heathen farm, in the woods where he had been caught, beaten, lashed, and shot three times before. As the toubob's arm reared backward with the lash, Kunta's arm whipped forward with a viciousness that sent him falling sideways as his fingers released the rock.

He heard the toubob shout; then a bullet cracked past his ear, and the dogs were upon him. As he rolled over and over on the ground ripping at the dogs, Kunta glimpsed one toubob's face with blood running down it. Kunta was snarling like a wild animal when they called off the dogs and approached him with their guns drawn. He knew from their faces that he would die now, and he didn't care. One lunged forward and grabbed him while the other clubbed with the gun, but it still took all of their strength to hold him, for he was writhing, fighting, moaning, shrieking in both Arabic and Mandinka — until they clubbed him again. Wrestling him violently toward a tree, they tore the clothes off him and tied him tightly to it around the middle of his body. He steeled himself to be beaten to death.

But then the bleeding toubob halted abruptly, and a strange look came onto his face, almost a smile, and he spoke briefly, hoarsely to the younger one. The younger one grinned and nodded, then went back to his horse and unlashed a short-handled hunting ax that had been stowed against the saddle. He chopped a rotting tree trunk away from its roots and pulled it over next to Kunta.

Standing before him, the bleeding one began making gestures. He pointed to Kunta's genitals, then to the hunting knife in his belt. Then he pointed to Kunta's foot, and then to the ax in his hand.

When Kunta understood, he howled and kicked — and was clubbed again. Deep in his marrow, a voice shouted that a man, to be a man, must have sons. And Kunta's hands flew to cover his foto. The two toubob were wickedly grinning.

One pushed the trunk under Kunta's right foot as the other tied the foot to the trunk so tightly that all of Kunta's raging couldn't free it. The bleeding toubob picked up the ax. Kunta was screaming and thrashing as the ax flashed up, then down so fast — severing skin, tendons, muscles, bone — that Kunta heard the ax thud into the trunk as the shock of it sent the agony deep into his brain. As the explosion of pain bolted through him, Kunta's upper body spasmed forward and his hands went flailing downward as if to save the front half of his foot, which was falling forward, as bright red blood jetted from the stump as he plunged into blackness.

CHAPTER 50

For the better part of a day, Kunta lapsed into and out of consciousness, his eyes closed, the muscles of his face seeming to sag, with spittle dribbling from a corner of his open mouth. As he gradually grew aware that he was alive, the terrible pain seemed to split into parts — pounding within his head, lancing throughout his body, and searing in his right leg. When his eyes required too much effort to open, he tried to remember what had happened. Then it came to him — the flushed, contorted toubob face behind the ax flashing upward, the *thunk* against the stump, the front of his foot toppling off. Then the throbbing in Kunta's head surged so violently that he lapsed mercifully back into blackness.

573

The next time he opened his eyes, he found himself staring at a spider web on the ceiling. After a while, he managed to stir just enough to realize that his chest, wrists, and ankles were tied down, but his right foot and the back of his head were propped against something soft, and he was wearing some kind of gown. And mingled with his agony was the smell of something like tar. He had thought he knew all about suffering before, but this was worse.

He was mumbling to Allah when the door of the hut was pushed open; he stopped instantly. A tall toubob he had never seen came in carrying a small black bag. His face was set in an angry way, though the anger seemed not to be directed at Kunta. Waving away the buzzing flies, the toubob bent down alongside him. Kunta could see only his back; then something the toubob did to his foot brought such a shock that Kunta shrieked like a woman, rearing upward against the chest rope. Finally turning around to face him, the toubob placed his palm against Kunta's forehead and then grasped his wrist lightly and held it for a long moment. Then he stood up, and while he watched the grimaces on Kunta's drawn face, called out sharply, "Bell!"

A black-skinned woman, short and powerfully built, with a stern but not forbidding face, soon came inside bringing water in a tin container. In some peculiar way, Kunta felt that he recognized her, that in some dream she had been already there looking down at him and bending beside him with sips of water. The toubob spoke to her in a gentle way as he took something from his black bag and stirred it into a cup of the water. Again the toubob spoke, and now the black woman kneeled and one of her hands raised the back of Kunta's head as the other tilted the cup for him to drink, which he did, being too sick and weak to resist.

His fleeting downward glance enabled him to catch a glimpse of the tip of the huge bandaging over his right foot; it was rust-colored with dried blood. He shuddered, wanting to spring up, but his muscles felt as useless as the vile-tasting stuff that he was permitting to go down his throat. The black woman then eased his head back down, the toubob said something to her again, and she replied, and the two of them went out.

Almost before they were gone, Kunta floated off into deep sleep. When next he opened his eyes late that night, he couldn't remember where he was. His right foot felt as if it were afire; he started to jerk it upward, but the movement made him cry out. His mind lapsed off into a shadowy blur of images and thoughts, each of them drifting beyond his grasp as quickly as they came. Glimpsing Binta, he told her that he was hurt, but not to worry, for he would be home again as soon as he was able. Then he saw a family of birds flying high in the sky and a spear piercing one of them. He felt himself falling, crying out, desperately clutching out at nothingness.

When he woke up again, Kunta felt sure that something terrible had happened to his foot; or had it been a nightmare? He only knew that he was very sick. His whole right side felt numb; his throat was dry; his parched lips were starting to split from fever; he was soaked in sweat, and it had a sickly smell. Was it possible that anyone would really chop off another's foot? Then he remembered that toubob pointing to his foot and to his genitals, and the horrible expression on his face. Again the rage flooded up; and Kunta made an effort to flex his toes. It brought a blinding sheet of pain. He lay there waiting for it to subside, but it wouldn't. And it was unbearable — except that somehow he was bearing it. He hated himself for wanting that toubob to come back with more of whatever it was he put in the water that had given him some ease.

Time and again he tried to pull his hands free of the loose binding at his sides, but to no avail. He lay there writhing and groaning in anguish when the door opened again. It was the black woman, the yellowish light from a flame flickering on her black face. Smiling, she began making sounds, facial expressions, and motions that Kunta knew was an effort to make him understand something. Pointing toward the hut's door, she pantomimed a tall man walking in, then giving something to drink to a moaning person, who then broadly smiled as if feeling much better. Kunta made no sign that he understood her meaning that the tall toubob was a man of medicine.

Shrugging, she squatted down and began pressing a damp, cooling cloth against Kunta's forehead. He hated her no less for it. Then she motioned that she was going to raise his head for him to sip some of the soup she had brought. Swallowing it, he felt flashing anger at her pleased look. Then she made a small hole in the dirt floor into which she set a round, long, waxy thing and lighted a flame at the top of it. With gesture and expression, she asked finally if there was anything else he wanted. He just glowered at her, and finally she left.

Kunta stared at the flame, trying to think, until it guttered out against the dirt. In the darkness, the kill-toubob plotting in the big canoe came into his mind; he longed to be a warrior in a great black army slaughtering toubob as fast as his arms could swing. But then Kunta was shuddering, fearful that he was dying himself, even though that would mean he would be forevermore with Allah. After all, none had ever returned from Allah to tell what it was like with Him; nor had any ever returned to their villages to tell what it was like with the toubob.

On Bell's next visit, she looked down with deep concern into Kunta's bloodshot and yellowing eyes, which had sunken farther into his fevered face. He lay steadily shuddering, groaning, even thinner than when he had been brought here the week before. She went back outside, but within an hour was back with thick cloths, two steaming pots, and a pair of folded quilts. Moving quickly and — for some reason — furtively, she covered Kunta's bared chest with a thick, steaming poultice of boiled leaves mixed and mashed with something acrid. The poultice was so blistering hot that Kunta moaned and tried to shake it off, but Bell firmly shoved him back. Dipping cloths into her other steaming pot, she wrung them out and packed them over the poultice, then covered Kunta with the two quilts.

She sat and watched the sweat pour from him onto the dirt floor in rivulets.

With a corner of her apron, Bell dabbed at the sweat that trickled into his closed eyes, and finally he lay entirely limp. Only when she felt the chest cloths and found them barely warm did she remove them. Then, wiping his chest clean of all traces of the poultice, she covered him with the quilts and left.

When he next awakened, Kunta was too weak even to move his body, which felt about to suffocate under the heavy quilts. But — without any gratitude — he knew that his fever was broken.

He lay wondering where that woman had learned to do what she had done. It was like Binta's medicines from his childhood, the herbs of Allah's earth passed down from the ancestors. And Kunta's mind played back to him, as well, the black woman's secretive manner, making him realize that it had not been toubob medicine. Not only was he sure that the toubob were unaware of it, he knew that the toubob should never know of it. And Kunta found himself studying the black woman's face in his mind. What was it the toubob had called her? "Bell."

With reluctance, after a while, Kunta decided that more than any other tribe, the woman resembled his own. He tried to picture her in Juffure, pounding her breakfast couscous, paddling her dugout canoe through the bolong, bringing in the sheaves of the rice harvest balanced on her head. But then Kunta reviled himself for the ridiculousness of thinking of his village in any connection with these pagan, heathen black ones here in the toubob's land.

Kunta's pains had become less constant now, and less intense; it hurt now mostly when he tried to strain against the bonds in his desperate achings to move around. But the flies tormented him badly, buzzing around his bandaged foot, or what was left of it, and now and then he would jerk that leg a little to make the flies swarm up awhile before returning.

Kunta began to wonder where he was. Not only was this not his own hut, but he could also tell from the sounds outside, and the voices of black people walking by, that he had been taken to some new farm. Lying there, he could smell their cooking and hear their early-night talking and singing and praying, and the horn blowing in the morning.

And each day the tall toubob came into the hut, always making Kunta's foot hurt as he changed the bandage. But when Bell came three times daily — she brought food and water, along with a smile and a warm hand on his forehead. He had to remind himself that these blacks were no better than the toubob. This black and this toubob may not mean him any harm — though it was too soon to be sure — but it was the black Samson who had beaten him almost to death, and it was toubob who had lashed him and shot him and cut his foot off. The more he gained in strength, the deeper grew his rage at having to lie there helpless, unable to move anywhere, when for all of his seventeen rains he had been able to run, bound, and climb anywhere he wanted to. It was monstrous beyond understanding or endurance.

When the tall toubob untied Kunta's wrists from the short stakes that had held them at his sides, Kunta spent the next few hours trying futilely to raise his arms; they were too heavy. Grimly, bitterly, relentlessly, he began forcing usefulness back into his arms by flexing his fingers over and over, then making fists — until finally he could raise his arms. Next he began struggling to pull himself up on his elbows, and once he succeeded, he spent hours braced thus staring down at the bandaging over his stump. It seemed as big as a "punkin," though it was less bloody than the previous bandagings he had glimpsed as the toubob took them off. But when he tried now to raise the knee of that same leg, he found that he couldn't yet bear the pain.

He took out his fury and his humiliation on Bell when she came to visit him the next time, snarling at her in Mandinka and banging down the tin cup after he drank. Only later did he realize that it was the first time since he arrived in toubob's land that he had spoken to anyone else aloud. It made him even more furious to recall that her eyes seemed warm despite his show of anger.

One day, after Kunta had been there for

nearly three weeks, the toubob motioned for him to sit up as he began to unwrap the bandaging. As it came nearer to the foot, Kunta saw the cloth stickily discolored with a thick, yellowish matter. Then he had to clamp his jaws as the toubob removed the final cloth — and Kunta's senses reeled when he saw the swollen heel half of his foot covered with a hideous thick, brownish scab. Kunta almost screamed. Sprinkling something over the wound, the toubob applied only a light, loose bandaging over it, then picked up his black bag and hurriedly left.

For the next two days, Bell repeated what the toubob had done, speaking softly as Kunta cringed and turned away. When the toubob returned on the third day, Kunta's heart leaped when he saw him carrying two stout straight sticks with forked tops; Kunta had seen hurt people walk with them in Juffure. Bracing the stout forks under his arms, the toubob showed him how to hobble about swinging his right foot clear of the ground.

Kunta refused to move until they both left. Then he struggled to pull himself upright, leaning against the wall of the hut until he could endure the throbbing of his leg without falling down. Sweat was coursing down his face before he had maneuvered the forks of the sticks underneath his armpits. Giddy, wavering, never moving far from the wall for support, he managed a few awkward, hopping forward swings of his body, the bandaged stump threatening his balance with every movement.

When Bell brought his breakfast the next morning, Kunta's glance caught the quick pleasure on her face at the marks made by the ends of the forked sticks in the hard dirt floor. Kunta frowned at her, angry at himself for not remembering to wipe away those marks. He refused to touch the food until the woman left, but then he ate it quickly, knowing that he wanted its strength now. Within a few days, he was hobbling freely about within the hut.

CHAPTER 51

In many ways, this toubob farm was very different from the last one, Kunta began to discover the first time he was able to get to the hut's doorway on his crutches and stand looking around outside. The black people's low cabins were all neatly whitewashed, and they seemed to be in far better condition, as was the one that he was in. It contained a small, bare table, a wall shelf on which were a tin plate, a drinking gourd, a "spoon," and those toubob eating utensils for which Kunta had finally learned the names: a "fork" and a "knife"; he thought it stupid for them to let him have such things within his reach. And his sleeping mat on the floor had a thicker stuffing of cornshucks. Some of the huts he saw nearby even had

586

small garden plots behind them, and the one closest to the toubob's big house had a colorful, circular flower patch growing in front of it. From where he stood in the doorway, Kunta could see anyone walking in any direction, and whenever he did, he would quickly crutch back inside and remain there for some time before venturing back to the doorway.

Kunta's nose located the outhouse. Each day, he held back his urges until he knew that most of them were out at their tasks in the fields, and then — carefully making sure that no one was nearby — he would go crutching quickly across the short distance to make use of the place, and then get safely back.

It was a couple of weeks before Kunta began to make brief ventures beyond that nearby hut, and the hut of slave row's cooking woman, who wasn't Bell, he was surprised to discover. As soon as he was well enough to get around, Bell had stopped bringing him his meals — or even visiting. He wondered what had become of her — until one day, as he was standing in his doorway, he caught sight of her coming out the back door of the big house. But either she didn't see him or she pretended not to, as she walked right past him on her way to the outhouse. So she was just like the others after all; he had known it all along. Less often, Kunta caught glimpses of the tall toubob, who was usually getting into a black-covered buggy that would then go hurrying away, with its two horses being driven by a black who sat on a seat up front.

After a few more days, Kunta began to stay outside his hut even when the field workers returned in the evening, shambling along in a tired group. Remembering the other farm he had been on, he wondered why these black ones weren't being followed by some toubob with a whip on a horse. They passed close by Kunta — without seeming to pay him any attention at all — and disappeared into their huts. But within a few moments most of them were back outside again going about their chores. The men did things around the barn, the women milked cows and fed chickens. And the children lugged buckets of water and as much firewood as their arms could carry; they were obviously unaware that twice as much could be carried if they would bundle the wood and balance it, or the water buckets, on their heads.

As the days passed, he began to see that although these black ones lived better than those on the previous toubob farm, they seemed to have no more realization than the others that they were a lost tribe, that any kind of respect or appreciation for themselves had been squeezed out of them so thoroughly that they seemed to feel that their lives were as they should be. All they seemed to be concerned about was not getting beaten, having enough to eat and somewhere to sleep. There weren't many nights that Kunta finally managed to fall asleep before lying awake burning with fury at the misery of his people. But they didn't even seem to know that they were miserable. So what business was it of his if these people seemed to be satisfied with their pathetic lot? He lay feeling as if a little more of him was dying every day, that while any will to live was left to him, he should try to escape yet again, whatever the odds or the consequences. What good was he anymore — alive or dead? In the twelve moons since he was snatched from Juffure — how much older than his rains he had become.

It didn't help matters any that no one seemed to have found any kind of useful work for Kunta to do, though he was getting around ably enough on his crutches. He managed to convey the impression that he was occupied sufficiently by himself and that he had no need or desire to associate with anybody. But Kunta sensed that the other blacks didn't trust him any more than he trusted them. Alone in the nights, though, he was so lonely and depressed, spending hours staring up into the darkness, that he felt as if he were falling in upon himself. It was like a sickness spreading within him. He was amazed and ashamed to realize that he felt the need for love.

Kunta happened to be outside one day when the toubob's buggy rolled into the yard with the black driver's seat shared by a man of sasso borro color. When the toubob got out and went into the big house, the buggy came on nearer the huts and stopped again. Kunta saw the driver grasp the brown one under his arms to help him descend, for one of his hands seemed to be encased in what looked like hardened white mud. Kunta had no idea what it was, but it seemed likely that the hand was injured in some way. Reaching back into the buggy with his good hand, the brown one took out an oddly shaped dark box and then followed the driver down the row of huts to the one at the end that Kunta knew was empty.

Kunta was so filled with curiosity that in the morning he made it his business to hobble down to that hut. He hadn't expected to find the brown one seated just inside his doorway. They simply looked at each other. The man's face and eyes were expressionless. And so was his voice when he said "What you want?" Kunta had no idea what he was saying. "You one of dem African niggers." Kunta recognized that word he'd heard so often, but not the rest. He just stood there. "Well, git on, den!" Kunta heard the sharpness, sensed the dismissal. He all but stumbled, wheeling around, and went crutching in angry embarrassment back on up to his own hut.

He grew so furious every time he thought about that brown one that he wished he knew enough of the toubob tongue to go and shout, "At least I'm black, not brown like you!" From that day on, Kunta wouldn't look in the direction of that hut whenever he was outside. But he couldn't quell his curiosity about the fact that after each evening's meal, most of the other blacks hastened to gather at that last hut. And, listening intently from within his own doorway, Kunta could hear the voice of the brown one talking almost steadily. Sometimes the others burst into laughter, and at intervals he could hear them barraging him with questions. Who or what was he, Kunta ached to know.

In midafternoon about two weeks later, the brown one chanced to be emerging from the privy at the very moment Kunta was approaching it. The brown one's bulky white arm covering was gone, and his hands were plaiting two cornshucks as the furious Kunta rapidly crutched on past. Sitting inside, Kunta's head whirled with the insults he wished he could have expressed. When he came back outside, the brown one was calmly standing there, his matter-of-fact expression as if nothing had ever happened between them. Still twisting and plaiting cornshucks between his fingers, he beckoned with his head for Kunta to follow him.

It was so totally unexpected — and disarming — that Kunta found himself following the brown one back to his cabin without a word. Obediently, Kunta sat down on the stool the brown one pointed to and watched as his host seated himself on the other stool, still plaiting. Kunta wondered if he knew that he was plaiting much the same as Africans did.

After a while more of reflective silence, the brown one began speaking: "I been hearin' 'bout you so mad. You lucky dey ain't kilt you. Dey could of, an' been inside de law. Jes' like when dat white man broke my hand 'cause I got tired of fiddlin'. Law say anybody catch you 'scapin' can kill you and no punishment for him. Dat law gits read out again eve'y six months in white folks' churches. Looka here, don't start me on white folks' laws. Startin' up a new settlement, dey firs' builds a courthouse, fo' passin' more laws; nex' buildin's a church to prove dey's Christians. I b'lieve all dat Virginia's House of Burgess do is pass more laws 'gainst niggers. It's a law niggers can't carry no gun, even no stick that looks like a club. Law say twenty lashes you get caught widdout a travelin' pass, ten lashes if'n you looks white folks in dey eyes, thirty lashes if'n you raises you hand 'gainst a white Christian. Law say no nigger preachin' less'n a white man dere to listen; law say can't be no nigger funeral if dey think it's a meetin'. Law say cut your ear off if'n white folks swear you lied, both ears if dey claim you lied twice. Law say you *kill* anybody white, you hang; kill 'nother nigger, you jes' gits whipped. Law say reward a Indian catchin' a 'scaped nigger wid all de tobacco dat Indian can carry. Law 'gainst teachin' any nigger to read or write, or givin' any nigger any book. Dey's even a law 'gainst niggers beatin' any drums — any dat African stuff.''

Kunta sensed that the brown one knew he couldn't understand, but that he both liked to talk and felt that Kunta's listening might somehow bring him at least closer to comprehension. Looking at the brown one's face as he spoke, and listening to his tone, Kunta felt he almost *could* understand. And it made him want to both laugh and cry that someone was actually talking to him as one human being to another.

'' 'Bout your foot, looka here, it ain't jes' foots and arms but dicks an' nuts gits cut off. I seen plenty ruined niggers like dat still workin'. Seen niggers beat till meat cut off dey bones. Nigger women's full of baby gits beat layin' face down over a hole dug for dey bellies. Niggers gits scraped raw, den covered with turpentine or salt, den rubbed wid straw. Niggers caught talkin' 'bout revolt made to dance on hot embers 'til dey falls. Ain't hardly nothin' ain't done to niggers, an' if dey die 'cause of it, ain't no crime long as dey's owned by whoever done it, or had it done. Dat's de law. An' if you thinks dat's bad, you ought to hear what folks tell gits did to dem niggers dat some slaveboats sells crost the water on dem West Indies sugar plantations.''

Kunta was still there listening — and trying to understand — when a first-kafo-sized boy came in with the brown one's evening meal. When he saw Kunta there, he dashed out and soon returned with a covered plate for him, too. Kunta and the brown one wordlessly ate together, and then Kunta abruptly rose to leave, knowing that the others would soon be coming to the hut, but the brown one's gesture signaled Kunta to stay.

As the others began arriving a few minutes later, none were able to mask their surprise at seeing Kunta there — particularly Bell, who was one of the last to show up. Like most of the rest, she simply nodded — but with the trace of a smile, it seemed to Kunta. In the gathering darkness, the brown one proceeded to hold forth for the group as he had done for Kunta, who guessed that he was telling them some kind of stories. Kunta could tell when a story ended, for abruptly they would all laugh — or ask questions. Now and then Kunta recognized some of the words that had become familiar to his ears.

When he went back to his own hut, Kunta was in a turmoil of emotion about mingling with these black ones. Sleepless late that night, his mind was still tumbling with conflicts, he recalled something Omoro had said once when Kunta had refused to let go of a choice mango after Lamin begged for a bite: "When you clench your fist, no one can put anything in your hand, nor can your hand pick up anything."

But he also knew that his father would be in the fullest of agreement with him that, no matter what, he must never become anything like these black people. Yet each night, he felt strangely drawn to go among them at the hut of the brown one. He resisted the temptation, but almost every afternoon now, Kunta would hobble over to visit with the brown one when he was alone.

"Git my fingers back to workin' right

to fiddle again,'' he said while weaving his cornshucks one day. "Any kin' of luck, dis massa here go 'head an' buy me an' hire me out. I done fiddled all over Virginia, make good money for him an' me both. Ain't much I ain't seen an' done, even if'n you don't know what I'm talkin' 'bout. White folks says all Africans knows is livin' in grass huts an' runnin' 'roun' killin' an' eatin' one 'nother.''

He paused in his monologue, as if expecting some kind of reaction, but Kunta just sat there watching and listening impassively and fingering his saphie charm.

"See what I means? You got to put away all dat stuff,'' said the brown one, pointing to the charm. "Give it up. You ain't goin' nowheres, so you might's well face facks an' start fittin' in, Toby, you hear?''

Kunta's face flashed with anger. "Kunta Kinte!'' he blurted, astonished at himself.

The brown one was equally amazed. "Looka here, he can talk! But I'm tellin' you, boy, you got to forgit all dat African talk. Make white folks mad an' scare niggers. Yo' name Toby. Dey calls me Fiddler.'' He pointed to himself. ''Say dat. Fiddler!'' Kunta looked at him blankly, though he understood exactly what he meant. ''Fiddler! I's a fiddler. Understan' — fiddler?'' He made a sawing motion across his left arm with the other hand. This time Kunta wasn't pretending when he looked blank.

Exasperated, the brown one got up and brought from a corner the oddly shaped box that Kunta had seen him arrive with. Opening it, he lifted out an even more oddly shaped light brown wooden thing with a slender black neck and four taut, thin strings running almost its length. It was the same musical instrument he had heard the old man play at the other farm.

''Fiddle!'' exclaimed the brown one.

Since they were alone, Kunta decided to say it. He repeated the sound: ''Fiddle.''

Looking pleased, the brown one put the fiddle away and closed the case. Then, glancing around, he pointed. ''Bucket!'' Kunta repeated it, fixing in his head what that thing was. ''Now, water!''

Kunta repeated it.

After they had gone through a score or more of new words, the brown one pointed silently at the fiddle, the bucket, water, chair, cornshucks, and other objects, his face a question mark for Kunta to repeat the right word for all of them. A few of the names he promptly repeated; he fumbled with a few others and was corrected; and some sounds he was unable to say at all. The brown one refreshed him on those, then reviewed him on them all. "You ain't dumb as you looks," he grunted by suppertime.

The lessons continued through the following days and stretched into weeks. To Kunta's astonishment, he began to discover that he was becoming able not only to understand but also to make himself understood to the brown one in a rudimentary way. And the main thing he wanted him to understand was why he refused to surrender his name or his heritage, and why he would rather die a free man on the run than live out his life as a slave. He didn't have the words to tell it as he wished, but he knew the brown

600

one understood, for he frowned and shook his head. One afternoon not long afterward, arriving at the brown one's hut, Kunta found another visitor already there. It was the old man he'd seen now and then hoeing in the flower garden near the big house. With a glance at the brown one's affirming nod, Kunta sat down.

The old man began to speak. "Fiddler here tell me you run away four times. You see what it got you. Jes' hopes you done learned your lesson like I done. 'Cause you ain't done nothin' new. My young days, I run off so much dey near 'bout tore my hide off 'fore I got it in my head ain't nowhere to run to. Run two states away, dey jes' tell about it in dey papers an' sooner later you gits cotched an' nearly kilt, an' win' up right back where you come from. Ain't hardly nobody ain't thought about runnin'. De grinnin'est niggers thinks about it. But ain't nobody I ever knowed ever got away. Time you settled down and made de best of things de way dey is, 'stead of wastin' yo' young years, like I did, plottin' what cain't be done. I done got ol' an' wore out now.

Reckon since you been born I been actin' like de no-good, lazy, shiftless, head-scratchin' nigger white folks says us is. Only reason massa keep me here, he know I ain't got no good auction value, an' he git more out of me jes' halfway doin' de gardenin'. But I hears tell from Bell massa gwine put you to workin' wid me tomorrow."

Knowing that Kunta had understood hardly any of what the gardener had said, the fiddler spent the next half hour explaining what the old man had told him — only slowly and more simply, in words Kunta was familiar with. He had mixed feelings about nearly everything the gardener had said. He understood that the old man meant well by his advice — and he was beginning to believe that escape was indeed impossible — but even if he never got away, he could never pay the price of giving up who and what he had been born in order to live out his years without another beating. And the thought of spending them as a crippled gardener filled him with rage and humiliation. But perhaps just for a while, until he got his strength back. And it might be good to get his mind off himself and his hands in the soil again — even if it wasn't his own.

The next day, the old gardener showed Kunta what to do. As he chopped away at the weeds that seemed to spring up daily among the vegetables, so did Kunta. As he plucked tomato worms and potato bugs from the plants and squashed them underfoot, so did Kunta. They got along well, but apart from working side by side, they didn't communicate much, either. Usually the old man would only make grunts and gestures whenever Kunta needed to be shown how to do some new task, and Kunta, without responding, simply did as he was told. He didn't mind the silence; as a matter of fact, his ears needed a few hours' rest each day between conversations with the fiddler, who ran his mouth every minute they were together.

That night after the evening meal, Kunta was sitting in the doorway of his hut when the man called Gildon — who made the horse and mule collars and also shod the black people — walked up to him and held out a pair of shoes. At the orders of the "massa," he said he had made them especially for Kunta. Taking them and nodding his thanks, Kunta turned them over and over in his hands before deciding to try them on. It felt strange to have such things on his feet, but they fit perfectly — even though the front half of the right shoe was stuffed with cotton. The shoemaker bent down to tie the lacings, then suggested that Kunta get up and walk around in them to see how they fit. The left shoe was fine, but he felt tiny stinging sensations in his right foot as he walked awkwardly and gingerly around outside his hut without the crutches. Seeing his discomfort, the shoemaker said that was because of the stump, not the shoe, and he would get used to it.

Later that day, Kunta walked a bit farther, testing, but the right foot was still uncomfortable, so he removed a little of the cotton stuffing and put it back on. It felt better, and finally he dared to put his full weight on that foot, and there wasn't any undue pain. Every now and then he would continue to experience the phantom pain of his right toes aching, as he had nearly every day since he started walking around, and he would glance downward — always with surprise — to find that he didn't have any. But he kept practicing walking around, and feeling better than he let his face show; he had been afraid that he would always have to walk with crutches.

That same week the massa's buggy returned from a trip, and the black driver, Luther, hurried to Kunta's hut, beckoning him down to the fiddler's, where Kunta watched him say something, grinning broadly. Then with gestures toward the big house and with selected key words, the fiddler made Kunta nod in understanding that Massa William Waller, the toubob who lived in the big house, now owned Kunta. "Luther say he just got a deed to you from his brother who had you at first, so you his now." As usual, Kunta did not let his face show his feelings. He was angry and ashamed that anyone could "own" him; but he was also deeply relieved, for he had feared that one day he would be taken back to that other "plantation," as he now knew the toubob farms were called. The fiddler waited until Luther had left before he spoke again — partly to Kunta and partly to himself. "Niggers here say Massa William a good master, an' I seen worse. But ain't none of 'em no good. Dey all lives off us niggers. Niggers is the biggest thing dey got."

CHAPTER 52

Almost every day now, when work was done, Kunta would return to his hut and after his evening prayer would scratch up the dirt in a little square on his floor and draw Arabic characters in it with a stick, then sit looking for a long time at what he had written, often until supper. Then he would rub out what he had written, and it would be time to go down and sit among the others as the fiddler talked. Somehow his praying and his studying made it all right to mix with them. That way, it seemed to him he could remain himself without having to remain *by* himself. Anyway, if they had been in Africa, there would have been someone like the fiddler to go to, only he would have been a wandering musician and griot traveling from one village to the next and singing as he played his kora or his balafon in between telling of fascinating stories drawn from his adventures.

Just as it had been done in Africa, Kunta had also begun to keep track of the passing of time by dropping a small pebble into a gourd on the morning after each new moon. First he had dropped into the gourd 12 rounded, multicolored stones for the 12 moons he guessed he'd spent on the first toubob farm; then he had dropped in six more for the time he'd been here on this new farm; and then he had carefully counted out 204 stones for the 17 rains he'd reached when he was taken from Juffure, and dropped them into the gourd. Adding them all up, he figured that he was now into his nineteenth rain.

So as old as he felt, he was still a young man. Would he spend the rest of his life here, as the gardener had, watching hope and pride slip away along with the years, until there was nothing left to live for and time had finally run out? The thought filled him with dread — and determination not to end up the way the old man had, doddering around in his plot, uncertain which foot to put before the other. The poor man was worn out long before the midday meal, and through the afternoons he was only able to pretend that he was working at all, and Kunta had to shoulder almost all the load.

Every morning, as Kunta bent over his rows, Bell would come with her basket — Kunta had learned that she was the cook in the big house — to pick the vegetables she wanted to fix for the massa that day. But the whole time she was there, she never so much as looked at Kunta, even when she walked right past him. It puzzled and irritated him, remembering how she had attended him daily when he lay fighting to survive, and how she would nod at him during the evenings at the fiddler's. He decided that he hated her, that the only reason she had acted as his nurse back then was because the massa had ordered her to do it. Kunta wished that he could hear whatever the fiddler might have to say about this matter, but he knew that his limited command of words wouldn't allow him to express it right — apart from the fact that even asking would be too embarrassing.

One morning not long afterward, the old man didn't come to the garden, and Kunta guessed that he must be sick. He had seemed even more feeble than usual for the past few days. Rather than going right away to the old man's hut to check on him, Kunta went straight to work watering and weeding, for he knew that Bell was due at any moment, and he didn't think it would be fitting for her to find no one there when she arrived.

A few minutes later she showed up and, still without looking at Kunta, went about her business, filling her basket with vegetables as Kunta stood holding his hoe and watching her. Then, as she started to leave, Bell hesitated, looked around, set the basket on the ground, and — throwing a quick, hard glance at Kunta — marched off. Her message was clear that he should bring her basket to the back door of the big house, as the old man had always done. Kunta all but exploded with rage, his mind flashing an image of dozens of

Juffure women bearing their headloads in a line past the bantaba tree where Juffure's men always rested. Slamming down his hoe, he was about to stamp away when he remembered how close she was to the massa. Gritting his teeth, he bent over, seized the basket, and followed silently after Bell. At the door, she turned around and took the basket as if she didn't even see him. He returned to the garden seething.

From that day on, Kunta more or less became the gardener. The old man, who was very sick, came only now and then, whenever he was strong enough to walk. He would do a little something for as long as he felt able, which wasn't very long, and then hobble back to his hut. He reminded Kunta of the old people in Juffure who, ashamed of their weakness, continued to totter about making the motions of working until they were forced to retreat to their pallets, and finally were rarely seen out any more at all.

The only new duty Kunta really hated was having to carry that basket for Bell every day. Muttering under his breath, he would follow her to the door, thrust it into her hand as rudely as he dared, then turn on his heel and march back to work, as fast as he could go. As much as he detested her, though, his mouth would water when now and then the air would waft to the garden the tantalizing smells of the things that Bell was cooking.

He had dropped the twenty-second pebble into his calendar gourd when — without any outward sign of change — Bell beckoned him on into the house one morning. After a moment's hesitation, he followed her inside and set the basket on a table there. Trying not to look amazed at the strange things he saw everywhere around him in this room, which they called the "kitchen," he was turning to leave when she touched him on the arm and handed him a biscuit with what looked like a piece of cold beef between the slices. As he stared at it in puzzlement, she said, "Ain't you never seed a san'wich befo'? It ain't gonna bite you. You s'posed to bite *it*. Now git on outa here."

As time went on, Bell began to give him more than he could carry in his hand —

usually a tin plate piled with something called "cornpone," a kind of bread he had never tasted before, along with boiled fresh mustard greens in their own delicious potliquor. He had sown the mustard's tiny seeds himself — in garden soil mixed with rich black dirt dug from the cow pasture — and the tender greens had swiftly, luxuriously sprung up. He loved no less the way she cooked the long, slender field peas that grew on the vines coiling around the sweet corn's stalks. She never gave him any obvious meat of the pig, though he wasn't sure how she knew that. But whatever she gave him, he would always wipe off the plate carefully with a rag before returning it. Most often he would find her at her "stove" — a thing of iron that contained fire — but sometimes she would be on her knees scrubbing the kitchen floor with oak ashes and a hard-bristled brush. Though at times he wanted to say something to her, he could never muster a better expression of his appreciation than a grunt — which now she returned.

One Sunday after supper, Kunta had

gotten up to stretch his legs and was walking around the fiddler's hut idly patting himself on the belly when the brown one, who had been talking steadily all through the meal, interrupted his monologue to exclaim, "Looka here, you startin' to fill out!" He was right. Kunta hadn't looked — or felt — better since he left Juffure.

After months of incessant plaiting to strengthen his fingers, the fiddler, too, felt better than he had in a long time — since his hand was broken — and in the evenings he had begun to play on his instrument again. Holding the peculiar thing in his cupped hand and under his chin, the fiddler raked its strings with his wand — which seemed to be made of long, fine hairs — and the usual evening audience would shout and break into applause when each song had finished. "Dat ain't nothin'!" he would say disgustedly. "Fingers ain't nimble yet."

Later, when they were alone, Kunta asked haltingly, "What is nimble?"

The fiddler flexed and wiggled his fingers. "Nimble! Nimble. Get it?"

Kunta nodded.

"You a lucky nigger, what you is," the fiddler went on. "Jes' piddlin' 'roun' eve'yday in dat garden. Ain't hardly nobody got a job dat sof' 'cept on plantations whole lot bigger'n dis."

Kunta thought he understood, and he didn't like it. "Work *hard*," he said. And nodding at the fiddler on his chair, he added, "Harder dan *dat*."

The fiddler grinned. "You awright, African!"

CHAPTER 53

The "months," as they called moons here, were passing more quickly now, and before long the hot season known as "summer" was over and harvest time had begun along with a great many more duties for Kunta and the others. While the rest of the blacks — even Bell — were busy with the heavy work out in the fields, he was expected to tend the chickens, the livestock, and the pigs in addition to his garden. And at the height of the cotton picking, he was called upon to drive the wagon along the rows. Except for having to feed the filthy swine, which almost made him ill, Kunta didn't mind the extra work, for it made him feel less of a cripple. But it was seldom that he got back to his hut before dark — so tired out that he sometimes even forgot to eat his supper. Taking off nothing but his frayed straw hat and his shoes — to relieve the aching of his half foot — he would flop down on his cornshuck mattress, pulling his quilt of cotton-stuffed burlap up over him, and within moments he would be sound asleep, in clothes still wet with sweat.

Soon the wagons were piled high with cotton, then with plump ears of corn, and the golden tobacco leaves were hanging up to dry. The hogs had been killed, cut into pieces, and hung over slowly burning hickory, and the smoky air was turning cold when everyone on the plantation began preparing for the "harvest dance," an occasion so important that even the massa would be there. Such was their excitement that when Kunta found out that the black people's Allah didn't seem to be involved, he decided to attend himself — but just to watch.

By the time he got up the courage to join the party, it was well under way. The fiddler, whose fingers were finally nimble again, was sawing away at his strings, and another man was clacking two beef bones together to keep time as someone shouted, "Cakewalk!" Dancers coupled off and hurried out before the fiddler. Each woman put her foot on the man's knee while he tied her shoestring; then the fiddler sang out, "Change partners!" and when they did, he began to play madly, and Kunta saw that the dancers' footsteps and body motions were imitating their planting of the crops, the chopping of wood, the picking of cotton, the swinging of scythes, the pulling of corn, the pitchforking of hay into wagons. It was all so much like the harvest dancing back in Juffure that Kunta's good foot was soon tapping away on the ground — until he realized what he was doing and looked around, embarrassed, to see if anyone had noticed.

But no one had. At that moment, in fact, almost everyone had begun to watch a slender fourth-kafo girl who was dipping and whirling around as light as a feather, her head tossing, her eyes rolling, her arms describing graceful patterns. Soon the other dancers, exhausted, were moving to the sides to catch their breaths and stare; even her partner was hard put to keep up.

When he quit, gasping, a shout went up, and when finally even she went stumbling toward the sidelines, a whooping and hollering engulfed her. The cheering got even louder when Massa Waller awarded that girl a half-dollar prize. And smiling broadly at the fiddler, who grinned and bowed in return, the massa left them amid more shouting. But the cakewalk was far from over, and the other couples, rested by now, rushed back out and went on as before, seemingly ready to dance all night.

Kunta was lying on his mattress thinking about what he had heard and seen when suddenly there came a rapping at his door.

"Who dat?" he demanded, astonished, for only twice had anyone ever come to his hut in all the time he'd lived there.

"Kick dis do' in, nigger!"

Kunta opened the door, for it was the voice of the fiddler; instantly he smelled the liquor on his breath. Though he was repelled, Kunta said nothing, for the fiddler was bursting to talk, and it would have been unkind to turn him away just because he was drunk.

"You seen massa!" said the fiddler. "He ain't knowed I could play dat good! Now you watch an' see if'n he don't 'range for me to play for white folks to hear me, an' den hire me out!" Beside himself with happiness, the fiddler sat on Kunta's three-legged stool, fiddle across his lap, and went on babbling.

"Looka here, I second fiddled with the best! You ever hear of Sy Gilliat from Richmond?" He hesitated. "Naw, 'course you ain't! Well, dat's de fiddlin'est slave nigger in de worl', and I fiddled wid him. Looka here, he play for nothin' but big white folks' balls an' dances, I mean like the Hoss Racin' Ball every year, and like dat. You oughta see him wid dat gold-painted fiddle of his an' him wearin' court dress wid his brown wig an' Lawd, dem manners! Nigger name London Briggs behin' us playin' flute an' clarinet! De minuets, de reels, de congos, hornpipes, jigs, even jes' caperin' 'bout —

don't care what it was, we'd have dem white folks dancin' up a storm!''

The fiddler carried on like this for the next hour — until the alcohol wore off — telling Kunta of the famous singing slaves who worked in Richmond's tobacco factories; of other widely known slave musicians who played the "harpsichord," the "pianoforte," and the "violin" — whatever they were — who had learned to play by listening to toubob musicians from someplace called "Europe," who had been hired to come to plantations to teach the massas' children.

The following crispy cold morning saw the starting of new tasks. Kunta watched as the women mixed hot melted tallow with wood-ash lye and water, boiling and stirring, then cooling the thick brown mixture in wooden trays to let it set for four nights and three days before they cut it into oblong cakes of hard, brown soap. To his complete distaste, he saw men fermenting apples, peaches, and persimmons into something foul-smelling that they called "brandy," which they put into bottles and barrels. Others mixed gluey red clay, water, and dried hog hair to press into cracks that had appeared in their huts. Women stuffed some mattresses with cornshucks like Kunta's, and some others with the moss he had seen drying; and a new mattress for the massa was filled with goose feathers.

The slave who built things from wood was making new tubs in which clothes would be soaked in soapy water before being boiled and lumped onto a wooden block to be beaten with a stick. The man who made things with leather — horse collars, harnesses, and shoes — was now busily tanning cows' hides. And women were dyeing into different colors the white cloth the massa had bought to make clothes with. And just as it was in Juffure, all of the nearby vines, bushes, and fences were draped with drying cloths of red, yellow, and blue.

With each passing day, the air became colder and colder, the sky grayer and grayer, until soon the ground was covered once again with snow and ice that Kunta found as unpleasant as it was extraordinary. And before long the other blacks were beginning to talk with great excitement about "Christmas," which he had heard of before. It seemed to have to do with singing, dancing, eating, and the giving of gifts, which sounded fine — but it also seemed to involve their Allah, so even though Kunta really enjoyed by now the gatherings at the fiddler's, he decided it would be best to stay to himself until the pagan festivities were safely over. He didn't even visit the fiddler, who looked curiously at Kunta the next time he saw him, but said nothing about it.

Thence swiftly came another springtime season, and as he knelt planting among his rows, Kunta remembered how lush the fields around Juffure always looked at this time of year. And he recalled as a second-kafo boy how happily he had gone prancing out behind the hungry goats in this green season. Here in this place the black "young'uns" were helping to chase and catch the *baaaing,* bounding "sheep," as the animals were called, and then fighting over whose turn was next to sit on the head of a desperately struggling sheep while a man snipped off the thick, dirty wool with a pair of shears. The fiddler explained to Kunta that the wool would be taken off somewhere to be cleaned and "carded into bats," which then would be returned for the women to spin woolen thread from which they would weave cloth for the making of winter clothes.

The garden's plowing, planting, and cultivating went by for Kunta in a sweating blur of dawns to darks. Early in the midsummer month they called "July," those who worked out in the fields would return exhausted to their huts every night as they pressed to complete the last hoeing of grass from around the waist-high cotton and corn that was heavy with tasseled heads. It was hard work, but at least there was plenty to eat in the storehouses that had been filled to overflowing the past fall. At this time in Juffure, Kunta thought, the people's stomachs would be aching as they made soup from roots, grubworms, grass, and anything else they could find, because the crops and fruits so lushly green were not yet ripe.

The "laying by" had to be finished

before the second "Sunday" in July, Kunta learned, when the blacks from most of the plantations in this area — which was called "Spotsylvania County" — would be permitted to travel someplace to join in some kind of "camp meetin'." Since, whatever it was, it had to do with their Allah, no one even suggested that Kunta go along with the more than twenty of them who left very early that Sunday morning, packed into a wagon whose use Massa Waller had approved.

Nearly everyone was gone for the next few days — so many that few would have been there to notice if Kunta had tried to run away again — but he knew that even though he had learned to get around all right and make himself fairly useful, he would never be able to get very far before some slave catcher caught up with him again. Though it shamed him to admit it, he had begun to prefer life as he was allowed to live it here on this plantation to the certainty of being captured and probably killed if he tried to escape again. Deep in his heart, he knew he would never see his home again, and he could feel something precious and irretrievable dying inside of him forever. But hope remained alive; though he might never see his family again, perhaps someday he might be able to have one of his own.

The publishers hope that this Large Print Book has brought you pleasurable reading. Each title is designed to make the text as easy to see as possible. G. K. Hall Large Print Books are available from your library and your local bookstore. Or you can receive information on upcoming and current Large Print Books by mail and order directly from the publisher. Just send your name and address to:

G. K. Hall & Co.
70 Lincoln Street
Boston, Mass. 02111